AMERICA AT WAR SINCE 1945

AMERICA AT WAR SINCE 1945

POLITICS AND DIPLOMACY IN KOREA, VIETNAM, IRAQ, AND AFGHANISTAN

GARY A. DONALDSON

Carrel Books may be purchased in bulk at special discounts for sales promotion, corporate gifts, fund-raising, or educational purposes. Special editions can also be created to specifications. For details, contact the Special Sales Department, Carrel Books, 307 West 36th Street, 11th Floor, New York, NY 10018, or carrelbooks@skyhorsepublishing.com.

Carrel Books® is a registered trademark of Skyhorse Publishing, Inc.®, a Delaware corporation.

Visit our website at www.carrelbooks.com.

10 9 8 7 6 5 4 3 2 1

Library of Congress Cataloging-in-Publication Data is available on file.

Cover design by Rain Saukas
Cover photo credit: Library of Congress

ISBN: 978-1-63144-064-9
Ebook ISBN: 978-1-63144-065-6

Printed in the United States of America.

CONTENTS

INTRODUCTION

In 1945 the United States came away from World War II as a victor over an obvious evil, a world leader, and prepared to put behind it the horrors of war. In fact, between V-J Day and June 1950, when the Korean War started, America began a predictable slip back into its historic isolationism, insisting it had no interests (as it had insisted for nearly two centuries) in the petty conflicts of the world. But the rising specter of communism changed all that. Americans began to see the spread of communism as a cancer that must be limited and contained. The fear played well in the American political arena—used by politicians as an issue to further their careers and enhance their opportunities for election. By the time North Korea invaded South Korea in June 1950, the nation's political situation virtually demanded that United States president Harry Truman move immediately to stop the invasion—and America was involved in its second war in five years. When the Chinese attacked later that fall (implementing their own brand of containment), the U.S. forces found themselves in rapid retreat against the massive Red Army. Only after three years of intense negotiations did the United States finally extricate itself from that conflict—claiming little more than a stalemate.

Did the United States learn any lessons in Korea? Would it again allow itself to become involved in a land war that the American people did not fully support, in a far-off place that had little significance to the defense of the nation? In Vietnam, the French defeat in 1954 meant the collapse of anticommunist forces there—something that Washington could not allow in the still politically charged era of the anti-Communist 1950s. America's involvement in Southeast Asia grew slowly through the late 1950s and the early 1960s. President John Kennedy, however, strongly believed that it was important to show the American people that he was not soft on communism and that in at least someplace in the world he was sending troops to fight for freedom. But the war in Vietnam was not so much a war against communism as a war against Vietnamese nationalism, a political force (and ultimately a military force) that was nearly unstoppable. By the mid-1960s the United States was again caught in an enormous quagmire of a war, against a force it could not defeat, in a far-off region of the world that really meant little to American defense—or the American people. But once U.S. leaders came to see that fact clearly, they found that extricating the nation's fighting force from the region was nearly impossible—at least from a political standpoint. As in Korea, the war dragged into stalemate, soldiers died, and America's place in the world order slipped proportionately. In addition, the nation divided over the war and the ghosts of Vietnam haunted the nation for decades.

In both wars, the United States fought to show the world that it would stand up to the evils of communism, that it could be counted on (with money, advisors, or even a major military effort if necessary) to halt the Communist advance. The United States set itself up as the major defender of anticommunism, the leader of the free world. Both wars, however, showed that the United States was militarily vulnerable, that the American people often did not stand behind their nation's foreign policy, and that the U.S. involvement often came with a price tag that was too high to pay. At home, Americans lost faith in their government and in their military. But in 1990, as the Gulf War was about to begin, President George H.W. Bush insisted there would be no more Vietnams—just as his critics argued that the war in Iraq might turn into another Korea-like stalemate. Bush, however, saw an opportunity to place the United States back into its old post-World War II position of prominence. The cold war was over, and the Soviets (and their proxies) were no longer a threat of any significance. Madmen like Saddam Hussein, however, still persisted, and there was still a need, so it seemed, for the United States to protect the world's weak nations against tyranny and aggression. Thus, in 1990, the United States would become what it had been in 1945: a world leader and the defender of freedom. For Americans, the Gulf War was a relief, a breath of fresh air. When the one hundred hours of fighting ended in the Iraqi desert, President Bush said privately that the nation had finally kicked the Vietnam Syndrome, that the many ghosts of Vietnam and Korea had finally stopped haunting the nation.

Not unlike his father, George W. Bush would be defined by his reaction to crises. And those crises would come; first in the September 11 attacks, and then in the wars on terror in Afghanistan and Iraq. Americans would follow him into battle, throwing their support to his initiatives against terrorists. But many Americans quickly grew tired of the wars. They questioned the initial reasoning for going to war and the manner in which the wars were being fought. Then they began asking the all-important questions, the questions that had been first asked in Korea and then in Vietnam: what is the strategy for withdrawing, and when? Bush's answers were unsatisfying, and Americans found themselves in two wars, fought in far-off parts of the world, while soldiers and civilians died in alarming numbers.

Even the most critical of observers tried to avoid comparisons with Vietnam, because there were certainly important differences—but there were obvious parallels. If it is true that George Bush, the father, had seen the ghosts of Vietnam when he fought Saddam Hussein in the early 1990s, George Bush, the son, was not similarly haunted. He found himself propping up an unstable government and fighting an irregular army on a battlefield that was not defined, and for reasons that were not entirely clear to the American people. In a 2007 speech, the president stepped back into the Vietnam quagmire by insisting that the United States should not have left Vietnam, that had the nation stayed the course, it would have won. *Newsweek* called the remark "an abuse of historical fact."

There were a number of other events in the Bush administration that showed that the United States was not invulnerable, that despite its great power, it could still be attacked, could still get bogged down in an expensive war, and could fall out of favor with the world and even diminish its leadership role. It was a frustrating time. Polls reflected a lack of confidence in the government. In 2007, over 70 percent of those polled said they did not like the direction the nation was headed—an amazing number, considering the strength of the economy and relative security at home. The president's approval ratings occasionally dipped below 30 percent; approval ratings for Congress often dropped below 20 percent.

Both political parties began asking themselves: What do the people want? As the 2008 presidential campaign approached, both candidates, senators Barack Obama and John McCain, focused their campaigns on the issue of change. Eight years later, the presidential candidates Donald Trump and Hillary Clinton, continued to call for change—and a new direction for the nation.

This book was first published in 1996. The focus then was on the ghosts of Vietnam, and how that war (and the war in Korea before it) had shaped U.S. foreign policy clear through the 1990s. America's second involvement in the Middle East under George W. Bush was a different conflict, but the lessons of Korea and Vietnam were still there, still a factor in U.S. foreign policy.

PART I
KOREA

I

ORIGINS AND INVOLVEMENT

The United States became involved in the Korean War in June 1950, just five years after World War II ended. For most Americans, the war in Korea, at first, represented the proper response to what seemed to be the onward march of world communism and the impending decline of American influence abroad if lines were not drawn and defended. Certainly, in 1950 Americans were of the opinion that their nation's military force could deal with the situation in Korea, just as it had dealt with the great powers of Germany and Japan only a few years earlier. And, as the war was presented to the American people (as a "police action" under the guise of the United Nations), it seemed less the war that it would become, and more the job of America to ferret out and push back the tyrants of world communism. So it was that America became involved in another war just five years after the end of World War II.

The end of World War II brought to America what appeared to be a clean-cut victory over a palpable evil. If anyone in the world doubted that, there was the striking evidence of the Nazi prison camps and the Japanese atrocities against its Asian neighbors. For most of America, World War II had been a good war, a war in which sacrifices had paid off handsomely in a complete military and moral victory, leaving the United States free of any serious enemies and free to turn its now-huge military-industrial complex into peaceful production that would bring jobs, products, and ultimately prosperity to the people of the nation. Satisfied in their victory and rich beyond compare in the new world order, Americans could now turn their attention to peace and prosperity. The war's duration had finally come.

However, the end of the war simply brought on a new series of international problems, the most serious of which was the postwar disposition of the German and Japanese empires. There were now huge power vacuums in Asia and Europe, and somehow those power vacuums would have to be filled. Deciding the future of these areas was to be the focus of several big-power conferences during the war. Korea had been a part of the Japanese Empire since the early decades of the century; its fate would be decided at these conferences.

Korea first came under Japanese rule as a result of Russia's defeat in the Russo-Japanese War that ended in 1905. Korea had looked to Russia for assistance against Japanese encroachments, and with Russia's defeat, Japan took the opportunity to force Korea into its sphere of influence. In the Treaty of Portsmouth, Japan's leaders received much less than they believed their decisive victory over Russia warranted, but they did obtain a controlling influence in Korea, and from there the Japanese hoped to extend their authority into the mineral-rich region of Manchuria, the real prize on the Asian mainland and Japan's ultimate objective through the next decades. In 1910 Japan annexed Korea and gave the peninsula its ancient name of "Chosen." Japan's appetite for greater influence and imperial conquests on the Asian mainland eventually brought it into conflict with China in the 1930s, and that ultimately precipitated the Pacific war that drew in the United States in December 1941.

The disposition of postwar Korea was first dealt with at the Cairo Conference in 1943 in which the United States, England, and China planned for Korea's freedom in what was vaguely termed "due course." Two years later at the Yalta Conference, Franklin Roosevelt proposed that after the war Korea should be placed under an international trusteeship that would ultimately guide the country toward independence.

Roosevelt was an ardent anti-colonialist, and he hoped that a postwar Asia would be free from the suppression of Western colonial domination. The French colony of Indochina and the Dutch colonies in the East Indies had all come under Japanese control during the war, and Roosevelt hoped that as the Japanese armies withdrew from these areas following Tokyo's impending surrender, the old Western colonies would become free and independent nations. In that same vein, Roosevelt also pressured England to grant independence to its Asian colonies after the war. England's prime minister, Winston Churchill, however, believed strongly in maintaining the English colonial system, and for much of the war the two world leaders found themselves at odds over the question of postwar colonialism in Asia. FDR's anti-colonial stance seemed noble, but it was only partly aimed at granting self-determination to the peoples of Asia. Roosevelt also intended that an Asia free of Western colonial networks would open the vast Asian markets to American manufacturers after the war. An Asia free of colonial rule would greatly benefit America's postwar economy.

Certainly, the largest power vacuum left by Japan's defeat would be in China, and plans for a postwar Asia could not go forward without some consideration for the most populous nation in the world. Before World War II expanded into the Pacific, China had been embroiled in a bitter civil war between the Guomindang Nationalist forces led by Generalissimo Jiang Jieshi (Chiang Kai-shek) and the Communist armies of Mao Zedong. When China's war with Japan broke out in 1937, Mao and his forces went into exile in the north, and Jiang became the sole recognized power in China. During the war, Japan came to control much of eastern China, while Jiang and the Guomindang fled west to Chongqing in Szechwan province and Mao and his forces remained concentrated in the north around Yan'an in Shaanxi province. These two Chinese contingencies remained in direct ideological conflict throughout the war, but faced with the common threat from the Japanese army, the two forces reluctantly formed the United Front against their common enemy. This United Front was uneasy and for the most part unsuccessful against the Japanese, and most of the world believed that the two forces were simply waiting out the war in their provincial strongholds, preparing to resume their own internal conflict once the war against Japan ended.

There was a great fear, particularly in Washington, that a resumption of the Chinese civil war following the withdrawal of Japanese troops might place the world's Communist forces against the world's non-Communist forces on the Chinese mainland—and that the United States and the USSR might be drawn into that conflict on opposing sides. The prospect of such a war clearly plagued Roosevelt, and he moved to disarm that postwar scenario at the Yalta Conference in February 1945.

Yalta had far-reaching implications for postwar America and the world. It was here that Josef Stalin, Churchill, and Roosevelt decided the fate of the postwar world. The future of Europe was the chief concern of the negotiators to be sure, but it was at Yalta that Korea's postwar destiny was planned as well—or at least plans were put into place for the disposition of postwar Asia, and Korea was made a part of those larger plans.

FDR went to Yalta hoping to achieve several goals. First, he wanted to ensure freedom for the Polish people after the war. Second, he wanted an assurance that the Soviets would participate enthusiastically in the planned international organization that would become the United Nations. And third, he wanted to convince Stalin to enter the war against Japan once Germany was defeated in the west. It was this last point that would ultimately affect the future of Korea.

In early 1945 it was clear to America's military leaders that an invasion of the Japanese mainland would be a mammoth undertaking, and that the cost in American lives of that invasion would be difficult to justify to the American public. Roosevelt hoped to convince Stalin to enter the war in the east after the defeat of the Germans in Europe and aid in administering the final blows to Japan by attacking the Japanese forces on the Asian mainland, particularly in Manchuria. It was a plan that would save the lives of thousands of American boys, but it was clear that Stalin would agree to such a plan only if he received major concessions. In fact, FDR was very much in a beggar's position with this proposal; from the time of America's entrance into the war in late 1941 until the D-Day invasion of 1944, Stalin had pleaded with FDR to open a second front in Europe to relieve the Soviet army of the burden of fighting the entire German army alone. America, weighed down with its own problems in the Pacific, failed to come to Stalin's aid in a significant way before the summer of 1944. Now it was Roosevelt who was asking Stalin to relieve the pressure and aid American forces in the Pacific. Stalin would want concessions, and FDR would have to give them.

In hindsight, of course, FDR did not need the assistance of Soviet troops to defeat Japan. But the success of the atomic bomb was months away, and the probability of such a device becoming workable before the war's end could not be factored into Roosevelt's plans at Yalta. It seems fairly clear now that the Japanese might well have surrendered before an American invasion of the home islands would have become necessary. However, working from what he knew in February 1945, FDR believed that he needed the mass of the Red Army to defeat Japan, and he acted and entreated on that premise.

Stalin's demands were considerable, but they did not stand in the way of FDR's postwar plans for a greater Asia. In exchange for entering the war against Japan within a certain time following the defeat of Germany, the United States would not oppose Soviet control of Outer Mongolia through a puppet government there, the Kuril Islands (then in Japanese hands), the southern half of Sakhalin Island, control of Port Arthur in Manchuria, and joint operation with the Chinese of the major rail lines in Manchuria. In exchange, Soviet troops would move into Manchuria and engage the Japanese army there. They would also move into northern Korea.

Another part of this agreement would also ultimately affect Korea. Roosevelt insisted, and Stalin agreed, that the Soviets sign a treaty of friendship and alliance with Jiang and the Nationalist Chinese. This was important to FDR's greater plan for the Far East because it denied Soviet support to Mao and the Chinese Communists—still holed up in northern China but preparing to move south into areas abandoned by the retreating Japanese army. Roosevelt wanted a coalition govern-ment in China, made up of Nationalists and Communists, or more properly, the moderates from both groups. He believed that if Soviet aid was denied to Mao and the Communists (by a Soviet-Guomindang treaty) the Communists would be forced to join such a coalition, and, of course, a postwar Chinese civil war would be averted. Ultimately, how-ever, Roosevelt's plan failed—mainly because of the insurmountable ide-ological differences between the two groups, but also because Mao had little need for Soviet support against Jiang and his already-crumbling Guomindang.

Roosevelt was also willing to make these concessions at Yalta because he feared that Stalin might move unilaterally in Asia if some sort of coop-erative arrangement was not reached with the Soviets before the end of the Asian war. With U.S. forces engaged no closer to the Asian mainland than Okinawa in the summer of 1945, it would be impossible for the United States to deter any unilateral Soviet acquisitions or aggressions in Manchuria or Korea. FDR's goals at Yalta, at least as far as Asia was concerned, were to reach an accord with Stalin and prevent an outbreak of a civil war in China.

But all this broke down when Roosevelt died two months later and Harry Truman moved into the White House—with no preconceived notions about cooperation with Stalin. Added to this was a mounting distrust of Stalin among the American people as the Soviets continued to strengthen their positions in Eastern Europe. At the same time, the need for Soviet aid against Japan ended abruptly when Truman was notified in late July 1945 that the atomic bomb was a success.

When the Asian war ended in August 1945, Truman issued General Order #1, designed to limit any unilateral advance by the Soviets: Japanese forces on the Asian mainland were to surrender to the forces of the Guomindang, not the Chinese Communists; and the United States was to occupy the Japanese home islands alone. A message from Ambassador Edwin Pauley in Moscow convinced Truman that the United States needed to move quickly to counter Soviet moves in Asia: "Conclusions I have reached," Pauley wrote, "lead me to the belief that our forces should occupy quickly as much of the industrial areas of Korea and Manchuria as we can, starting at the southerly tip [of Korea], and progressing northward."[1] As Soviet troops rushed into Manchuria and then into Korea, the United States feared Soviet control of the entire Korean peninsula and proposed to the Soviets an arbitrary division of Korea. The dividing line was set at the 38th parallel. To the surprise of U.S. military experts, the Soviets accepted the proposal and halted their advance. To enforce the arrangement, the United States flew in troops from Okinawa. They occupied the American half of the peninsula, below the 38th parallel, early in September 1945. This was America's first act of containment in Asia; for the first time, the United States had drawn a line that was designed to contain Soviet expansion.

The final blow to the Yalta accords, and to Roosevelt's grand plan for a postwar Asia, came with the resumption of fighting between the Chinese Communists and the Guomindang Nationalists. When the Japanese war ended, both sides moved in to claim territory abandoned by the retreating Japanese troops. The Communists had their greatest successes in the countryside and in the north, while the Guomindang moved to occupy the infrastructure of China—its cities, ports, and railroads. Through 1946 it was clear that both sides were preparing for a resumption of their conflict, and despite attempts by Truman's special envoy, General George Marshall, to mediate a settlement, fighting broke out the next year. After two years of fighting, Jiang and the armies of the Guomindang were finally routed and crushed by Mao and his Red Army. Seeing that a Communist victory was inevitable, and being fed up with the graft and corruption in Jiang' s government, Truman distanced himself from the collapse. Jiang and his supporters escaped to the island of Formosa, and on October 1, 1949, Mao declared the People's Republic of China.

The fall of China to the Communists had a great impact on American politics for the next two and a half decades. Truman was forced to bear the blame for not coming to the aid of Jiang, a loyal ally in World War II, and for allowing the Communists to take over in China. Truman and the Democrats, the Republicans claimed, had "lost" China to the Communists. In response to this, and to other Republican attacks, Truman signed executive orders requiring oath-taking and investigations of suspected Communists employed by the federal government. All of this played hard on American politics and foreign policy in the postwar years. The Republicans continued to increase their pressure on the president to do something about the growing Communist menace, whether real or imagined, which led to an increase in get-tough rhetoric and get-tough action by the administration against the Soviets. America was moving toward the political center in the postwar years, becoming more politically moderate, and it soon became clear to Truman and his advisors that if the Democratic party was to remain in power through the decade they would have to jump on the anti-Communist bandwagon—at least to some degree. Politically it was the right move, and the strategy was partly responsible for Truman's surprising 1948 election victory. But diplomatically it was a mistake. Truman's anti-Communist belligerence exacerbated the already growing problems between the United States and the Soviets, and it was instrumental in pushing the world into a cold war.

In addition, several of Truman's advisors wanted a get-tough-with-Stalin stance and counseled the president to move unilaterally in Europe and Asia to head off what appeared to be Soviet expansionist tendencies. In a memo, written for the president in September 1946, a young Clark Clifford, then special counsel to the president, wrote:

> A direct threat to American security is implicit in Soviet foreign policy which is designed to prepare the Soviet Union for war with the leading capitalistic nations of the world. Soviet leaders recognize that the United States will be the Soviet Union's most powerful enemy if such a war as that predicted by Communist theory ever comes about and therefore the United States is the chief target of Soviet foreign and military policy.[2]

Clifford drew the information for this memo from several leading members of the foreign affairs constabulary in Washington. It was the first peacetime interagency foreign policy review of U.S.-Soviet relations, and it clearly carried a great deal of weight with Truman. At the same time, much of the same advice was coming from other corridors. In July 1947, in an article in the foreign policy journal *Foreign Affairs*, George F. Kennan wrote of the evils of Soviet communism, and of the USSR's desire to expand its borders and its influence. The United States, he wrote, should employ "a long-term, patient but firm and vigilant containment of Russian expansive tendencies" through the "application of counter-force at a series of constantly shifting geographical and political points." He went on to call for restraint and balance in this policy, but few paid attention to that aspect of Kennan's remarks.[3] The focus instead was now on the new catchword: "containment." Certainly, by 1950, when the Korean War broke out, rabid anticommunism was a pervasive factor in American society and politics, and in the administration's foreign policy.

There was a great deal of political unrest in Korea immediately after the war. A nationalist revolution broke out there, and forces of the Right and Left often fought for control of the government in the South. General Douglas MacArthur (governing the American sector of Korea from Tokyo) set up a military government in Seoul under General John Hodge. Hodge feared being blamed for a Communist takeover in the

South, and in response to that fear allied himself with the Far Right in the Korean internal conflict. He also kept the Japanese occupation system intact in the U.S. zone, which included making use of a brutal secret police force that had become the paramilitary arm of the right-wing. In the eyes of many Koreans this placed Hodge and his American troops in much the same position as the Japanese occupiers; and it also placed the Americans at odds with the political Left in the South. The result was that Hodge allowed the political Right to organize the government, restore order in the streets, and suppress the Left. By the end of 1945 Hodge had effectively crushed both the Left and Center, and had established a pro-American right-wing police state in the southern occupation zone of Korea.

Before the end of 1945 the U.S. military force in Korea was reduced to a sparse 45,000 men, reflecting Washington's postwar policy of military cutbacks; but it also exhibited a lack of concern for the events taking shape on the Korean peninsula. Hodge responded to the troop reductions by building a Korean constabulary force under the control of a group of right-wing military officers. It was this army (along with the police force) that would control the American occupation zone from the Far Right in the immediate postwar years.

Through 1946 several attempts were made to unify Korea, oddly enough as both sides became more and more ingrained and established in their own occupation zones. The first plan was an agreement for a five-year trusteeship under a united provisional government. But the U.S.-supported right wing in the South opposed this plan as just another form of imperialism, and rejected it outright. The North, however, supported the plan. In early 1947, the United States proposed free elections throughout the peninsula. The Soviets rejected this idea, but they presented their own plan for a single united legislative body designed to give the Communists in the North a majority. That plan was rejected by the Americans.

As the two sides distanced themselves from one another, the United States brought in Syngman Rhee to give some legitimacy to its occupation of the southern zone. Rhee was a fierce Korean nationalist and an ardent anticommunist who had spent most of his life working unsuccessfully to free Korea from Japan's imperialistic clutches. He was chosen because he had spent the war outside of Korea and had not collaborated with the Japanese, as had many political figures on the Right. In December 1946 a legislative assembly was set up in the South with Rhee and the Far Right in control.

Across the 38th parallel, the shape of things to come was also taking form. The Soviets, for the most part, kept their hands out of the affairs of northern Korea's government, although they did work to place pro-Soviet Communists into high office. Their main figure was Kim II Sung, a staunch Communist and ex-guerrilla commander in the war against Japan. He had definite ties to the Soviets, but none to Mao and the Chinese Communists. This was important in Kim's rise because the Soviets were suspect of those Korean Communists who had served with Mao, whom they considered an adventurer working outside the Marxist-Leninist guidelines as defined by Moscow. Kim was poorly educated (although he may have attended Soviet military schools) and easily manipulated by the Soviets. But as events would show, he was not a dupe of Moscow.

As the two governments, North and South, formed under their local leaders, the last attempts at unification failed. In September 1947 the fledgling United Nations took on the task of unifying Korea. A temporary commission was set up to observe a nationwide election on the peninsula, but when the commission was denied entrance into North Korea it recommended elections in the South only. That finally occurred on May 10, 1948, with Rhee and his rightists winning a large majority. On August 15, 1948, Rhee proclaimed the Republic of Korea and denounced the North for its obstruction of the unification process. In December the new nation received a seat in the United Nations as the only legitimate Korean government. The North responded in kind by creating the Democratic People's Republic of Korea with its capital at Pyongyang and Kim as its president. In his inaugural address Kim declared his government to be the only legitimate Korean government, and then denounced the South for obstructing Korean unification. The country was divided: Two opposing governments were set up, one right-wing and capitalist, the other Communist. They were antagonists, each led by a belligerent dictator who hoped to unite the country under his personal leadership. And each was backed by one of the opposing super forces in the growing cold war.

By 1947 further budget concerns in Washington had forced an additional cut in U.S. troop numbers in Korea. Hodge responded by making it clear to the Pentagon that his depleted force was not strong enough to maintain a military post on the Asian mainland in the face of the huge Red Army assembled across the 38th parallel. The Joint Chiefs in Washington agreed and responded by planning for a complete unilateral withdrawal of American forces from Korea; in the event of an outbreak of hostilities on the Korean peninsula, the Joint Chiefs concluded that the United States could rely on its superior air force, then based at Okinawa, to deal with the problem. But just as that decision was being made in Washington in September 1947, the Soviets proposed a bilateral withdrawal of forces from both sides. This provided the United States with an easy way out of the growing mess in Korea: hand the whole problem over to the UN for settlement. It was decided in Washington that the occupation of Korea had become more expensive than the situation there warranted—and it was a time when the cold war in Europe was taking priority over situations else-where in the world. In addition, the Joint Chiefs (which included Dwight Eisenhower as the Army Chief of Staff) concluded that Korea really had little strategic value, and stated in a report that military action in the defense of South Korea would be "ill-advised." This report, however, also suggested that in the event of a North Korean invasion of the South, the United States might become one part of a UN-sponsored police action that would include other nations.[4] It was clear that South Korea held little strategic importance for the Joint Chiefs in mid-1948, and that they had no intention of unilaterally committing U.S. forces to a military struggle with the Communists on the Asian mainland.

The withdrawal of troops from the two sides began in September 1948. In place of the departing soldiers, both the United States and the Soviet Union created local armies to hold the line against the other side. The last Americans left in the summer of 1949, leaving behind a force of 50,000 U.S.-trained Korean soldiers, as well as some small arms, some obsolete artillery, and a few trucks. The departing Americans were instructed by Washington not to leave behind tanks or aircraft. Clearly, Washington did not trust Rhee. He had promised often, in a number of belligerent speeches, that given the chance he would invade the North and unite Korea under his own leadership.

The U.S. military withdrawal was accompanied by little fanfare. It had no effect on the presidential election of 1948—a time when it was popular for a candidate to tag his opponent as soft on Communism. For most Americans in the summer and fall of 1948, Korea was remote, poverty stricken, and generally worthless—not worth defending. Besides, the United States had successfully built a perimeter of friendly nations around the Soviet Union in Asia, with defenses in Alaska, the Aleutian Islands, Japan, Formosa, and then to the south in the Philippines. There was no need, so it seemed, for the United States to have troops on the Asian mainland.

But the character of the cold war changed in 1949 when America's monopoly on the atom bomb came to an abrupt end and China fell to Mao and the Chinese Communists. America's power was no longer uncontested, and the world's most populous nation had joined the Communist bloc. The result was a general fear that these Communist victories were the result of a conspiracy of international communism, and that communism was slowly eating away at the free world, bit by bit. Although Truman was blamed for the "loss" of China, Americans began to see the wisdom in the president's policy of containment. Now, with the bomb and China both in Soviet hands, it seemed clear that the United States must move forward to contain the evils of expanding communism.

In April 1950 President Truman was presented with a document that significantly changed the course of American foreign policy; it also became an important focal point for U.S. operations in Korea. National Security Council Paper Number 68, or NSC-68, was to become one of the key documents in American foreign policy for the next twenty years.

Written by Secretary of State Dean Acheson and Paul Nitze of the State Department's policy planning staff, NSC-68 argued that "any substantial further extension of the area under the domination of the Kremlin would raise the possibility that no coalition adequate to confront the Kremlin with greater strength could be assembled." The report asserted, "The assault on free institutions is world-wide now and in the context of the present polarization of power a defeat of free institutions

North Korean Offensive
(June 25, 1950)

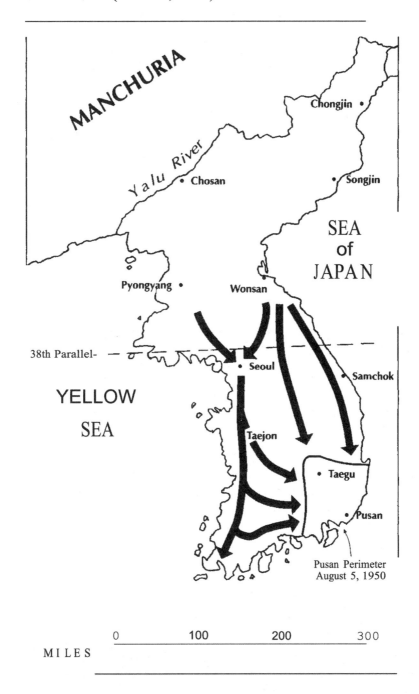

anywhere is a defeat everywhere." NSC-68 also evoked the old myth of monolithic communism, that Communists worldwide were of one mind, which was directed from the Kremlin; and of one goal: to control the world. "The Soviet Union is developing the military capacity to support its design for world domination," the report claimed. The definitive proof, so it seemed, was the Sino-Soviet alliance signed between Stalin and Mao in February 1950. NSC-68, with its myth of monolithic communism, would be the basis of the mistaken belief by American foreign policy experts that the North Korean invasion (just three months away) must have been commanded directly from Moscow. NSC-68 also argued that the United States must not allow the Soviet Union to thwart the actions of the United Nations; at the same time it gave Truman and his advisors the justification for using the United Nations as a tool of American foreign policy to contain Soviet expansion wherever possible. "The overthrow . . . of a regime established under the aegis of the UN would . . . constitute a severe blow to the prestige and influence of the UN; in this respect the interests of the US are parallel to, if not identical with, those of the UN." The document also said that controlling certain Soviet strong points would no longer be adequate, that the United States must employ a much stronger defensive perimeter system made up of friendly nations surrounding, and thus containing, the Communist bloc. All this, of course, would take a massive military rebuilding, considerable tax increases, and "a government-created 'consensus' on the necessity of 'sacrifice' and 'unity' by Americans."[5]

The Joint Chiefs agreed with NSC-68, but Truman, beset by severe budget constraints, brushed the report aside as too costly. However, in September, three months after North Korea launched its invasion, Truman accepted NSC-68, and it became the point guard of American foreign policy for the next twenty years.

It seems clear today that Acheson and Nitze exaggerated the Soviet threat to the West. Soviet intentions were much more defensive than offensive during this period; in addition, the concept of monolithic communism proved to be a myth. The entire document oversimplified the situation and drew dangerously alarmist conclusions when none were apparent. Possibly, one of the most tragic aspects of this era is that the framers of NSC-68 counseled U.S politicians and diplomats that the

United States should shun negotiations with Moscow—at the very time when the Soviets were rapidly moving toward a policy that would later be called "peaceful co-existence." But in 1950, Americans had developed a great fear of the growing menace of communism, and NSC-68 reflected that fear. The result of NSC-68 was an immediate mass armament buildup, and within a year the first cold war arms race was well under way.

In the last few months before the outbreak of the war in Korea, American foreign policy was ambiguous at best, sending mixed signals to the world. The Truman Doctrine (now the institutionalization of the containment policy) had stated firmly that the United States would aid any nation fighting communism. However, in January 1950 at the National Press Club in Washington, Secretary of State Acheson told his audience of influential newsmen that the United States had succeeded in establishing a defense perimeter in the Far East that included the Aleutian Islands in the north, as well as Japan, Okinawa, and the Philippines—thus excluding both Korea and Formosa. The rest of Asia, he said, could not expect American military support. They should instead look to "the commitment of the entire civilized world under the Charter of the United Nations which so far has not proved a weak reed to lean on by any people who are determined to protect their independence against outside aggression."[6] It seemed evident that Korea, Formosa, and the rest of Asia were now excluded from the U.S. defense perimeter and would have to defend themselves any way they could. Acheson's speech might well have been a clear message to the North Koreans that the United States would not run to the defense of South Korea.

In these days of fiscal austerity before the adoption of NSC-68, Acheson's speech certainly reflected the administration's budget considerations, along with a new foreign policy revelation that the United States simply could not afford to defend the entire free world. Congress and the president in this period were under great pressure from the electorate to cut spending and move toward a balanced budget, and it was on military spending that the budget axe was falling the hardest. "While the Russians put half their total effort into creating military power," Acheson recalled later, "our air force no longer had a monopoly of atomic weapons; our army had been demobilized and our navy put in mothballs."[7] Budget constraints had forced the administration to remove U.S. troops from

South Korea and then finally to abandon Korea and Formosa entirely. But when the war in Korea broke out all that changed. NSC-68 took over as the foreign policy directive in Washington, and economic considerations quickly took a backseat to a containment-at-all-costs policy and an accompanying tremendous American military buildup.

The attack by the North Koreans on June 25, 1950, caught policy makers in the West completely off guard. Apparently MacArthur, at his headquarters in Japan, was aware that there was a sizable military buildup, as well as troop movements north of the 38th parallel; and the State Department had received word in April that Communist military activity was heightening somewhere in Asia—but they had eliminated North Korea because they believed Kim would not attack.[8] If there was to be a Communist military thrust in Asia, Washington analysts agreed, it would probably come in Formosa or Indochina, areas perceived as much more volatile than Korea. The signals had not set off any alarms in Seoul, Tokyo, or Washington. Much of the South Korean army was off on furlough, and only one lone rifle company was stationed near the 38th parallel on the day of the invasion.

The timing of the attack is still a mystery. Kim had made numerous trips to Moscow to convince Stalin that the people in the South would join him if he attacked. In addition, he argued, the United States would not intervene because it had not helped Jiang against Mao in 1949. Kim convinced Stalin and was given the weapons of the Soviet 25th Army, but was told, however, to look to Beijing for additional aid if, as Stalin told him, "you are kicked in the teeth."[9] In January, the Soviet Union had walked out of the UN Security Council in protest over U.S. demands that Formosa (rather than Mao's mainland China) be recognized by the United Nations. Consequently, there was no Soviet Security Council veto to stop a UN-sponsored military response to the North Korean invasion. Clearly, the Soviets had been left in the dark as to the timing of the North Korean attack. Even the North Koreans were only partially prepared for the invasion. Mobilization of their army at the 38th parallel was incomplete and several scheduled Soviet weapons shipments had not yet arrived. Possibly Kim realized the importance of a surprise attack and concluded in June that if he waited an additional two months to move his entire army into position his intentions would be discovered. That would give the United

States enough time to gauge its own public opinion and then respond from Japan, either with its own troops or possibly by strengthening ROK (Republic of Korea) forces with tanks, artillery, U.S.-piloted aircraft, and advisors. If, however, he affected a lightning attack and unified the peninsula before the United States could respond, the Americans might allow the unification to stand without a military response.

Nikita Khrushchev wrote in his memoirs that Stalin had acquiesced in the North Korean attack on the South, but the time for the attack had not been set.[10] Stalin was certainly sympathetic to Kim's desire to unify his nation and to bring Communism to the rest of Korea. He must also have realized that the fall of South Korea would do little to damage Washington's anti-Soviet defense perimeter in East Asia. To the rest of the world, however, another American loss on the Asian mainland would demonstrate clearly that it was the Soviets in Moscow, and not the Americans in Tokyo, who would be dictating the future of the Far East.

Truman's decision to intervene was made quickly—some have said possibly too quickly. However, faced with a foreign policy stance and a domestic political climate that left him little room for contemplation or reflection, it should be no surprise that his decision to intervene was a quick one. He was notified by Acheson of the invasion at his home in Independence, Missouri, on Saturday evening, June 24, 1950. The next afternoon he was in Washington. In that intervening time Acheson and other State Department operatives had decided that intervention through the UN was the best course of action. Truman quickly agreed. UN Secretary-General Trygve Lie was notified and he too approved the plan. While Truman was still in Independence, the UN Security Council met and approved a resolution condemning the North Korean action and calling on the North Koreans to withdraw. Within twelve hours, Truman was back in Washington, and plans were already being drawn up to get U.S. troops on the Korean peninsula as quickly as possible. Acheson met the president at National Airport in Washington. "By God," Truman told Acheson, "I am going to let them have it."[11] In the limousine on the way from the airport, Truman told Secretary of Defense Louis Johnson that he intended to "hit them hard."[12] Clearly, Truman had made his decision.

On Sunday evening Truman met with the chief military and foreign affairs figures from the Pentagon and the State Department at Blair House, where the president and his family had been shuffled during White House renovations. The situation in Korea was blurred by the insistence of the American ambassador in Seoul, John Muccio, that the army of the ROK was the best army in Asia and that eventually it would push the North Koreans back north of the 38th parallel. The United States, he advised, need only supply ammunition and air support to the ROK army.

Many of those at the Blair House meeting, however, were looking at the bigger picture. The chairman of the Joint Chiefs, General Omar Bradley, speculated that the Korean invasion was a feint to draw U.S. troops into farthest eastern Asia while the main thrust against U.S. and Allied forces was planned for Western Europe; or that Korea was simply the first of a number of hot spots that were about to open up all over the world, including Formosa, Indochina, Iran, Turkey, and Greece. Bradley, moreover, argued, "We must draw the line somewhere," and Korea "offered as good an occasion for drawing the line as anywhere else."[13] Acheson agreed. But both men expected that Communist thrusts against Indochina and Formosa could come at any moment.[14]

Following the Blair House meeting, Acheson showed Truman a letter from newly appointed State Department consultant John Foster Dulles. Dulles had recently returned from Korea, and he had speculated in a letter to Acheson that North Korea might launch an attack on the South. If the Republic of Korea cannot repulse an attack from the North, Dulles wrote, "U.S. force should be used even though this risks Russian countermoves. To sit by while Korea is overrun by [an] unprovoked armed attack would start a disastrous chain of events leading most probably to world war."[15] Dulles's letter fit well into Truman's own analysis of the situation.

Why should Truman react to the situation in Korea with the full force of the U.S. military when just months before he had allowed mainland China to fall into Communist hands with barely a protest? It was, in fact, just because Truman had "lost" China to the Communists that he felt compelled to use aggression in Korea. By the summer of 1950 American domestic politics had become a major factor behind Truman's decision to intervene in Korea. In February, Wisconsin senator Joseph McCarthy had made his first charges that Communists had infiltrated the State Department—and the nation's second Red Scare in the twentieth century quickly accelerated. Alger Hiss had been tried for espionage before the nation. The trial of spy Klaus Fuchs in England had led to the exposure of Julius and Ethel Rosenberg as spies in the United States. At the same time, the Republicans (looking for a big victory in the 1950 congressional elections) had joined forces with the powerful Formosan-based anti-Communist interest group known as the "China Lobby" to make it as clear as possible to American voters that Truman and the Democrats had "lost" China to communism. McCarthy and his associates had accused Truman of being "soft on communism," and Acheson of "harboring Communists at the State Department." By the summer of 1950 anti-Communism had developed into the most powerful political issue of the time. In this charged political climate, the politics of McCarthyism and the politics of Korea became one and the same. From this standpoint, Truman could do little else but intervene.

But there were other factors. Truman also feared for the future of the United Nations. If something was not done to halt the North Korean invasion, the president believed, the UN would lose credibility and possibly its future would be jeopardized. "We can't let down the UN," he told an aide.[16] Truman told a chief advisor that he would not stand by and allow the UN to go the way of the League of Nations.[17] In his memoirs he wrote: "The foundations and the principles of the United Nations were at stake unless this unprovoked attack on Korea could be stopped."[18] After all, the UN was an American creation; its credibility would have to be protected. For the United States to allow the UN to be undermined in Korea might undermine anti-Communist forces elsewhere in the world, such as in Indochina.

Truman was also looking at those now-ingrained lessons of World War II: the Munich Syndrome and appeasement. To General Hoyt Vandenburg, Air Force chief of staff, Truman wrote: "The present Russian feeler in Korea is an exact imitation of Japan in Manchuria; Hitler in the Rhineland and Mussolini in Ethiopia."[19] In his memoirs he wrote of his thoughts while flying from Independence to Washington on that Sunday afternoon, the day after the invasion:

> Communism was acting in Korea just as Hitler, Mussolini, and the Japanese had acted ten, fifteen, and twenty years earlier. I felt that if South Korea was allowed to fall Communist leaders would

be emboldened to override [other] nations. . . . If the Communists were permitted to force their way into the Republic of Korea without opposition from the free world, no small nation would have the courage to resist threats and aggression by stronger Communist neighbors. If this was allowed to go unchallenged it would mean a third world war, just as similar incidents had brought on the second world war.[20]

Truman was also concerned about America's place in the new postwar world order. The nations of the new emerging world had to be shown that the United States was willing to stand up, as it had promised it would, to Communist aggression anywhere in the world. Not to intervene in Korea was to admit that America's promises had been empty threats. And empty threats, Truman believed, would have simply invited further Communist aggressions. Also, the United States had just orchestrated the formation of the North Atlantic Treaty Organization (NATO) in Europe. Truman could not let down America's new partners. He had to show force against the Communists in Korea if he was to maintain U.S. prestige worldwide.

The Korean attack also seemed to prove that NSC-68 was right on target, that the Communists were trying, in fact, to expand their borders and that if the United States did not move to stop that expansion the result would be devastating for America and for the future of the free world. Truman did not approve NSC-68 until September, but immediately after the North Korean invasion in June he began a massive buildup of the type called for in NSC-68 to confront Communist aggressions throughout the world.

Truman was being pushed from two sides to intervene in Korea. His foreign policy, based on Clifford's memo, NSC-68, and his own Truman Doctrine, called for containment of Communist aggressions. At the same time, political pressures from the Republicans and the anti-Communists in his own party pushed him hard to stand up to Communist expansion. His "loss" of China had hurt him badly in the polls. Truman, in his own mind, had no choice but to intervene in Korea. It is no wonder that his decision came quickly.

Support from the United Nations came in the form of two resolutions. The first called for a North Korean withdrawal; the second recommended that the "members of the United Nations furnish such assistance to the Republic of Korea as may be necessary to repel the armed attack and to restore international peace and security in the area."[21] This was to be the legitimization of hostilities against the North by the United States and its allies. These resolutions allowed the United States to use the UN as a vehicle for intervention in Korea and to further the objectives of its own foreign policy of containment as stated in the Truman Doctrine and then expanded in NSC-68. The war would be fought under U.S. direction to achieve American ends.

The American attitude toward Korea had changed in just a few hours. Korea had been, generally, an area of the world somewhere outside the U.S. strategic perimeter. It had little strategic value because of budget constraints in Washington that demanded military cutbacks—with the result that Korean defenses had been cut to the bone. There had been no effort to maintain forces in Korea, or even to establish an effective defense on the peninsula. It was not one of the hot spots of the growing cold war like Berlin, Iran, or Southeast Asia. But once attacked in June 1950, Korea became, in the minds of American policy makers, the first domino, the first line of defense. It evoked the memory of Munich and the disastrous diplomacy of "peace in our time," and appeasement. Policy makers also believed that the situation in Korea was an example—a message to be sent to the rest of the world that the United States would be the one to put a stop to Communist aggression; it would show other nations that they could rely on the forces of the United States if they were attacked by the forces of communism, and that other nations would not now be allowed to go the way of China. America's prestige was at stake, and of all the reasons the United States intervened in Korea in 1950, the maintenance of U.S. credibility with the rest of the world was by far the most important. America intended to become the world leader after World War II; Moscow challenged that aspiration. But U.S. action in Korea was designed to prove to the world that America, and not the Soviet Union, was the most deserving of that leadership role.

The Korean War was a new stage in the cold war. At home Americans again felt confident that they were fighting on the right side and for the right reasons. Allied and UN involvement legitimized the actions. The U.S. military, it seemed, was again leading the world against the dark forces of aggression.

2

ACROSS THE PARALLEL AND INTO STALEMATE

On Monday, June 26, Truman met again with his Pentagon and State Department advisors at Blair House. On that day Ambassador Muccio had wired from Korea that things there were not going quite as he expected. Rhee had fled Seoul in advance of the approaching North Korean tanks, and the situation was disintegrating rapidly. MacArthur wired even worse news:

> South Korean units unable to resist determined Northern offensive. Contributory factor exclusive enemy possession of tanks and fighter planes. South Korean casualties as an index to fighting have not shown adequate resistance capabilities or the will to fight and our estimate is that a complete collapse is imminent.[1]

Truman reacted to these grim reports by allowing air strikes into South Korea (but not above the 38th parallel). Unknown to the president, however, MacArthur had already ordered U.S. bombing raids in the South. MacArthur's actions here were a foreshadowing of problems to come between the president and his commanding officer.

Truman resisted sending in ground forces immediately because his Air Force generals insisted that the invasion could be repulsed through the sole use of air power. It was the beginning of a conflict that would rage on in all of America's Asian wars: Could the conflict be won through the exclusive use of air power, and thus reduce U.S. casualties? The Air Force would always insist that it could. The Army would argue that ground forces alone are capable of dislodging an enemy and occupying land. Truman soon began listening to his Army generals, particularly MacArthur, who convinced him that the war ultimately would be won on the ground. The enemy would have to be removed from South Korea, MacArthur argued, if the United States were to achieve its goals there. Truman quickly realized that the consequences of failure in Korea were too great; he decided to send in troops. Deferring to the fears of Acheson and Bradley that Korea was only one of several Communist thrusts to come, Truman authorized both financial aid and a military mission to the French in Indochina—the nation's first commitment to the Indochina war. Truman also ordered the 7th Fleet to the straits between Formosa and mainland China. There had been reports that Mao was massing troops across the straits from Formosa and was planning to invade the island should the United States become occupied in Korea; others feared that Jiang, on the other end, might choose the occasion to invade the mainland. Truman wanted to guard against both. A second outbreak of war on the Asian continent might necessarily involve the United States and divide the American effort. Chinese premier Chou Enlai issued a public statement calling the U.S. action "armed aggression against the territory of China."[2] But in fact Mao probably welcomed the U.S. interposition. It allowed him to transfer some 30,000 troops from Fujian province on the Formosa Strait to Liaoning province in the north, just across the Yalu River from North Korea.

Truman understood immediately the necessity of a limited response in Korea, that America could not become involved in an all-out war of the type it had fought so successfully in World War II. It was the right decision, and the Joint Chiefs supported him completely. However, he would be criticized severely for restraining American power, for not using all of the nation's resources in an effort to achieve total victory. But Truman realized the need for a limited war because of the possibility of Chinese and Soviet countermoves, and ultimately the outbreak of a third world war. "We must be damned careful," he said. "We want to take any steps we have to push the Koreans behind the line, but I don't want to get us overcommitted to a whole lot of other things that could mean war."[3]

He also knew that the Soviet and Chinese troop strength was massive, outnumbering anything the Americans could put into the field in Asia— or anywhere. Despite the U.S. advantages in air power, a ground war against the Soviets and their Chinese ally would have been devastating, possibly leading to a nuclear confrontation.

Truman's idea of how the war in Korea should be fought clashed with those of MacArthur, and several others on the political Right and many within the military constabulary. Eisenhower wrote in his diary as the Korean situation began to escalate in the last days of June: "An appeal to force cannot, by its nature, be a partial one."[4] The limited war in Korea also set the standard by which the Vietnam War would be fought. It was a war strategy that few understood in 1950. It was a war strategy necessitated by politics and foreign policy, and not by raw military power.

Then what kind of war was it? The Constitution was clear; Congress (and only Congress) had the power to declare war. Would Truman declare war on North Korea? On June 29 at his press conference announcing American involvement in Korea, Truman referred to the war as a "police action."[5] The United States had been involved in police actions before, particularly in South and Central America, but as casualty lists began coming in from Korea, and war photographs began appearing in press reports, it became obvious that Truman's police action was nothing less than a war of major magnitude and consequences. The president, of course, never conceded that it was anything more than a police action, but he was haunted by the term until he left office. It also raised questions for the future. Would the United States become involved in similar police actions throughout the world? Was the United States destined to become the policeman of the world? Such a thought seemed like an ominous responsibility to many Americans in 1950.

On June 30, Truman authorized the use of American ground combat forces, at MacArthur's request, as the only method to halt the rapid advance of Kim's army. In just five days Truman had committed the United States to a war in Korea. Among Truman's advisors there were no dissenters. The only question being bandied around by policy makers was whether the Communists had broader intentions than simply the attack over the 38th parallel, or was this an isolated conflict? The Soviet reply to the U.S. action in Korea was characteristically bellicose and stern, but the responses from Moscow also made it clear that the Soviets had no intention of intervening on the part of the North Koreans so long as the war did not expand or threaten Soviet integrity. However, George Kennan and a number of other advisors in the State Department and the Pentagon warned throughout the war that the Soviets might in fact intervene should the United States carry the war into North Korea. The Chinese responded to American intervention in the conflict with more fervor, immediately making threats to intervene under certain circumstances. Within a week, Truman and his advisors were certain that the Soviets would not intervene as long as the war was contained, and that the Chinese had little desire to do so. Acheson and Bradley had been wrong; there was no Communist grand design, no concert of Communist power preparing to attack U.S. interests from all sides on two continents.

By June 30, Truman was confronted with a question, the magnitude of which he could not have fathomed. Should he ask Congress for approval to go to war in Korea? The same question would confront Lyndon Johnson in 1964, George H. W. Bush in 1990, and George W. Bush in 2001. Truman discussed the question with Senator Tom Connally, who advised the president: "You might run into a long debate . . . which would tie your hands completely."[6] Connally also advised Truman that under the UN charter the president had no obligation to consult Congress. The same advice came from General Bradley and Secretary of Defense Louis Johnson. All agreed that most congressmen approved of the action anyway, and that a small minority opposing intervention might slow the congressional mandate, and that would be dangerous to America's effective action in Korea and to the nation's morale in the face of the crisis. Truman took the advice and chose not to ask Congress for an authorization to send in U.S. troops. However, when the war went sour the nation placed the blame at Truman's feet. It would be a lesson for the future.

Another mistake was the failure of the administration to establish simple war objectives. Would the United States settle for containment, whereby the enemy would be pushed back behind the 38th parallel into North Korea; or would the United States try to do what Syngman Rhee wanted and unite North and South Korea, thus risking Communist Chinese or even Soviet intervention? These questions were apparently never asked—and consequently never answered. John Foster Dulles pushed Truman and the administration hard, as early as the end of July, to authorize U.S. troops to attack into North Korea and unite the peninsula. Warren Austin, the U.S. representative on the UN Security Council, agreed, often referring to the impossibility of leaving Korea "half slave and half free." But George Kennan and other moderate-minded diplomats at the State Department believed that the United States should not go beyond bringing an end to the fighting at the 38th parallel. Kennan later recalled that there simply was not a policy in Washington, no goals or objectives had been set: "The Korean attack had stirred us all up like a stone thrown into a beehive. People went buzzing and milling around, each with his own idea of what we were trying to do. . . . Never before," he entered in his diary in mid-August, "has there been such utter confusion in the public mind with respect to U.S. foreign policy."[7] The lack of objectives in Korea would bring indecision later, and serve as a lesson for the future.

Just forty-eight hours after the invasion, the ROK troops were already beginning to disintegrate. The North Korean Soviet-made T-34 tanks, about 120 to 150 in all, were crushing the South Koreans and forcing rapid retreats south. There was nothing in the ROK arsenal to defend against such advanced mechanized power. In addition, the North Koreans were well trained, and were even experienced in the type of war being fought on the Korean peninsula. Fully one third of the North Korean soldiers had fought with Mao's Communists against the Chinese Nationalists, and many were veterans of the guerrilla war fought in China and Korea against Japan. The North Korean army probably crossed the 38th parallel at about 135,000 strong, softening the enemy ahead with heavy artillery and mortar fire. They also had air support from about 180 Soviet-built planes. They were a formidable force.

In the South, the army of the ROK numbered about 95,000. They had no tanks, no antitank weapons, no heavy artillery, and no air support. They had some artillery, mostly obsolete U.S. World War II surplus—and small compared to the firepower of the North Koreans. This weakness reflected America's distrust of Syngman Rhee, who had often threatened to invade North Korea in the name of Korean unity. American policy makers opposed such a move, so they refused to provide Rhee with the means to carry out his plans. It also reflected budget constraints in Washington, and the State Department's contention that Korea was not strategic to the United States' defense perimeter in Asia. And it showed that the United States had not seriously considered an attack from the North.

At MacArthur's request two U.S. divisions were rushed into Korea from Japan on July 1. But in the summer of 1950 the United States armed forces were hardly the answer to South Korea's military problems. Foreign policy and military planners in Washington had come to rely on the atomic bomb as the nation's first line of defense, while conventional forces had been allowed to atrophy. Underfunded, undersupplied, and less than well trained, the U.S. Army in 1950 was not what it had been just five years earlier. In 1945 there were over eight million men in uniform; in 1950 there were less than 600,000. Washington spent only $5 billion on the military in 1950, less than one-tenth of what was spent in 1945. And with the exception of jet fighters, the United States had little that was new in fighting equipment. In fact, through the greater part of the war in Korea, U.S. forces fought mostly with World War II surplus matériel. NSC-68 would change much of this, but in the summer of 1950 America was weak in its ability to deter a conventional ground offensive, particularly one on the Asian mainland.

The North Koreans, attacking across the 38th parallel on June 25 (June 24 in the United States), advanced with their greatest force from the west and made a dash for Seoul, passing first through Munsan and Uijongbu. Seoul fell on June 27. The main North Korean force then headed south, where it met and pushed back the U.S. 24th Infantry Division near Osan. From there, one force moved west along Korea's west coast to Kunsan, while the main thrust veered off to the southeast in pursuit of the 24th Infantry toward Taejon. At the same time, two secondary pushes held the North Korean flanks in the east. One of these attacked initially through Chunchon and then moved south through the central mountains to Wonju and Yechon, pushing back ROK forces with little difficulty as it advanced. A third force followed the eastern coastline, almost unopposed to Yongdok. As the main force moved to take Taegu in the last days of July, the three North Korean forces converged in an arc around Pusan in the southeast corner of the peninsula.

They pushed back the U.S. 24th and 25th Infantry Divisions and the 1st Cavalry Division in the west, and ROK divisions in the north. On August 5, U.S. forces held the west flank of what became known as the "Pusan Perimeter." The army of the ROK held the northern end of the arc.

MacArthur's man on the ground was Lieutenant General Walton H. Walker, known to his men as "Johnnie." A veteran of World War I and one of General George Patton's corps commanders in World War II, Walker was about as tough as they came in the U.S. Army. He was not liked by his junior officers, and he often gave stand-or-die orders to his men in the field. He hated the press, and he often let the press know it. The unifying factor in Walker's personality was his stubbornness. It is Walker and this stubbornness that is usually credited with holding the Pusan Perimeter through the late summer of 1950.

With little difficulty, UN pilots quickly gained control of the skies over both North and South Korea. The U.S. Navy took control of the shorelines, also with little resistance. But it was the ground war that defined the war in Korea, and it was on the ground that UN forces were having the most difficulty. Their main problem was the T-34 tanks, probably the most formidable tank built for its time. The army of the ROK made no pretense of stopping these monsters, and the first American forces were no more effective, as the tanks lumbered southward nearly unopposed.

Inside the Pusan Perimeter, U.S. and ROK forces numbered about 92,000 combat soldiers. The North Koreans, outnumbered now but still on the offensive, had been reduced to about 70,000.

U.S. troops had fared badly in combat. Walker often complained of the difficulty in keeping his men on the battle line. In these first months of the war, American soldiers were often accused of fleeing the battlefield, even leaving wounded soldiers on the field in their wake. The fast-moving North Koreans often tore through American lines. On July 29, as the enemy began its last surges toward Pusan, Walker ordered his men to hold their positions or die trying. "There will be no more retreating, withdrawal, or readjustment of lines or any other terms you choose." Defeat at Pusan, he added, "would be one of the greatest butcheries in history. We must fight until the end. . . . If some of us must die, we will die fighting together."[8] It was clear that major engagements were coming, and Walker would need every man on the line.

In August the North Koreans made several big pushes, intent on breaking through the Pusan Perimeter. On August 5, the North Korean 4th Division pushed hard against the southern end of the perimeter near the confluence of the Naktong and Nam rivers. After two weeks of on-and-off fighting, the reinforced 25th Infantry Division pushed the North Koreans out of the area. In the second week of August, the North Koreans hit hard at ROK forces in the center of the perimeter near Taegu and Waegwan. But the ROK, with U.S. reinforcements, held the charge. Near Yongdok along the east coast, North Korean troops began moving south toward the U.S. airfield at Yonil. It looked like they might break through there, but they withdrew after only minor resistance, apparently low on matériel and too far from their supply lines. By mid-August, UN forces and supplies began flooding into the Pusan Perimeter, including U.S. tanks and antitank weapons. On September 1, the North Koreans made one last desperate attempt to push through the perimeter lines. But by then it was clear that the tide had changed in favor of the UN forces. There were now eight American divisions in the perimeter and several regimental combat teams. Walker began planning his counteroffensive.

Truman's decisiveness in handling the situation in Korea sat well with the American people. The enemy was shown to be evil: reports of North Korean atrocities were spread liberally in the news, and there was the important factor that the United States was fighting as one of many nations in a "police action" or resolving a "conflict" under the UN flag. Americans saw the enemy as a clear and present aggressor, and to add to this villainy North Korea was a Communist aggressor trying to spread its disease to the rest of the world. Generally, Republican dissension quieted, and Truman's ratings rose steadily in the polls. Korea had all the ingredients of a good war.

In July the UN asked Truman to name a commander of all the UN forces in Korea, and Truman chose MacArthur. Because of MacArthur's past achievements and his reputation among the nation's soldiers, it can hardly be called a bad decision. In fact, Truman would have had a difficult time choosing another man for the job; there was no one in 1950 who knew more about the Asian theater than MacArthur. Despite the multinational character of the Allied war in Korea, MacArthur's command was clearly an American affair from the beginning. The other fifteen UN nations that sent forces had little effect on the outcome of the war, or even on the day-to-day events. MacArthur directed the war entirely, and his commanders in the field were all Americans. The other UN forces fought within their own outfits under their own commanders, but it was the Americans who ran the show on the military side, and from Washington in the diplomatic arena.

The Korean War proved to be the catalyst needed to implement NSC-68. When first submitted to Truman in April 1950, the president filed it away as an outrageously expensive plan. For the country to rearm as suggested by NSC-68 would take a significant tax increase, and the federal budget would be forced well out of balance. Such actions in times of peace were politically unwise. If nothing else, the American people would not support a tax increase. But Korea changed all that. There was an obvious need for a dramatic increase in military spending as American forces fought the forces of communism in Asia. By July 1950 Truman was preparing to spend the money necessary to conduct the war in Korea, and by September he officially implemented NSC-68 as a statement of U.S. policy. In fiscal 1951 the president requested $13.5 billion for defense. The final authorization that year was over $48 billion. Government spending on defense would expand the economy and that expansion would pay for more arms. What has come to be known in America as the "military-industrial complex" had its origins here; the U.S. global buildup had begun.

Just as NSC-68 was being made a part of the official U.S. policy, U.S. forces were retreating down the Korean peninsula to the Pusan Perimeter. The situation seemed severe: the U.S. and ROK armies were being pushed back with their backs to the Sea of Japan. But the U.S. military strategists inside the perimeter had come to realize that the situation there was not quite as bad as it first appeared. The current situation on the peninsula had developed for three reasons: (1) the June invasion was a surprise; (2) the abilities of the army of the ROK had been greatly overestimated; and (3) the North Korean tanks had given the enemy a significant battlefield advantage. The UN forces had overcome the first problem; the second was no longer a factor now that reinforcements had arrived; and it would not be long before U.S. tanks and antitank weapons would solve the last problem. Despite significant progress toward turning the war around, U.S. newspapers continued to report that UN troops were seriously outnumbered and seriously out-gunned. But the North Korean troops were clearly exhausted and far from their lines of supply—and those lines were being battered daily by U.S. air power. They had also lost nearly one-fourth of their tanks, and attrition had reduced their manpower on the front lines. Although MacArthur was calling for more and more reinforcements to hold the line against the invaders, most military leaders had come to believe by mid-July that it was only a matter of time before the United States could get the troop numbers, the air support, and the tanks necessary to push the North Koreans back. In Washington, as early as the end of July, John Foster Dulles, Dean Rusk, Warren Austin, and others, seeing victory ahead, were already arguing for an advance across the 38th parallel into North Korea.

The United States had created a dictatorship and a police state in South Korea under Syngman Rhee. He was, at best, an uncomfortable partner. Before the invasion, and before U.S. troops arrived to aid the South, Rhee's atrocities against his own citizens, and his bellicose statements made in the name of Korean nationalism and unification could be brushed off as the workings of a sovereign head of state and out of U.S. hands. After all, Korea was an independent nation. But when the war began in June 1950, Rhee became an American partner, in fact an American puppet, and in many ways the United States became responsible for his actions.

In the summer of 1950, as his government began its fall back to Pusan with the retreating U.S. forces, Rhee went on a reign of terror that left as many as 50,000 Korean "subversives" dead. The North Koreans found mass graves as they advanced through Taejon, and they used that information to their advantage. These incidents, however, were never reported in the American press, which was often flooded with examples of North Korean atrocities against South Korean civilians as the Communists advanced south. Clearly, both sides committed atrocious acts of terror against their enemy. Rhee would remain an embarrassment to the United States throughout the war.

By mid-August the balance had turned for the U.S. forces, now holding up (and building up) inside the Pusan Perimeter. The North Korean offensive around the perimeter on the first day of September was weak compared to the August attacks, and it was easily pushed back by U.S. and ROK troops. It was time for a counteroffensive. On July 23, well before the Pusan Perimeter was secure, MacArthur met with representatives from the Joint Chiefs of Staff in Tokyo to deal with the question of a counteroffensive. MacArthur proposed a daring amphibious landing at Inchon, some twenty miles from Seoul and far behind the North Korean lines. The Joint Chiefs, including their chairman, Omar Bradley, were at best skeptical of the idea. But MacArthur was difficult to turn down. After all, he had initiated a number of daring amphibious assaults in the western Pacific in World War II that defeated the Japanese Empire. Still, the Joint Chiefs remained reluctant. This was an attack over a seawall and into an occupied city, not a beach landing. But MacArthur was adamant. He argued that the North Korean supply lines ran through a bottleneck at Seoul, and if he could cut that bottleneck the entire North Korean army to the south would have to retreat. In addition, if U.S. troops could liberate Seoul, the morale boost for the entire Allied operation would be great, while the North Koreans would be demoralized. It was a good argument. The representatives of the Joint Chiefs reported back to Washington and the plan was approved. In the second week of September, MacArthur was given free rein to carry out the assault on Inchon.

The invasion began on September 10 with the bombing of a strategic harbor island, Wolmi-do. On September 15 marines took the island and the next day marine units hit the beach at Inchon, crossed the wall, and entered the city. By the next morning, Inchon was in U.S. hands. The landing was a success, and casualties were minimal: fewer than two hundred, including twenty dead. The marines moved on to take the airfield at Kimpo, then toward the Han River and Seoul. Considering what was expected, the landing was relatively painless for the marines. Certainly it was a major success.

The next day, UN forces under Walker's command pushed out of the Pusan Perimeter. This move was designed initially to keep the North Koreans from shifting their forces to the Inchon front, but it quickly

Inchon Landing and UN Advance into North Korea

(September 15 to November 24, 1950)

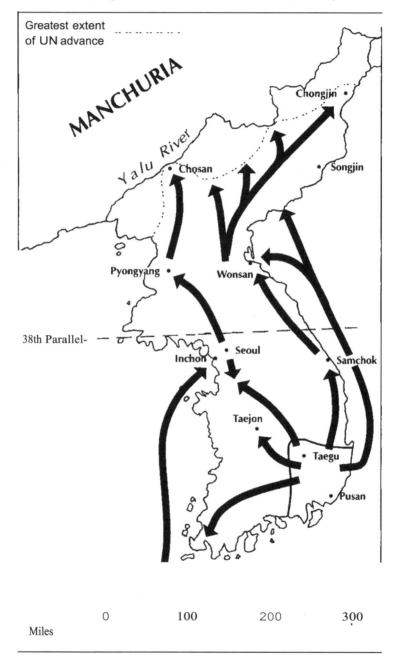

became clear that the enemy was in rapid retreat in front of the UN advance. By September 22, the North Koreans were falling back quickly, fleeing, even breaking up and dissolving, as the UN troops broke one North Korean stand after another. With U.S. tanks leading the way, UN forces moved northward, often unopposed, capturing scores of prisoners as they advanced. On September 26, the force moving north from Pusan met up with the force moving south from the Inchon invasion. The tables had been turned in just two months.

The liberation of Seoul, however, proved difficult. All marine advances on the city from Kimpo were blocked by stubborn North Korean troops, and the Han River. But by September 25, the North Koreans were beginning to evacuate the city. MacArthur announced the liberation of Seoul on that day, just nine days after the landing at Inchon. It all had been a success. The enemy was evaporating. The war, it seemed, was nearly over.

The questions were immediate. Should the U.S. and UN forces cross the 38th parallel in pursuit of the rapidly retreating North Korea troops? Should the United States and its allies take on the responsibility of uniting Korea? Nearly every one of Truman's advisors at the Pentagon and in the State Department agreed that the UN forces should cross the parallel and unite Korea under a single, popularly elected government. Acheson agreed, as did George Marshall, the newly appointed secretary of defense. Bradley agreed as well, and of course MacArthur stood ready. These were men revered by Truman. He thought MacArthur was a genius, and he had called Marshall "the greatest living American." Also, Eisenhower stated publicly that the UN forces should cross the parallel. Ike was clearly moving toward a presidential nomination in 1952, and that put pressure on Truman to be aggressive. Eisenhower, after all, had won the war in Europe; MacArthur had won the war in the Pacific. Their advice carried great weight with Truman and the nation in 1950.

At the same time, in the political arena Truman was still being chastised for having "lost" China to the Communists, and McCarthyism was gaining momentum—along with public support. There was a midterm election coming up, and a quick military victory in Korea would help Democratic candidates running for office at all levels all over the country. To stop at the 38th parallel when U.S. troops had the enemy on the run would have brought a great deal of criticism from those who believed that the only objective worth achieving in war was a complete victory. Also, there was a feeling in America that if the North Korean government (and its army) were allowed to survive, the military effort would have been in vain, and possibly U.S. troops would have to return at a later date to fight a stronger, more mechanized North Korean force. And of course, American boys had died. Truman had to punish the offenders. The president soon came to believe he had to finish the job in Korea.

On the day of the Inchon landing, September 15, MacArthur was told by the Joint Chiefs to begin preparations for an attack north of the 38th parallel. But the UN would have to give its support for the offensive to maintain the appearance of a multilateral action. The British approved the plan for many of same reasons that influenced Truman. The government of Prime Minister Clement Attlee would gain a great deal in prestige and votes from such a cold war initiative. So it was the British, and not the Americans, who pushed through the resolution in the UN. The final language was wide sweeping; for the most part it could be interpreted any way Truman and MacArthur wanted. It called for all appropriate steps to be taken to secure stability in all of Korea, for the holding of elections, and for "the establishment of a unified, independent and democratic Government in the sovereign state of Korea."[9] The government of India opposed it on the grounds that it exceeded the original UN mandate and did, in effect, constitute an aggressive act: the invasion of North Korea. The resolution passed the General Assembly on October 7, just six days after the People's Republic of China celebrated its first National Day, the first anniversary of the establishment of the nation under Communist rule.

While the UN, the United States, and its allies were making these decisions, Beijing was sending clear signals that if U.S. forces crossed the 38th parallel, China would enter the war. Acheson had been in contact with Chou Enlai through intermediaries in the Indian government, and Chou, through September, had continued to express China's peaceful intentions. In addition, the prevailing wisdom at the State Department was that Mao would not intervene because of China's massive economic problems. But on October 3, Chou changed his stance and told the Indian Ambassador to China that Beijing would intervene if the United States crossed the 38th parallel into North Korea. At the same time, the Soviets made a peace proposal in the UN to end the fighting at the 38th parallel. The United States refused to heed the Chinese warning or accept the Soviet's peace initiative. To Acheson it was merely an eleventh-hour attempt to save the collapsing North Korean government. In his memoirs, Acheson wrote: "Chou's words were a warning, not to be disregarded, but, on the other hand, not an authoritative statement of policy."[10] Chou's words should not have been disregarded.

On October 9 the UN coalition had amassed some 230,000 combat troops and an additional 70,000 support personnel on the 38th parallel in preparation for the move into the North. On October 1 South Korean forces first crossed into North Korea; UN troops crossed the 38th parallel eight days later. The North Koreans put up considerable resistance in the early going, but they quickly collapsed and retreated ahead of the advancing UN troops.

On October 15, Truman and MacArthur met at Wake Island in the Pacific to bask in the glory of their successes. To the American people, the enemy was once again on the run. As at the Battle of Midway in the Pacific in 1942 and in Europe at Normandy in 1944, the United States had turned the tide against a noxious foe and was rolling the enemy back. The leaders met to plan their final thrusts, and their final defeat of the enemy. In October 1950 the war in Korea was progressing as it should.

The Wake Island meeting between the president and his Far Eastern commander was short, cordial, and politically motivated. The celebrated issue of whose airplane would land first, and who then would wait subordinately on the ground for the other, seems to be one of myth. The only real significant detail of the meeting was MacArthur's insistence that the Chinese would not enter the war. But if they did, he promised Truman, "there would be the greatest slaughter."[11] The statement has gone down as one of history's great miscalculations, but in fact it was the prevailing wisdom of the time, in both Korea and Washington.

One important aspect of the Wake Island meeting was the friction that was beginning to develop between the conflicting concepts of total war and limited war. Truman saw the need to contain the war in Korea. Although he was willing to expand it into North Korea, he did not want a confrontation with either the Chinese or the Soviets. And he tried to make that clear to MacArthur at Wake Island. MacArthur, on the other hand, was from the school of total war. He believed, as did many other military men of the time, that a limited involvement was against all basic military principles. He also believed that the North Koreans were not the real enemy, that the enemy lay north of the Yalu River, and even beyond that in Moscow. He had no stomach for limited warfare—or the political and diplomatic realities that went along with it. America had entered a new period after World War II; MacArthur was from another time. When Truman returned to San Francisco, he said in a press conference: "I also felt that there was pressing need to make it perfectly clear—by my talk with General MacArthur—that there is complete unity in the aims and conduct of our foreign policy."[12] Clearly there was not.

In July, American intelligence picked up information that the Chinese were beginning to amass troops around Shenyang in Manchuria. By late August it was estimated that over 200,000 Chinese troops were being moved into northeastern China. Three weeks later that number had actually doubled, although U.S. intelligence was not aware of that increase. In October, prisoners captured by UN forces were identified as Chinese. For some reason, these incidences triggered no alarms in Washington or Tokyo. If the Joint Chiefs at this time had any misgivings about MacArthur's rapid advance north, or that the result might be a Chinese intervention, they did not voice them. On October 26, an ROK unit, moving faster than the others, reached the Yalu River. Marine landings on the Korean west coast at Wonsan and Iwon pinched out any retreating North Koreans. Victory was close.

As the UN forces advanced north they somehow bypassed nearly 250,000 Chinese soldiers who had managed to infiltrate into North Korea. This mass movement of troops, moving at night and remaining camouflaged during the day, also managed to escape U.S. intelligence. In fact, through much of October, U.S. and ROK troops often fought Chinese armies in sparring, hit-and-run affairs, and did not realize it. Obviously, no one was expecting a Chinese attack; the UN, Tokyo, Seoul, and Washington still did not consider China's intervention a real possibility.

The Chinese had not been greatly concerned by the events in Korea over the summer. As the decision makers in Washington had perceived, Mao had more than he could handle in trying to deal with China's economic troubles at home. The last thing he needed was a costly war with the West. However, when Truman decided to position the 7th Fleet in the Formosa Strait, Beijing called it an act of aggression, and it was not long before large anti-American rallies were being held in Beijing and other major Chinese cities. In August, MacArthur met with Jiang Jieshi in Formosa, and that meeting was used by Beijing to show the Chinese people that the United States and its allies were conspiring, through the war in Korea, to attack China and put Jiang back in power on the mainland. By early September it became clear to the Chinese that it was only a matter of time before the UN forces would push the North Koreans back beyond the 38th parallel, and the leaders in Beijing began to implement their own policy of containment against the impending encroachment. The Chinese had little concern over a strong South Korea as long as a friendly North Korea remained as a buffer on their border. But once it became obvious that the UN, U.S., and ROK troops were preparing to move north and unite Korea under the anticommunist Syngman Rhee, the Chinese felt compelled to make a move. Such an enemy on their northern border would be unacceptable. They probably feared that scenario more than the possibility that the UN forces would continue on beyond the Yalu and invade Manchuria.

On November 4 MacArthur again assured the president and the Joint Chiefs back in Washington that the Chinese would not intervene. His armies, unaware of the onslaught that was about to come, continued north to meet up with other coalition troops that had reached within thirty miles of the Yalu in the west near Sinuiju. The war now seemed little more than a mopping-up campaign.

The first Chinese attack came on October 25 against the ROK 6th Division—and virtually wiped it out. At Unsan, ROK and U.S. troops were surrounded, and then ambushed as they tried to fight their way out. The 8th Cavalry pushed through to reinforce the stranded units, but it was nearly destroyed in the attempt, losing almost six hundred men in the battle. Surprised and dazed, the UN forces pulled back to the Chongchon River. The Chinese troops then withdrew, pulling back into the mountains—disappearing as quickly as they had appeared, and leaving U.S. field commanders wondering just what had happened. In the east, ROK and U.S. forces continued on toward the Yalu, unaware of the situation to the west. On that same day, October 25, Russian MiG-15 jets made their first appearance in the skies over Korea.

The end of October brought a three-week lull in the fighting as MacArthur paused to bring up supplies from the South in preparation for his final assault to the Yalu, which he believed would win the war and unite Korea. His forces were poised, for the most part, across the narrow neck of the peninsula. The Chinese attack of late October had not been at full strength; possibly as few as 20,000 soldiers were engaged. And their quick withdrawal encouraged MacArthur. He became convinced that the Chinese had been stung and then retreated, possibly back across the Yalu into Manchuria. Through this period of late October and early November, MacArthur continued to insist in communiques to the Joint Chiefs that the enemy before him was not resisting, that the Chinese would be destroyed if they joined the war in any strength, and that the war would be over in just a few weeks.

On November 5 MacArthur announced (without prior consultation with the president or the Joint Chiefs) that he planned to bomb the bridges over the Yalu to slow the movement of any additional Chinese troops into Korea—despite explicit orders from Washington not to invade the air space of China or the Soviet Union. On November 5 MacArthur told George Strademeyer, commander of the U.S. Air Force in the Far East, to "isolate the battlefield" (specifically that area between his advancing UN troops and the Yalu River) and to "destroy every means of communications and every installation, factory, city, [and] village" in it.[13] MacArthur's order pushed the Joint Chiefs to pull in the reins a bit on their Far East commander, and for the first time they countermanded one of his orders and forced MacArthur to postpone all bombing within five miles of the Yalu River.[14] MacArthur's reply was explosive. "Every hour that [the bombing of the Yalu bridges] is postponed will be paid for dearly in American . . . blood."[15] The next day, November 7, MacArthur continued to complain that he was being restrained from winning the war, and he went a step further by insisting he be allowed to bomb enemy sanctuaries in Manchuria. "The present restrictions imposed on my area of operations provide a complete sanctuary for hostile air immediately upon their crossing the Manchuria-North Korean border. . . . Unless measures [are] promptly taken," MacArthur added, "the air problem could assume serious proportions."[16] MacArthur's plan would violate Chinese and possibly even Soviet airspace—a situation that could quickly widen the war well beyond anything Washington wanted.

MacArthur's demands were a serious problem for Truman and the Joint Chiefs. MacArthur was a towering figure among Washington's military constabulary and presidential advisors—and an extraordinarily popular figure among the American people. To pull him back from what he and others (like George Marshall at this time) perceived as America's first military victory over the evils of communism, was nearly impossible in the politically charged atmosphere of 1950. To stop MacArthur's advance now and begin negotiations with the enemy would undoubtedly open the door to a long-term political disaster for the Democrats. MacArthur still rode the success of Inchon, and, for that matter, the successes of an entire lifetime on the top rung of the U.S. military ladder. He continued to argue eloquently for an advance to the Yalu and victory. If Truman had any misgivings at this point he did not voice them. He refused to allow MacArthur to bomb into Manchuria, but he gave the go-ahead to the Joint Chiefs to permit MacArthur to bomb the Yalu bridges.

At this time several players in Washington and at the UN began to feel uneasy about the Chinese intervention. Word of the late October attack had leaked to the press, and questions were beginning to be raised, particularly by the British, who had no stomach for a broader war with the Chinese. They began arguing for a ceasefire at the Korean neck and a search for a negotiated settlement. Acheson was also beginning to worry. He suggested that a ten-mile demilitarized zone on each side of the Yalu might be a point to begin negotiations with the Chinese. Policy makers in the Pentagon, at the State Department, and in the White House began to explore the political ramifications and diplomatic possibilities of halting MacArthur's advance at the Korean neck. The biggest fear was that the Chinese attack was intended as a diversionary strike that would soon be followed by a major surge against Western Europe—where most military strategists believed the real battle against the enemy would be fought. On November 7, the Democrats took a beating in the congressional elections, losing control of the Senate and effectively bringing to an end most of Truman's domestic agenda for the next two years. Although redbaiting from the McCarthyites was most likely the reason for the Democrats' defeat, many believed that the intervention of the Chinese hurt the Democrats as well—that American voters had come to believe the Republican claim that the administration was bungling the war. Finally, on November 8 the Joint Chiefs cabled MacArthur that his mission "may have to be re-examined in the light of the Chinese intervention."[17] MacArthur's response the next day was scathing. He referred to any plan to restrict his offensive as "fatal." "Any program short of [uniting all of Korea to the Yalu] would completely destroy the morale of my forces and the psychological consequences would be inestimable." He predicted that the forces of South Korea might, in fact, turn against his own forces; and that the Chinese (appeased in being allowed to control parts of North Korea) would attack further south against the UN forces. "To give up any portion of North Korea to the aggression of the Chinese Communists," he added, "would be the greatest defeat of the free world in recent time." He went on to denounce the British plan as appeasement, with "its historical precedent in the action taken at Munich. . . . [W]e should press on to complete victory," he concluded, "which I believe can be achieved if our determination and indomitable will do not desert us.[18]

Faced with such limited options from their commander on the scene, the Joint Chiefs relented, and that afternoon they informed MacArthur that he could begin his offensive to unite Korea to the Yalu—but that he was not to bomb into Manchuria. The stage was set for one of the biggest military blunders in American history. MacArthur had gotten his way. Riding on his reputation and popularity, he moved his forces slowly forward toward the Yalu River on November 24. He promised it would all be over by Christmas, and indeed it appeared that way.

The decision to allow MacArthur to begin his offensive was a mistake, and in the years afterward many of those who were in on the decision agreed. Omar Bradley wrote:

> We read, we sat, we deliberated and, unfortunately, we reached drastically wrong conclusions and decisions. . . . The [Joint Chiefs] should have taken firmest control of the Korean War and dealt with MacArthur bluntly. . . . At the very least the chiefs should have canceled MacArthur's planned offensive. Instead we let ourselves be

misled by MacArthur's wildly erroneous estimates of the situation and his eloquent rhetoric, as well as too much wishful thinking of our own. [19]

Acheson came up with much the same analysis: "All the president's advisors in this matter, civilian and military, knew that something was badly wrong, though what it was, how to find out, and what to do about it, they muffed. . . . None of us, myself prominently included, served [the president] as he was entitled to be served."[20] Truman gave his own analysis ten years later: "What we should have done was stop at the neck of Korea. . . . But [MacArthur] was the commander in the field. You pick your man, you've got to back him up. That's the only way a military organization can work. I got the best advice I could and the man on the spot said this was the thing to do. So I agreed. That was my decision—no matter what the hindsight shows."[21]

But the United States was headed for a disaster. What had begun as a good war was about to take a horrible turn. MacArthur was overconfident, and his forces were divided as they prepared to head for the Yalu with no real idea of what stood before them: one million Chinese Communists were preparing a massive, devastating attack. In Washington, Truman was not getting good counsel from his advisors, civilian or military, mainly because MacArthur had failed to provide the correct information from the battlefield. The war, in the last days of November 1950, would soon enter a new phase: large-scale limited warfare—America's first Asian quagmire.

3

CHANGING OBJECTIVES AND THE ACCORDION WAR

Opposing the American and UN troops was a massive Chinese army, experienced and battle hardened by years of fighting Jiang's Nationalists and the Japanese. It was well organized, well equipped, and well led. This was no citizen's army drafted from the masses. This formidable army was under the command of General Zhu De, the brilliant commander who took the Communist forces to victory over the Nationalists, and the builder of the People's Liberation Army in the 1930s and 1940s. His deputy was Peng Dehui. Under their command in the field were Lin Biao, at the head of the Chinese 4th Army, and Chen Yi, in command of the 3rd Army. The 4th Army had crossed into North Korea in October and had conducted the first attacks against the UN forces later that month; the 3rd Army had followed about two weeks later. What remained of the North Korean army was quickly absorbed by the Chinese, and by some accounts it ceased to exist. It was, for all intents and purposes, a Chinese war after October 28.

The Chinese plan was to split the UN forces down the middle. MacArthur had, in fact, managed to do that himself by spreading his advancing army thinly in the face of what he believed to be light opposition. The west flank of the UN forces was separated from the east flank by a fifty-mile gap, a gap that Chinese intelligence operations had discovered. The Chinese hoped to push a large force between the two UN armies and (in classic Chinese military tradition) surround them, push them back to the sea, and destroy them. It was a good plan, particularly since the element of surprise was still theirs, even though they had kept several hundred thousand soldiers in the vicinity of the UN armies for nearly six weeks. MacArthur had let the world know his plans of attack through press conferences and open letters in the press. Through their own intelligence system, the Chinese also knew that MacArthur had been denied permission to attack into Manchuria, and that allowed them to move their support bases up to the Yalu River.

When MacArthur resumed his offensive on November 24, intelligence estimates showed that the advancing UN troops might be facing some 80,000 North Korean troops and between 40,000 and 80,000 Chinese troops. Such opposition would not have been an insurmountable obstacle for the far superior UN forces. However, by then the Chinese force south of the Yalu had grown to some thirty divisions—over 300,000 soldiers.

MacArthur ordered his troops to spread out from just north of Sinuiju on the Yellow Sea in the west to the east coast near Chongjin. On the left, the 24th, 25th, and 2nd Infantry divisions were now on the banks of the Chongchon River, pushed back to that point by the first Chinese strike a month earlier. The center was held by the 1st Marine Division, which had been ordered to move forward toward the Chosen Reservoir. The 24th Infantry, on the left flank, met little opposition to its advance on the first day. The right flank also made headway without stiff resistance. But the next day, November 25, Chinese troops hit hard on the west and center flank of the UN advance. The 6th, 7th, and 8th divisions of the ROK II Corps were overwhelmed and torn apart by the Chinese in a matter of hours. The Chinese also attacked the U.S. 24th, 25th, and 2nd Infantry Divisions to the west, but with lighter force.

The next day, the Chinese armies hit again. This time it was the 25th Infantry (to the west of the ROK II Corps, which had been destroyed the day before) that received the brunt of the attack. Walker responded by first sending in an aggressive Turkish brigade of some 5,000 soldiers to try to plug up the Chinese advance, then he sent in the U.S. 1st Cavalry, followed by the British Commonwealth Brigade. The Chinese were simply too strong; Walker began a long retreat south.

On the right flank, the X Corps was prepared to move forward (on November 27) despite the action to the west the day before. Winter had just blown in from Siberia and the armies would have to face temperatures that occasionally reached only zero during the day, and often dropped to thirty and forty degrees below zero at night. That night, as the temperature dropped, the Chinese launched an offensive at the Chosen Reservoir against the X Corps, and pushed the Americans back east toward the Sea of Japan. On November 28, again after dark, the Chinese threw six divisions against the 1st and 7th marines east of the Chosen Reservoir. The Americans held their positions until December 1, but retreating from that position would be another matter.

By November 28 it was clear in Washington that the situation in Korea was deteriorating rapidly and the UN forces were on the verge of retreating in the face of vastly superior numbers. That day, MacArthur finally admitted he had been wrong and telegraphed the Joint Chiefs that he believed he was facing as many as 200,000 Chinese troops, and that he would need reinforcements to deal with the power in his front. "We face," he said, "an entirely new war."[1] Bradley reported the information to Truman. The Chinese have "come in with both feet," he told the president.[2] This realization brought on a turning point in the war. From then on the Truman administration would begin reining in on the powers it had given MacArthur; but more importantly, the administration would start looking for a way out of the war. "We could not defeat the Chinese in Korea," Acheson recalled in his memoirs, "because they could put in more men than we could afford to commit there." At a meeting of the National Security Council on November 28, Acheson suggested that some means be found to establish a ceasefire line or a demilitarized zone and bring an end to the fighting as quickly as possible. Truman recalled that Acheson "was of the opinion that we should find some way to end it," and that Korea could become "a bottomless pit" that could "bleed us dry." General Marshall agreed with Acheson's assessment that the United States should not get involved in a war with the Chinese. The United States, he said, must find a way to "get out" of Korea "with honor."[3] Within four days (between November 24 and November 28) the U.S. strategy had changed from uniting Korea to cutting losses.

Chinese Attack and UN Withdrawal
(November 1950 to January 1951)

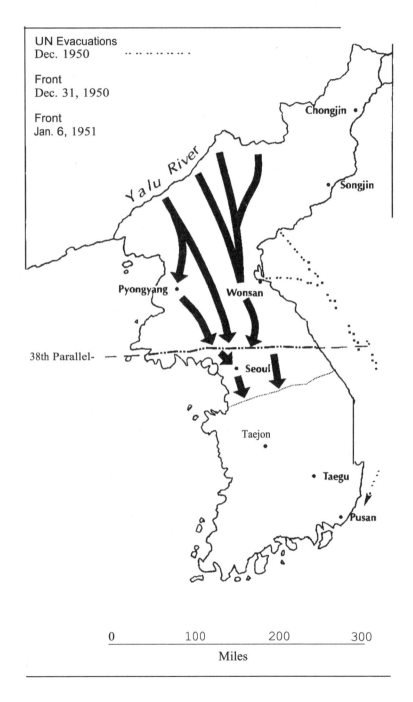

UN Evacuations
Dec. 1950 ·· ·· ·· ·· ·· ·

Front
Dec. 31, 1950

Front
Jan. 6, 1951

Chongjin ·

Yalu River

· Songjin

Pyongyang ·

Wonsan

38th Parallel-

· Seoul

Taejon
·

· Taegu

· Pusan

0   100   200   300

Miles

Acheson had convinced many of the policy makers in Washington in late 1950 that the world stood on the brink of World War III. Walter Bedell Smith, the director of the CIA in this period, agreed. The Communists would, Smith told Truman, try to "bleed us to death," and then, presumably, attack into Western Europe.[4] In late November the Joint Chiefs ordered a study to determine the feasibility of an atomic attack on the Soviet Union or China should the Soviets intervene, or if large numbers of American soldiers were pushed back to the sea and poised for slaughter by the Chinese. On November 30, Truman told a bevy of reporters that the atomic bomb was under "active consideration" by the administration for use in the escalating Asian war.[5] This statement is usually seen as a classic Trumanesque blunder. But it is more likely that it was a threat to the Chinese that the United States would not stand by while retreating American soldiers were slaughtered. It also may have been intended as a signal to the USSR that the United States would react strongly if it intervened in the war.

On December 3 Truman sent the Army chief of staff, General J. Lawton Collins, to Tokyo to talk to MacArthur about the situation in Korea. On that day MacArthur wired the Pentagon that the X Corps was in full retreat toward Hamhung on the Sea of Japan, and that Walker and the 8th Army were being pushed south so fast that Walker did not believe he could hold the North Korean capital of Pyongyang. Walker, MacArthur relayed, believed his best option was to withdraw to Seoul. It was now impossible, MacArthur continued, to unite the two wings of his army. They were in full retreat and being chased down the peninsula.

MacArthur's army had been split by the Chinese; one half was retreating east, the other west. MacArthur continued to complain to Washington that he did not have the force necessary to draw up a line of defense across Korea, and that unless he received reinforcements immediately his only alternative would be to continue his retreat south. "This small command," he wrote, "actually under present conditions is facing the entire Chinese nation in an undeclared war and unless some positive and immediate action is taken, hope for success cannot be justified and steady attrition leading to final destruction can reasonably be contemplated." The enemy he was facing, he added with some surprise, "are fresh, completely organized, splendidly trained and equipped and apparently in peak condition for actual operations."[6]

MacArthur used the meeting with Collins in Tokyo to lay out his needs and demands to fight this new force before him. He made it clear that the United States could either win or lose the war; it could choose between victory or defeat, a role in the future of world affairs or not. To win, to choose victory, MacArthur wanted a naval blockade of China, air attacks on Chinese forces and their installations in Manchuria, considerable reinforcements, the use of Jiang Jieshi's troops from Formosa, and a free hand to use nuclear weapons if necessary. Clearly, MacArthur was prepared to carry the United States into a full-scale war with the Chinese, and possibly the Soviets. The question of limited war versus total war again confronted Truman and MacArthur, the conflict that was pushing the president and the general to an ultimate break.

Truman and his advisors, civilian and military, realized that MacArthur's plan would bring on something that no one wanted: total war. There had been, since the beginning of the war in Korea, speculation by several of Truman's advisors (particularly Acheson) that the Chinese intervention was part of a greater scheme that threatened to lead to all-out war if the United States pursued the possibility. Clearly, any escalation by the United States would bring a matched escalation from either the Chinese or the Soviets—leading to a global war. Consequently, the U.S. command in Washington went on the defensive.

The Marine 5th and 7th Divisions pushed south from the Chosen Reservoir on December 1 in a retreat to catch up to the rest of the UN forces being evacuated toward the Korean east coast. General Oliver Smith, using language that might be considered indicative of the Marine character, told his troops: "Retreat? Hell, we're just attacking in another direction." The enemy was blocking their advance to the UN lines in the south, and to fight their way out they had to attack south. By the evening of December 7, Smith's forces had concentrated at Koto-ri, outside of the enemy trap. They were pursued for two more days until they finally returned to friendly territory.

By December 5, Walker's forces had been pushed south of the North Korean capital of Pyongyang. At Chinnampo, thirty miles south of Pyongyang, UN and ROK forces were being evacuated off the coast by the U.S. Navy. Between December 7 and January 5, the Navy evacuated nearly 70,000 UN personnel, 60,000 tons of supplies, and some 1,400 vehicles. On the east coast, troops, supplies, vehicles, and even some 91,000 Korean civilians demanding asylum were also evacuated by the Navy. The Chinese halted their assault to allow the evacuation to take place. The U.S. press compared it to Dunkirk.

By mid-December, Walker had drawn his forces up at the 38th parallel in hopes that a *status quo ante* would bring an end to the war. In response, so it seemed, the Chinese attacks appeared to wane. The prevailing opinion in Washington, Tokyo, and Korea was that the Chinese had simply implemented their own policy of containment and they would be satisfied to keep the UN invasion forces south of the 38th parallel. Other policy makers thought the Chinese were preparing for another frontal attack, or infiltrating to the east in an attempt to encircle the UN forces. Walker had devised a plan to move back into the old Pusan Perimeter and hold that line if it became necessary; and he hoped that the Chinese supply lines would become open to bombing from the air. At year's end the 38th parallel line held.

On December 23, Walker was killed in a jeep accident. He was replaced by General Matthew Ridgway, a man who understood Washington's need to fight a limited war in Korea. He was also liked and trusted by MacArthur. As he prepared to take control of his command, now poised at the 38th parallel, he was told by intelligence sources that he was facing some 174,000 enemy soldiers across the border. A more accurate figure was around a half-million. At least on the level of intelligence and enemy troop estimates, the United States forces were still operating in the dark. At the same time, it was clear to Ridgway that his forces were deeply demoralized and poised for retreat and defeat. And it was bitterly cold. It was a very bad situation in Korea for the U.S. and UN troops as the year end approached.

The war in Korea, now six months old, still made no strategic sense. The U.S. offshore defense of Asia was anchored in Japan and the Philippines, with Okinawa holding the center. The United States did not need Korea to maintain its Asian defense perimeter. At the same time, Washington policy makers were still of one mind that the real focal point of the cold war was in Europe, and that the war in Korea was impeding the European buildup of U.S. forces. The action in Korea was a Communist diversion at best, an American blunder into a military hole at worst. Few in Washington believed that Korea warranted such a tremendous (and expanding) U.S. commitment. But the United States involvement in Korea had little to do with U.S. strategic interests in Asia. America was there to show the world that it would intervene with military force to stop Communist aggressions. Even in areas of minimal U.S. strategic concern, like Korea, America could be counted on no matter what the cost.

Both MacArthur and Ridgway had correctly concluded that the Chinese would attack at the 38th parallel on New Year's Eve. Ridgway tried desperately to prepare his men for what was coming, but morale remained low and the Chinese attack pushed the UN forces back easily and quickly on nearly all fronts. As had been the case in the earlier attacks, the Chinese army picked on the ROK divisions first, this time the ROK 1st and 6th Divisions on the western front. At the same time, the Chinese pushed hard at the ROK forces in the center while totally bypassing the strong U.S. 24th and 25th Divisions. With many of his troops in flight south, Ridgway ordered a general withdrawal to Seoul. But the Chinese army quickly breached a gap in the center of the Allied line south of the Hwachon Reservoir and was threatening to move south of Seoul and surround the UN troops drawing up there. Ridgway had to abandon Seoul and retreat farther south to a position called Line D— from Samchok in the east to Pyongtaek in the west.

On January 15, a turnabout in the war occurred when a probe from the U.S. infantry divisions on the left encountered no enemy activity in their front. Further probes all along the line to the east showed that the Chinese had pulled back for some reason. On January 25 Ridgway ordered a general advance on the left, and his forces there moved up to the Han River, just south of Seoul. However, on February 12, the Chinese launched their fourth offensive, this time against the UN center, now north of Wonju. The attack was repulsed, and for the first time since the Chinese entered the war in October 1950 the UN forces held the initiative. Seoul was liberated (again) on March 15. By early April, Ridgway was making headway back toward the 38th parallel, and under

MacArthur's orders, the UN forces began a slow grind northward. The Chinese no longer seemed invincible.

Not surprisingly, there was very little discussion in Washington this time about the wisdom of proceeding north of the parallel. The UN successes, however modest, had brought most of Truman's advisors to begin thinking of negotiations and bringing an end to this messy war. Of course, it had been unthinkable to negotiate with the Chinese while UN troops were in retreat, as they had been for over four months. But now in March, it appeared that the UN forces again held at least some initiative. China had shown that it would not allow North Korea to be destroyed, and the United States had made the same point clear about the South. All hoped the war would end where it had begun, at the 38th parallel.

On March 19, the president and his advisors drafted a statement that the UN was willing to begin talks. MacArthur was sent a draft of the message, as were the leaders of the Allied nations. Everyone involved believed that this would be the start of peace negotiations and that the war nobody wanted would be over quickly. The UN, Truman planned to say, "is preparing to enter into arrangements which would conclude the fighting and insure against its resumption. Such arrangements would open the way for a broader settlement for Korea, including the withdrawal of foreign forces from Korea."[7] But while Truman prepared to hold out an olive branch, MacArthur held out a sword. On March 24, he issued his own statement on the situation in Korea which, in effect, sabotaged the administration's peace initiative. MacArthur wrote of China's "exaggerated and vaunted military power." "The enemy," he added, "must by now be painfully aware that a decision of the United Nations to depart from its tolerant effort to contain the war to the area of Korea, through an expansion of our military operations to its coastal areas and interior bases, would doom Red China to the risk of imminent military collapse."[8] The two statements by the president and his military commander were direct contradictions: one called for limited warfare and a negotiated peace, the other for total war and complete victory. To Truman it was a conflict over the constitutional authority of the presidency, an attempted subversion of civilian rule. That, however, was really never challenged. The conflict was over how the war in Korea should be fought.[9]

UN Counteroffensive
(January 25 to April 21, 1951)

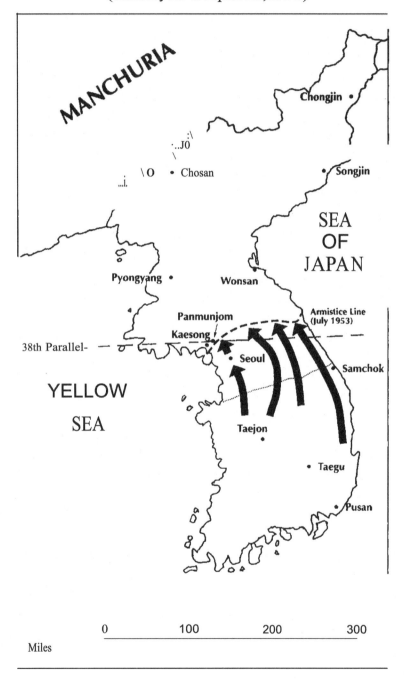

Truman responded immediately by telling MacArthur to keep such opinions to himself. It was clearly a final warning, and Truman later said he believed MacArthur had deliberately sabotaged the UN peace efforts. A few days later, on April 5, the Republican minority leader in the House, Joseph Martin, read an open letter from MacArthur on the floor of Congress. The real war against communism is in Asia, MacArthur wrote: "Here we fight Europe's war with arms, while the diplomats there still fight it with words. . . . We must win," he told Martin. "There is no substitute for victory."[10] Acheson called the letter "an open declaration of war on the Administration's policy."[11] If that was not enough, MacArthur gave an interview to a British news correspondent in which he offered his opinion on the conduct of the war in even clearer words. "The true object of a commander in war [is] to destroy the forces opposed to him," he was quoted as saying. But he was not being allowed to do that, he continued. "The situation would be ludicrous if men's lives were not involved."[12]

It was the last straw. On April 9, Acheson, Averell Harriman, George Marshall, and the members of the Joint Chiefs, including their chairman, Omar Bradley, met with the president. The decision was easy and unanimous: relieve MacArthur and replace him with Ridgway. Truman later wrote that MacArthur had made it clear at their meeting on Wake Island in October that he did not like the idea of a limited war in Korea. "I should have relieved MacArthur then and there," Truman wrote in his memoirs.[13] With MacArthur out of the way, President Truman, his advisors in Washington, and his commanders in Korea could move toward bringing an end to the war, their objective since November.

MacArthur became a symbol to those who believed that the Truman administration had fallen back on a policy of appeasing the Communists in Asia. They believed, as MacArthur had, that the real enemies were the Soviet Union and China, and that the United States, now provoked in Korea, should "finish the job," as the saying went at the time. Truman had become no less a traitor to the American way of life than the spies that McCarthy and his supporters were looking for (and not finding) in the government. Republican Senator William Jenner of Indiana, probably McCarthy's most ardent supporter, said that the Truman administration was made up of "a secret inner coterie which is directed by agents of the Soviet Union." McCarthy himself charged that Truman was drunk when he made the decision to fire MacArthur.[14] So, as the Republicans had once seized on anti-Communism as a political issue, they now seized on MacArthur's dismissal as one more issue that would paste onto the Democrats the label of "soft on Communism" and carry Republican candidates into the 1952 campaigns.

On April 11, the Republicans announced that they had invited MacArthur to speak before Congress. It was a brilliant political move. The Democrats could not object; MacArthur was by all accounts a national hero. They could only sit quietly as MacArthur made his way toward Washington, with huge "welcome home" parades in Honolulu, San Francisco, and then in Washington. The groundswell of support for him grew as he moved east. In his famous speech before Congress he reiterated his arguments for total war in Korea, and then closed with the celebrated line from an old army ballad, "Old soldiers never die; they just fade away." The chief spokesman for total war in a time of limited war was finally gone.

From May through August, the Senate carried on an investigation into the administration's policies in Korea. It largely vindicated Truman and his management of the war, but it also gave MacArthur a forum to argue his ideas about how the war should be fought, and how the United States should conduct its foreign policy. During the deliberations, MacArthur called limited warfare "appeasement," and said that the administration was retreating in the face of aggression at the cost of the lives of American boys. He added that in such a war of attrition, the Chinese could bottle up the U.S. military in Korea indefinitely at the cost of many lives. He again called for an escalation of the fighting by bombing China and by bringing in Jiang's troops from Formosa. The United States, he said, should use the maximum force available, and not hold back in the face of Communist aggression.

The administration argued that MacArthur's approach would plunge the nation into a global war. The Joint Chiefs argued individually that the United States was not prepared to go to war with China or the Soviet Union, and it certainly was not prepared to take on both at once. In addition, the use of Jiang's troops would further escalate the war unnecessarily, and Jiang's place in Asia was to defend Formosa, not fight in Korea.

In the final analysis, the Senate investigation committee split along party lines, with the Republicans filing a minority report.

The question of MacArthur's dismissal split America. Either MacArthur was a hero, or he had overstepped his bounds. Some realized the central issue—the question of limited versus total warfare—but most saw the conflict in the context of America's role in dealing with the expansion of worldwide Communism. Others saw it as necessary to the maintenance of civilian over military power. Truman's act, as necessary as it was, did his administration irreparable damage. He never again recovered popularity in the polls, and it gave the Republicans a groundswell of support that carried Eisenhower into the next election. The limited war that Truman had demanded (and MacArthur opposed) turned into a stalemate, a quagmire, as the two sides faced each other near the 38th parallel. Truman's lot was that he had gotten America into a war, and now he was unable to get the nation out.

The hearings on MacArthur's dismissal and (by its nature) on the conduct of the war itself probably did not move the public one way or the other on the issues. By 1951 the majority of Americans were fed up with what MacArthur had called "this accordion war." After spring 1951 there were important American victories over the Chinese, but they were victories only in the limited sense. The UN troops held the line, and occasionally pushed the Chinese back. For many Americans, however, this was not enough; they wanted a touchdown. Boys were being killed and wounded (nearly 70,000 battle casualties by the end of May) with little to show for it. Gallup polls continually showed that only about 30 percent of the U.S. public approved of the war. Although no antiwar movement emerged, it was clear that a strong dissenting opinion had developed among the American people as the war stalemated after the beginning of 1951. Americans had seen World War II as an all-out struggle against evil enemies; it had been a good war. Now they were fighting to sustain a corrupt government in a remote and strategically worthless area of Asia. And worse, they were fighting with the goal of achieving no more than the position they had held before the war began. Just as it would be in Vietnam, the concept of a limited war was a difficult commodity to sell to the American people.

With Ridgway in control in Korea there was no longer a divided command; consequently the conduct of the war changed rapidly. The administration and the general were now of one mind; they now knew where they were going, and goals and objectives were finally being set. In a National Security Council paper (NSC-48/5) the administration established its objectives for the remainder of the war. Approved by Truman in May 1951, while the MacArthur hearings were still underway, NSC-48/5 called for a unified Korea. However, that unity was to come as a result of "political, as distinguished from military, means." That is, the United States would be satisfied with a negotiated settlement to the war, and worry about unification later. In the absence of a settlement, the United States would pursue three goals in Korea: (1) inflict maximum losses on the enemy; (2) prevent the overrun of South Korea by military aggression; and (3) stop the spread of communism to other parts of Asia. In addition, if Communist aggression broke out elsewhere in Asia, the United States would resort to a MacArthur-like response by blockading Chinese ports, attacking "selected targets" in China, and making use of Jiang's army by giving them "the necessary operational assistance to make them effective."[15] Another important aspect of NSC-48/5 was the declaration that the United States would aid the nations of Southeast Asia in their fight to combat the spread of communism there. So, not only did NSC-48/5 establish goals in Korea, it also laid some of the groundwork for American involvement in Vietnam.[16]

While the Senate debated MacArthur's dismissal, Ridgway was conducting the administration's war with great success. Gone was the old MacArthur defeatism: that if I do not get what I want we will lose the war. Ridgway correctly believed that the enemy was embroiled in massive logistics problems. The Air Force was having tremendous success at destroying the enemy's supply lines, and apparently U.S. artillery had taken a toll as well. Ridgway believed the enemy was now weak, cold, hungry, and demoralized. In April and May, the Chinese attacked again. This time Ridgway's forces held, and then repulsed the enemy. He concluded that the Chinese were no longer capable of mounting a powerful assault south of the 38th parallel. It appeared the Chinese, like the North Koreans before them, were about to collapse under the weight of their own logistics nightmare—and U.S. firepower.

As if they had not learned their lessons, the Washington policy makers met at the White House on May 29 to discuss the possibility of attacking north of the 38th parallel with an Inchon-type landing near Tongchon on the east coast near the neck of Korea. The conferees included Acheson, Rusk, Nitze, Bradley, Harriman, Maxwell Taylor, and others. Bradley's argument prevailed. There would be no invasion of the North. In March, the Soviets had warned Washington that if the United States again approached the Yalu River they would intervene. The warning was taken seriously this time; the UN troops would hold along a line just north of the 38th parallel, and wage a war of "offensive defense." The orders to Ridgway were the same: inflict as much damage on the Chinese as possible—until they decide to call an end to the fighting.

Ridgway's man in the field was General James A. Van Fleet, a veteran of the anti-Communist action in postwar Greece. He arrived in Korea in mid-April, and at once began moving his troops forward to meet the enemy. It had become clear by spring 1951 that the Chinese were still capable of attacking in strength, but that now the attacks could not be sustained for long. Following an attack, the Chinese would retreat beyond UN artillery range and regroup, resupply, and bring up reinforcements to fill the gaps in their lines. When ready they would attack again. There was no mystery to it. As Van Fleet moved forward, the Chinese continued to retreat northward until they were again prepared to take the offensive. That offensive came on April 22, the Chinese "fifthphase offensive."

The Chinese military tactics had been designed by Zhu De and were similar to those used against Jiang's Nationalist troops just two years earlier. Chinese forces would attack in mass at what they had perceived to be a weak point in the enemy line, hoping to break through. If successful, they would push as many soldiers as possible through the hole. Moving rapidly, they would then attempt to move to the rear of the enemy force and either surround them or establish a block in the enemy's rear. A second wave from the original front would then push the enemy into the blocking position, crushing them easily. These frightening attacks nearly always came at night in Korea and were preceded by horns, whistles, drums, and flares. They were simplistic tactics, but they were also effective, making use of what the Chinese had the most: manpower. But by spring 1951, most Americans and the other troops on the lines were no longer frightened by the attacks, and by then they knew how to hold against them. The result was that the Chinese were beginning to take extremely heavy losses.

Also, by spring 1951 U.S. intelligence had finally begun to aid the UN action in Korea, with the result that Chinese troop numbers were at last becoming accurate—and surprising. Intelligence reports placed the Chinese force in North Korea at somewhere near 700,000 men, a spectacular mass of humanity. Everyone on the Allied side expected the next Chinese push to be a hard one. The Chinese fifth offensive came in late April and succeeded in breaking the UN line in two places. The breach came against the ROK 6th Division, and Van Fleet found himself nearly unable to close the gap as Chinese troops poured south; he was forced to order his army to fall back to protect its flanks. But by April 29, the Chinese had again extended themselves too far beyond their lines, and the U.S. Air Force had begun destroying the Chinese supply lines. The drive collapsed. As the Chinese withdrew north, the UN troops followed, pushing the Chinese at every opportunity.

On the night of May 15–16, the Chinese launched their sixth offensive. It was to be the attack that would bring them victory and push the imperialists off the Asian continent. They attacked with twenty-one Chinese divisions and nine North Korean divisions. Again, they aimed their attack at the weakest point in the UN line, near the Korean east coast all along the weak ROK III Corps line. The ROK forces collapsed, but the United States 3rd Infantry Division was raced in from I Corps near Seoul, clear across the Korean peninsula, to the Chinese front. The Chinese gained twenty miles, but the advance was stopped. Another attack against the X Corps' right also held.

By now knowledge of the Chinese tactics gave the UN commanders a significant advantage. Following the enemy's big push, they knew the Chinese were now overextended, exhausted, and unable to bring supplies forward because of pounding from U.S. air support. On May 20, Van Fleet started pushing back, and the Chinese began to collapse and retreat north. Within ten days UN forces were well above the 38th parallel and still moving. The Chinese had suffered a major defeat. UN forces were taking large numbers of prisoners and matériel, and intelligence concluded that the Chinese had suffered nearly 500,000 casualties since they entered the war, less than seven months before.

Now in the advantage, Ridgway took the opportunity to broadcast a message to North Korea that it was time to talk peace. "Upon receipt of word from you that such a meeting is desired," Ridgway said, "I shall be prepared to name my representative and suggest a date at which he could meet with your representative."[17] Beijing radio announced that Kim Il Sung and Peng Dehui (commander of the People's Volunteer Army) had accepted the offer. The acceptance surprised Washington, and it was considered a significant breakthrough. Most thought that a ceasefire would be agreed upon quickly, and the war would come to a speedy conclusion. Decision makers in Washington, however, concluded that a ceasefire would only allow the Chinese to rebuild their forces and prepare another attack. Foreshadowing Vietnam, the United States chose to continue fighting during the talks. The two sides met for the first time at Kaesong on July 10. They would not come to an agreement for two more years.

As the two great powers met to seek an accord over Korea, Kim Il Sung and Syngman Rhee found themselves excluded from the negotiations. Both men had vowed that Korea would be unified under their leadership, and in fact, the armies of both sides had fought and died with unification as their primary goal. But now that the United States and China had locked horns in a draw, the result would be a negotiated peace and a divided Korea—once again and for the future. Rhee certainly felt betrayed. Kim probably felt the same way.

The Truman administration insisted that negotiations be carried on through Ridgway in the field. There was a fear that if the negotiations were conducted in the UN, political issues—such as the status of Formosa, the recognition of China in the UN, and the status of Indochina—might be raised and muddy the waters. There was also some fear that the other nations fighting with the United States in Korea might not agree to certain issues, which might weaken the demands. In the field, U.S. commanders-as-negotiators would speak with one voice controlled from Washington and nowhere else.

The focus of the war, then, turned from the battlefield to the negotiating table in June 1951. For the men in the field, of course, the war continued; the enemy was apparent and dangerous. But there were no more dramatic attacks, no major advances or retreats. The accordion war was over, and the two sides settled down to a war of attrition—with goals designed only to affect their individual bargaining positions at the ceasefire talks.

4

FIGHTING WHILE NEGOTIATING

The two sides that met on July 10, 1951 at Kaesong represented widely divergent cultures, ideologies, and styles. Neither side had bothered to understand the other beyond its military tactics. Each side thought it was racially superior to the other, and both entered the negotiations thinking they had achieved at least a limited military victory. The Americans believed the Chinese would try to win at the negotiating table what they had failed to win on the battlefield, and undoubtedly the Chinese believed the same of the Americans. It was clear from the beginning that neither side was prepared to concede anything to the other.

At the same time, Ridgway himself added to Washington's problems as the negotiations unfolded. He believed that the peace talks were a ruse, a plan by the Chinese to buy time to prepare for another offensive, or for the Soviets to prepare to attack another American stronghold, possibly Japan or Western Europe. He was an outspoken Communist-hater, and his war against the Chinese had amplified his feelings. "With its compelling fear of the truth," he wrote in a press release squelched by the Joint Chiefs before it could be printed, "communist imperialism has sought repeatedly to obscure the long and loyal record of friendship between the Chinese and American peoples."[1] His antagonistic posture made the negotiations even more difficult. Ridgway was not the best man for the job of facing the Chinese Communists across the negotiating table. In Washington, Truman, Acheson, and the other policy makers were under great pressure to put an end to the fighting in Korea. Public support for the war was waning quickly—as was support for the Democratic party. Truman's inability to bring the war to an end was already being used effectively by the Republicans as an issue in the quickly approaching 1952 presidential campaign. The strategy of limited war had ended the possibility for a total victory in Korea, and for many Americans that simply was unacceptable.

Many Americans had also come to believe that the generation of soldiers fighting in Korea seemed to lack what it took to win that war. News began filtering home that American soldiers often refused to fight, particularly in the first stages of the war; that their morale was low; and that they "bugged out," or simply ran from the battle line when the going got tough. It was a common belief that U.S. soldiers in Korea were poorly trained, out of shape, soft, and coddled. This was, supposedly, the great American army that had pushed back the imperial forces of Germany and Japan and fought two total wars in two theaters against two tremendous powers. The United States had the world's largest Air Force and Navy—and it had the bomb. How did this great power get itself pinned down on an obscure Asian peninsula by an un-mechanized third-rate power? Many blamed the administration for rejecting MacArthur's plan of action. But others blamed the soldiers. In addition, American POWs, it seemed, had difficulty standing up to their captors. "Brainwashing" by the Chinese, Americans were told, produced twenty-one U.S. defectors to China. But really more important, it was widely believed that the Chinese "leniency" policy toward U.S. POWs led the Americans to a passive existence in the POW camps. Under pressure they informed on each other, and occasionally engaged in collaborative behavior with the enemy; their death rate was the highest in history; and not one American managed to escape from an enemy prison camp throughout the war. The assumption was that the American POWs in Korea were somehow morally weak and uncommitted to traditional American values and ideals. Some blamed "progressive" educational methods at home, others blamed the "new generation of youth," a group whose lives were soft compared to that of their parents and grandparents (whose cohorts had performed admirably as POWs in the two previous wars). Much of this was refuted by sociologists in the 1950s and 1960s; their research showed that POWs in Korea reacted much the same as POWs in preceding wars. But during the Korean War, a war that was not being won, the question of the American soldier's integrity was raised for the first time in the nation's history. It would be raised again in Vietnam.

For the first time in the twentieth century, African-American soldiers in the U.S. military fought alongside white soldiers. Plans for integrating the armed services had been moving slowly since the end of World War II. The Air Force and the Navy had made some headway toward integration, but the Army and the Marines had done nothing. Just before the 1948 election, Truman, hungry for African-American votes, promised African-American leaders that a committee would be established after the election to consider the integration of the armed services. The Fahy Committee, chaired by former U.S. Solicitor General Charles Fahy, concluded that integration was a necessity in the armed forces and advised the various divisions to begin implementation. Although the Army complained, it appeared that the Fahy Committee plan would finally be accepted just as the war in Korea broke out. The Army, however, insisted that it would not become a sociological experiment in time of national crisis, and the nation went into its third war of the century with a segregated force. But as the war dragged on and manpower demands increased, it became obvious that if the nation's fighting force in Korea was to be at full strength, integration would be necessary. Also, the influence of African-American votes from northern urban areas had begun to outweigh the influence of the South in the battle to see who had power in the Democratic party, and Truman (again eager for African American votes) pressured the military to give in to the demands for integration. A third reason was the influence of Ridgway, who had come to believe that an integrated Army would be more efficient. Segregation, he said, "is both un-American and un-Christian." By the end of 1954 segregation was virtually eliminated from the active military.[2]

Fighting alongside the U.S. and UN troops was the army of the ROK, not officially a part of the UN forces in Korea, but under the direct control of the UN command. The United States had tried to remake the army of the ROK in its own image, but with little success. As the war got hotter in fall 1951, it became apparent that the South Koreans were a weak link, unreliable in battlefield emergencies. The North Korean soldiers, on the other hand, proved that they were a formidable foe over and over again, and the question had to be asked: why did Communist Koreans fight better than non-Communist Koreans (or why did their Koreans fight better than ours)? One reason was the political corruption and favoritism that permeated the South Korean army's upper echelon. Family status and inheritance, not ability, determined the composition of the South Korean officer corps. Korean officers came from the privileged caste of Korea's society while the conscripts were drafted from the peasantry. The U.S. Army tried repeatedly to force changes in this area, but Rhee and the ROK government refused to make the reforms necessary to put competent commanders on the lines. When Rhee asked the United States for arms to equip ten additional units, Ridgway rejected the idea and in his explanation to the president wrote, "The basic problems with the ROK Army are leadership and training; not manpower and equipment. Lack of leadership extends throughout except in rare instances. . . . I estimate," Ridgway added, "that since the beginning of the Korean campaign equipment losses in [the] ROK Army have exceeded that necessary to equip 10 divisions; this without inflicting commensurate losses on the enemy and in some cases without the semblance of a battle."[3] In addition, and possibly more important, the ROK army had grown out of Japanese imperialism and could not be made to identify with the Korean people. This led to atrocities that, throughout the war, hurt the Allied cause and severely damaged the morale of the Korean people—who came to fear equally the wrath of both warring armies. There was also a great deal of corruption in the South Korean ranks. The enlisted men were fed from an allowance given their commanders. That money was often squandered, and the men on the line starved. Pay for enlistees was inadequate, and was often eaten up by inflation. As the war continued into 1952 and 1953, it appeared that the ROK army was improving on the line, but that turned out to be only a reflection of the static nature of the war in those last two years. In July 1953, the Chinese mounted a final offensive against the ROK II Corps and forced its collapse—as if to show the United States that the ally it had chosen was weak and crippled with corruption. The United States would face many of these same problems in dealing with the army of South Vietnam, another army that it tried to build in its own image—but failed.

The negotiations at Kaesong got off to a bad start—and then got worse. Kaesong was located in a neutral zone between the two armies, but once it was designated as the site of the talks, the Chinese immediately moved to surround the area, which gave them considerable control over the negotiations. The UN delegation, which arrived on July 10, was escorted five miles to the site of the negotiations (now within the Chinese lines) by the Chinese, and treated as a defeated enemy, even to the point of being taunted by Chinese soldiers along the way. There were conflicts over which side of the negotiating table each party should occupy (for the Chinese, the victor must sit on the south and the vanquished on the north), whose chairs should sit higher, and how large the respective flags should be.

The deal the UN placed on the table at Kaesong, once the haggling over trivialities was concluded, contained the following provisions: (1) a twenty-five-mile demilitarized zone would be established between the two armies (in their positions at the time of the ceasefire); (2) neither side would introduce reinforcements once the agreement was signed; (3) the ceasefire would be policed by both sides; and (4) POWs would be exchanged on a one-for-one basis. Acheson hoped that a ceasefire would "stop the fighting in a posture favorable to the defense [of South Korea] and, given the presence of U.N. troops over a considerable time, might harden into a maintainable peace."[4]

The Chinese plan was even less complicated: (1) the 38th parallel would be established as the central line of the demilitarized zone between the two armies; and (2) all foreign forces would be withdrawn from Korea. It seemed simple enough, but in fact neither condition was acceptable to the United States. First of all, the 38th parallel was a poor defensive position, and Ridgway, Acheson, and others refused to allow U.S. or ROK troops to be placed into such a vulnerable situation. U.S. negotiators instead demanded the present position of the troops, along or near the easily defended Kansas-Wyoming line, as it was called. The Chinese, however, had understood, through informal lines of communication, that the United States wanted a *status quo ante*—a resumption of the 38th parallel as the line of demarcation. "The Russians and the Chinese could well have been surprised, chagrined, and given cause to feel tricked," Acheson admitted in his memoirs. "[W]hen at Kaesong we revealed a firm determination as a matter of major principle not to accept the 38th parallel as the armistice line. . . . They found us demanding a new line for our sphere of influence, not only more militarily significant but involving considerable loss of prestige for them."[5]

The second point in the Chinese plan was also unacceptable because it became clear early on that the Chinese did not consider their army in North Korea to be a foreign army. Their force, they argued, was not directed by any national government. The soldiers from China who were fighting for the liberation of North Korea, they said, were "volunteers," fighting on their own recognizance with no direction from Beijing or any other foreign government. This, of course, would not wash with the UN delegation. If the Chinese had their way, the settlement would have meant an American unilateral withdrawal.

China's agenda frightened Syngman Rhee, who had come to the conclusion that the United States was about to cut its losses and leave South Korea in the hands of the ROK army with three quarters of a million Chinese poised to invade. Acheson and General Marshall both made public statements to reassure Rhee that the United States would not pull out of Korea until a peace agreeable to all parties was firmly established. When it became apparent to Rhee that the United States would not, in fact, leave him high and dry, he again began demanding that Korean unification be a condition of the settlement, which complicated and slowed the negotiating process even further.

Through late July and August, the UN and Chinese delegations continued to argue over the location of the demarcation line, with the Chinese pushing for a *status quo ante* at the 38th parallel while the UN delegation insisted that the line remain at or near the strong defenses along the Kansas-Wyoming line. On August 23 the Chinese charged that the United States had bombed Kaesong the night before. Ridgway denied the charge, but two days later U.S. aircraft accidentally did strafe Kaesong. The UN delegation accepted responsibility for the attack and apologized. At this point, however, all parties agreed that the talks should be moved to a neutral site. Panmunjom was chosen, a small village between the lines. Negotiations resumed there on October 7.

At home, desire for a truce was building. The American public had come to believe (with some justification, based on reports from Washington) that the talks in Korea would bring an end to the fighting almost immediately, that a ceasefire would be declared and then what-ever minor hagglings remained would be worked out later. The press had come to the same conclusion. By September, editorials began criticizing the administration for avoiding a ceasefire so as to attain small parcels of wasteland at the expense of American lives. It was a point well made: while the ceasefire line was under discussion, there were 60,000 UN casualties, of whom 22,000 were American boys. The American people were becoming impatient.

Under this pressure Ridgway was instructed to accept a ceasefire at the current line of contact, provided the Chinese agreed to sign the ceasefire within thirty days. The Chinese, however, refused to accept the deadline. The UN delegation relented and agreed to extend the deadline as long as progress was being made in other areas. On November 26 the line of demarcation was finally set. Rumors passed through the ranks that the war was about to end: newspapers predicted an end to hostilities on a daily basis. But the fighting went on, as the two armies continued to grind away at each other for nameless pieces of ground.

The two delegations went on to item three: post-armistice inspec-tion. Ridgway believed that this was necessary to ensure that South Korea would not be invaded in the future. However, the administration was anxious to get on with a settlement and instructed Ridgway to give some ground on this issue. The United States hoped that the main deterrent against a Communist attack from the North would be U.S. retaliation against the Chinese mainland. By December 27 the quibbling over item three was handed over to the sub-delegation level. Here they also con-sidered the question of rehabilitation of airfields in the North. It was U.S. air power that had been the real advantage against the Chinese, and Ridgway balked at the prospect of giving up that advantage. If the Chinese were allowed to establish an effective air force in North Korea, the American position in the Far East might be jeopardized. However, the UN delegation could not argue effectively that North Korea should be forced to remain without air power while the United States clearly intended to build up its air force in the South—and that point had to be conceded.

The teams then pressed on to the next agenda item: the exchange of POWs. At the beginning of the peace talks the UN delegation pushed hard for an exchange of POW lists, but the Chinese continually shoved the issue aside. Finally in late December they produced their list and then agreed to an "all-for-all" prisoner exchange. But the lists and numbers provided by the Chinese did not add up. The Chinese had boasted that they had captured some 65,000 UN and South Korean soldiers, while the UN forces and the army of the ROK counted over 100,000 missing. That difference alone was significant, but the list of POWs offered by the Chinese at the peace talks in December counted only 7,142 South Koreans, 3,198 Americans, 919 British, and a little over 200 other UN personnel—hardly the 65,000 they claimed to hold. At the time there was a fear that large numbers of POWs had either been killed or sent to prisons in China and the Soviet Union.[6]

Another problem emerged over voluntary repatriation. Many of the Chinese and North Koreans held by the UN did not want to return north after the war. The Chinese negotiators refused to accept this concept of voluntary repatriation, and insisted that the UN turn over all prisoners. But the situation was complicated. The UN held in its POW camps, besides the North Korean and Chinese POWs, Communist South Koreans, non-Communist North Koreans, and even Chinese who had fought for the Nationalists in the Chinese civil war and had been captured by the Communists and forced to fight on their side. There were Korean civilians who had been caught as spies, political prisoners of the South Korean government, and even common criminals. The UN refused simply to hand over the entire lot; the Chinese insisted, claiming that the Geneva Convention did not give the UN the right to decide which prisoners should be repatriated. Their argument was correct, but the Geneva Convention architects clearly did not foresee such a complex situation. The two sides locked over the issue.

In April 1952 the UN negotiators decided to classify their POWs into two groups: those who wanted to return to North Korea or China, and those who did not. Those who wanted to go would be exchanged in an all-for-all deal. The Chinese at Panmunjom seemed prepared to accept this as a solution to the problem, and both sides appeared on the verge of a final agreement. However, a large part of the UN prison at Koje-do had been taken over by a militant group of anti-Communist Chinese prisoners, and the prison was now well beyond the control of the UN military authorities. These militant anti-Communists used terror tactics to influence the decisions of other prisoners during the UN screening process to determine each prisoner's status. Consequently, many more prisoners than anyone expected demanded asylum as non-Communists. The UN prisoners in its custody totaled some 170,000. But the final tally from the UN screening showed that only 70,000 POWs in UN hands wanted to return home to North Korea or China. To the Chinese, the prospect that more than half of their soldiers did not want to return to their socialist homeland was either a crass propaganda ploy by the Americans or a very serious embarrassment and a criticism of their new society. They received the news in silence, and then abruptly broke off the talks. The two sides were meeting again by midsummer, but the only objective was to maintain contact. Nothing was resolved. It became the main sticking point that kept the war going.

As summer 1952 approached it was clear that the Korean War would significantly influence the coming national election—and that the election as well would affect the outcome of the war. Truman spent his last months in office with a popularity rating in the polls as low as 23 percent, the lowest of any modern president. He was saddled with the war, corruption in his administration, and accusations from McCarthy and the Republicans that he was soft on Communism. To the opposition, Truman's administration had become "that mess in Washington." Senator Karl Mundt of South Dakota came up with a formula for a Republican victory in 1952: K^1C^2—Korea, Communism, and corruption. Not even a miracle like the one Truman had pulled off in 1948 seemed possible. In March, he announced he would not seek another term.

The Republicans were chafing at the bit. They had congressional leadership and appealing candidates, and the issues were on their side as the 1952 election approached. Robert Taft seemed the front-runner early on, but soon Eisenhower emerged to take a commanding lead in the polls, with MacArthur (splitting the party's right wing with Taft) poised for a deadlock. Taft's demand for a victory in Korea frightened several of the UN allies, particularly the British; but many Americans saw Taft as an isolationist who might move the nation in the opposite direction, away from the Korean commitment. In fact, that was Taft's philosophy on Korea: either victory or withdrawal. Eisenhower, on the other hand, was perceived as a doer, a middle-of-the-road candidate, a believer in containment, and a proven soldier. If Ike could beat the Germans, he could end the war in Korea. Eisenhower won the nomination easily, and he kept the Republican Right in line by choosing Richard Nixon as his running mate. A hardliner who had made a career as a Communist hunter, Nixon would have more of an impact on the next war than on Korea. Late in the campaign, on October 24, Ike announced what many wanted to hear: that he would go to Korea to secure an honorable peace. It was a promise the Democrats could not match. Eisenhower and his foreign policy advisor John Foster Dulles spoke strongly and often during the campaign about the problems the Truman administration had caused in Korea, but, in fact, Eisenhower believed in containment, and he had supported Truman's decision to intervene in Korea. As president, he would come to believe in the necessity of limited warfare—no matter how distasteful it was.

The Democrats went to Adlai Stevenson, the governor of Illinois and a proven liberal. Stevenson tried to distance himself from the unpopular Truman administration, particularly on domestic affairs. But on foreign policy, Stevenson went down the line with his predecessor. Like Eisenhower, he believed in containment; and he also believed in the president's decision to intervene in Korea. He refused to endorse a policy of either unilateral withdrawal or escalation of the war, offering the voter more of the same.

Ike won a landslide victory that brought in a Republican Congress. Most Americans believed that he could and would bring an honorable settlement to the Korean War, and certainly many voted for him for that reason. As president-elect, Eisenhower kept his promise and went to Korea, where his physical image alone raised morale among U.S. troops in the field. But in Washington, as president, Ike would have to form a foreign policy that would bring the honorable settlement that he had promised American voters.

When Eisenhower resigned his NATO post to run for president, he was replaced in Europe by Ridgway. Ridgway's replacement in the Far East was General Mark W. Clark, a staunch anti-Communist who argued the MacArthur solution to the war, including the use of Nationalist Chinese forces and the bombing of Manchuria. The concept of a limited war remained a deep frustration to those commanders who had come out of the successes of World War II.

By 1952 the forces on the Korean peninsula had reached an equilibrium. The times of long sweeps, massive offensives, and decisive victories had passed. The two enemies settled down to digging in and making their positions stronger. The Chinese and North Koreans had about 300,000 men manning their frontline positions, and probably another 600,000 behind the lines and in Manchuria as reserves. Perhaps as many as 10,000 Soviet advisors, trainers, and technical personnel were also working behind the Chinese lines. The UN forces had placed about 250,000 soldiers on their front line, with an additional 450,000 behind the lines as reserves and support troops.

The action flared up occasionally, and both sides kept alert. But for the most part the war had settled into stalemate. In August 1952 the Air Force increased pressure on the North Koreans and the Chinese by hitting hard at the North Korean capital of Pyongyang. In September, the Chinese attacked all along the line, but they were thrown back at every instance. Nameless hills continued to change hands, back and forth, and there were occasional artillery duels, but the war in Korea was stalled. It rated little more than back-page news at home.

Syngman Rhee continued to embarrass the Americans by insisting on a unified Korea, by committing atrocities against his own people, and by spouting disconcerting anti-Communist rhetoric throughout the negotiations. In May 1952, he made the UN position appear even less defendable by arresting his leading political opponents and declaring martial law. By July, after some pressure from Washington, Rhee agreed to a compromise. He lifted the martial law and released the opposition from prison on the condition that he would be reelected indefinitely.

The war seemed in permanent stalemate until March 1953 when, just after Stalin died, there was a break. The negotiations, by then, had been suspended since October the year before, and the United States was looking for a way to reopen the talks without showing any weakness. In the last days of 1952 the Red Cross suggested that the two sides make an effort to exchange wounded and sick prisoners. General Clark agreed to the plan and informed the Chinese and North Korean commanders that he was ready to participate in such an exchange. Six weeks later, on

March 5, the Communists responded that not only were they prepared to exchange sick and wounded, but that they were ready to end the war. In addition, Chou Enlai announced in Beijing that China would seek a solution to the POW question by turning the matter over to a neutral nation to administer, and that China would abide by the results. By mid-April, the two sides had agreed to begin swapping their sick and wounded prisoners. The Communists agreed to release about 450 South Koreans and 150 UN soldiers; the UN agreed to release some 700 Chinese and 5,100 North Koreans. Ultimately, both sides released more than they originally planned.

It is difficult to analyze this decision. Clearly, the Soviets wished the war to continue. The United States was pinned down in an unwin-nable war, while at the same time, China was becoming more and more dependent on money and resources from Moscow. China, however, was clearly tired of the war. It no longer felt threatened by UN action along the Yalu, and the loss of its men on the line had become enormous com-pared to gains made elsewhere in propaganda and diplomacy. In addi-tion, China wanted badly to get on with its own domestic reconstruction and had neither the time nor the money to spend defending North Korea. Possibly Chou Enlai, on his visit to Moscow in October 1952, convinced the Soviets that China must get out of Korea if it were to make its socialist experiment a success.

That led to a definite thaw in the negotiations, but it left unanswered the central question of how to deal with those POWs in UN hands who did not want to return to Communism. After a great deal of squab-bling through April and May, it appeared that a settlement would be reached. However, there was a breakdown in the negotiations in May, and the United States reacted to the Chinese boycott by increasing its military pressure in an attempt to force the enemy back to the nego-tiating table. General Clark turned up the volume on the war by ini-tiating a plan to destroy the North Korean rice crop from the air. U.S. pressure of this sort had not worked before, and it would not work here; the Communists simply became more stalwart in their position. The month-long bombing campaign was considered a success by the Army; however, its only apparent result was a Chinese attack against the UN forces all along the line in mid-July. By then it was clear to both sides that negotiations at Panmunjom were on the verge of completion, and each side was attempting to improve its position and end the war on a note of victory. The Chinese attack proved to be the hottest point in the war since the Chinese sixth offensive in May 1951. Six Chinese divisions slammed into the ROK II Corps near the center and pushed them back six miles after three days of hard fighting. The Chinese succeeded in breaking the line in two places, and several ROK units were crushed. For a time the attack posed a real danger, but General Maxwell Taylor, who had replaced Van Fleet in February, filled the gaps and stopped the ROK retreat. Eventually the Chinese push ran out of energy.

The distinctive factor in this engagement was the air battle. Prior to this the air was largely controlled by the U.S. Air Force. Soviet MiGs had been present, but not in enough numbers to be a real threat. During the last year of negotiations, U.S. intelligence had reported a buildup of air power by the Chinese just over the Yalu. When the war heated up in summer 1953, the MiGs came out to challenge U.S. air power for the first time. But the big surprise was the Chinese use of Il-28s, a medium-range jet bomber with the capability of striking deep into South Korea.

The POW agreement was finally signed on June 8. There would be a five-nation repatriation commission under the direction of India. Through a plan of supervised interrogation, the Communists would be given up to 120 days to change the minds of their soldiers who had decided not to return north to Communism. The agreement would lead the way to a final truce; it would also lead the way to a final Chinese assault. The Chinese tried to push back a bulge in the center of the UN line that reached up north to Kumhwa, the most northern point of the UN lines. They hit the right flank of the IX Corps and the ROK II Corps. The Chinese had some success in pushing the UN lines southward, but at great cost.

While everyone moved toward a truce (and the armies fought to achieve better positions), Syngman Rhee, it appeared, sought to shackle the entire process. Caught between the major powers, each with its own agenda for Korea's future, Rhee pushed his own plans for the future of Korea. He continued to insist that the enemy receive no concessions, that Communism be pushed off the Korean peninsula, and that all of

Korea be united under his leadership. In addition, if the UN negotiators refused to present his demands to the enemy, he threatened not to honor the truce and to continue the war alone. In mid-June, after the POW agreement was signed and the final phases of negotiations were underway, Rhee told his senior commanders in the field that the ROK would fight on after the truce was signed.

Eisenhower responded to Rhee's threats by offering him a postwar defense treaty, support for a twenty-division ROK army, and billions of dollars in aid in exchange for his support of the armistice. If Rhee refused, Eisenhower threatened to pack up his forces and leave Korea to its own fate. Certainly, such a move would have been politically impossible for Eisenhower and the Republicans in 1953, and in Washington it was decided that if Rhee refused to accept the armistice, he would be removed from power and replaced with a U.S. ally. On July 26 the Communists launched one last offensive against the ROK lines and crushed a number of divisions. Taylor again brought up reinforcements and held the line, but it seemed to show Rhee that the army of the ROK would be easy prey in a war alone against the forces of the North. On July 9 Rhee announced he would cooperate fully with the UN and the United States in efforts to unite Korea politically.

With the last of the obstacles overcome, the two sides signed the armistice on July 27 at Panmunjom. The Korean War was over. In the days that followed, the POWs were finally exchanged, and the issue that had kept the two sides fighting for an additional two years was finally resolved. The Communists returned 12,773 prisoners, of whom 7,862 were South Koreans and 3,597 were Americans. The UN returned 75,823 prisoners. Of that number, only 5,640 were Chinese; the rest were North Koreans.

The tally of dead and wounded showed that the Korean War was expensive. The United States lost 54,246 killed, a few less than were killed in Vietnam. Of that number 33,629 were actual combat casualties. Over 50,000 South Korean soldiers were killed fighting in their civil war, which became a superpower conflict. The total number of UN soldiers killed, wounded, or missing was tallied at just under one million, of whom 94,000 were combat and noncombat-related deaths. On the other side, the total number killed, wounded, or missing has been put at 1.4 million, of whom 520,000 were North Koreans. These numbers, of course, do not reflect the real tragedy of war: civilian casualties. The numbers are truly staggering for a war that was fought to no strategic gain by either side, in an area of the world with little strategic significance.

But the Korean War had a number of important results. First of all, it forced the United States to reevaluate its cold war strategy against world Communism. Containment had become the basis of American foreign policy after World War II: the United States and its allies in the free world were pledged to hold back Communist expansion. But that strategy was originally directed at Europe where the Soviets seemed to have placed most of their energies. The outbreak of the war in Korea forced the United States to change its focus (at least temporarily) to the Far East, where the Communist governments in Beijing and Moscow appeared the most intent on expanding their empire. The same circumstances in Korea pushed the United States into rebuilding Japan to support U.S. military operations in Asia. Japan quickly became "fortress Japan," the primary U.S. outpost in northeastern Asia. What had once been a European-focused strategy was now shifted, at least in part, to Asia.

The Korean War also brought about a shift in U.S. military planning and foreign policy by making the provisions of NSC-68 the basis for the nation's future foreign policy strategy. To conduct such wars as the one in Korea, the United States began building a large conventional force (as opposed to relying simply on nuclear arms). The Korean War seemed to have taught the Americans a lesson, at least in this respect. The U.S. military was unprepared to fight in Korea, and thus was unable to carry the war to a quick conclusion. The U.S. conventional force in the future, it was decided, must be well trained, well equipped, always ready, and effective against the enemy. The result was a massive increase in military spending, and the development of what Eisenhower called the "military-industrial complex." It fueled the economy through the Vietnam War and after, and increased economic growth in the nation—and this in turn fed its own growth.

The Korean War also seemed to solidify in the American mind the concept of monolithic Communism—the idea that all Communists worldwide were of one mind, controlled from Moscow. To most

Americans, the Chinese and the North Koreans were fighting under direct orders from Moscow. This led to another belief: that the United States was not, in fact, fighting the real enemy in Korea—that the U.S. Army was wasting its time and energy against these proxies of the Soviet Union. Much of this was also spelled out in NSC-68, and this gave that document even more credence as the basis of the American foreign policy and military planning after the Korean War.

The Korean War also directed politics at home. McCarthyism, begun under its own steam as a domestic phenomenon, was fueled enormously by the Korean War. Communists, it seemed, were everywhere, and in Korea, American soldiers were being killed by Communists every day. To the American people the Korean War made Communism a real threat: not just some figment of Joe McCarthy's imagination, but Communists with guns, trying to take an area and being stopped by American troops. The war strengthened the Republican anti-Communist stance, and it allowed the Republicans to claim that the Democrats (who could not win the war) were "soft on Communism." By the time the war ended, the Republicans carried the national flag of anti-Communism while the Democrats were forced to sit on the bench on that issue—at least through the remainder of the 1950s.

The war in Korea, after its first year, became unpopular at home. Polls reflected that the American people were fed up with a war they could not win; but at the same time they were fearful of becoming involved in a greater war should the war escalate. It was a deep frustration that would be felt again in Vietnam. The war in Korea also gave the American people that first twinge that U.S. boys should not be dying in some far-off place for a purpose that was more ideological than specific. As negotiators haggled, soldiers died, and Americans grew more restive, more tired of the war.

However, the enemy maintained its role in the American mind as an evildoer, a concept that is important if the U.S. government is to maintain the public's support for war. There was plenty of evidence of atrocities committed by the enemy, stories of torture and "brainwashing" of UN POWs. After all, it was an era of strident anti-Communism in America, and most Americans believed in the government's argument that Communism was a dangerous thing that must be stopped before it spread too far. Consequently, the American people were willing to tolerate the war.

Eisenhower had fulfilled his campaign pledge; he had gone to Korea. It was not victory, but peace with honor. He had not wallowed in appeasement, but neither had he escalated the conflict. As a warrior who had won World War II, Eisenhower believed in total war as the only solution to a military conflict, as did MacArthur and others from the 1945 victory. But by the end of the war in Korea, Eisenhower had come around to the realities of the times. "Unlimited war in the nuclear age was unmanageable," he wrote, "and limited war [was] unwinnable."[7]

The Korean War also served to push the Chinese and the Soviets into a long-term relationship—a relationship that, in fact, established what the Americans had so feared since the Chinese revolution in 1949: a Sino-Soviet monolith in control of Central Asia. The face of the Sino-Soviet pact may have been smiling, but in fact, the Chinese and the Soviets did not get along well. The Soviets had supported Jiang and the Nationalists during the Chinese civil war (at the behest of Franklin Roosevelt), and Mao and his people maintained long memories. Also, the Soviets considered Mao a Communist reformer, even an adventurer who refused to toe the Moscow line, while the Chinese saw the Soviets as just another imperialist power. The Korean War served to push these natural antagonists into bed together: Soviet technology became aligned with Chinese manpower. It seemed an unbeatable military combination—and after the Korean War, it was America's worst nightmare.

It is true that the Chinese have long memories. They did not forget easily the U.S. involvement on the Asian mainland, and they did not forget easily their sons and husbands who died in Korea fighting the United States. Mao's oldest son, in fact, was killed in Korea. It would be a long time (if indeed it has yet happened) before the Chinese could come to trust the United States, and the two remained antagonists in the Far East—and then in the world for decades to come.

As a result of the Korean War the United States made it clear that it would maintain Jiang and the Chinese Nationalists (the Chinese Communists' enemy) on Formosa. And that, too, ingrained the growing distrust between the United States and China. America's China policy would keep China out of the UN and place the United States in the position of insisting that the Nationalists on Formosa somehow represented the one billion Chinese people living on the mainland under the obviously legitimate Beijing government of Mao Zedong. The United States argued this position until 1979 when President Jimmy Carter finally established full diplomatic relations with China and severed formal diplomatic ties with the Nationalists on Taiwan (Formosa).

The war also forced China to change its military tactics. China's army in Korea had been effective, especially early in the Chinese involvement, but the number of lives lost by the Chinese caused the military leaders in Beijing to pause. If they would again tangle with the Western powers in a conventional war, they came to believe, they would have to mechanize. Wars could not be won by throwing manpower against the highly mechanized Western armies. China looked to the Soviets for aid in this buildup, and the Soviets responded. Thus, as a result of the Korean War, China became a much stronger military force, and it also became more dependent on Soviet money and technology.

China's intervention in Korea would wreak havoc on the Vietnam War policy makers fifteen years later: would the Chinese intervene in Vietnam? Many thought they would if given the opportunity, or if U.S. forces invaded into North Vietnam. American policy in Vietnam was often based on what was called the "what if" problem of Chinese intervention. It was America's fear of war with Red China more than anything else that protected North Vietnam from a U.S. invasion.

Korea was America's first limited war, and it was a baptism by fire. It was also the battleground for the conflict between the old method of total war and the new limited warfare, fought now out of necessity, not desire. The old method of total war was personified in MacArthur, the military man who believed that a nation should put all its resources into victory or it should withdraw from the field. Limited war was anathema to him and many of those who had fought and won World War II. Truman represented limited war. As both president and politician, Truman had to look beyond military tactics and strategy. He saw that warfare in the world after World War II, with its threat of atomic power, could escalate quickly. He did not want total war with the Soviet Union, and he did all he could to avoid it. So it was, much to the disgust of MacArthur and military men like him who had fought World War II, that Truman was forced to contain the war in Korea. It was the right decision, but it was frustrating to America's military men and to the American people.

Consequently, the Korean War set the stage for Vietnam. The working mechanism was in place by the time the United States became deeply involved in Southeast Asia—put in place by the United States' conduct in Korea. National Security Council directives that mapped U.S. foreign policy in Asia made it clear that the United States government believed strongly that Communism, directed from Moscow, was attempting to spread throughout Asia, and that it was the mission of the United States to stop that spread through military means if necessary. NSC-68 spoke to the problem. NSC-48/5 made it clear that Southeast Asia was an area of the world where American aid was the most needed.

No sooner was the United States out of one bog on the Asian mainland than it became bogged down in another conflict there—for generally the same reasons, and in generally the same way. Eisenhower, as we will see, had learned the lessons of Korea. He recalled how the limited land war on the Asian continent had badly damaged the Democratic party and become unpopular with the American people. But to his successors Korea was a forgotten war, and its lessons were overshadowed by the greater complexities of the cold war itself. American foreign policy advisors and planners (many of the same people) began to look at Korea as a success rather than the failure that it was. As the situation began to unravel in Vietnam in the 1960s, the United States seemed to see itself again being needed to fulfill a mission to stop another Communist threat in Asia—as it had done in Korea. And the United States jumped in with both feet. Korea was not a U.S. victory, and U.S. military advisors and policy makers in Washington after 1961 should have seen Korea as a lesson.

In 1951, at the MacArthur hearings, the Joint Senate Armed Forces and Foreign Affairs Committee issued a report concerning one of the committee's major topics of discussion: the constitutionality of declaring war without congressional approval. The report stated that "the United States should never again become involved in war without the consent of Congress."[8] The committee's main fear was that the situation in Korea might set a precedent for U.S. involvement elsewhere in the world without the consent of the Congress and the American people. The debate has raged since. The Founding Fathers believed that the armed forces should not be committed (war should not be declared) without the consent of the people—through their Congress—and that such a devastating decision should not be left up to the president. Truman's decision to send troops to Korea without the consent of Congress was just the beginning of the debate that would not end with Vietnam, with the Gulf War, or with America's involvement in the Middle East after the 9/11 attacks.

It is important that the war in Korea set a precedent for using an international force to repel aggression. In Korea, the international character of the UN forces justified U.S. intervention in the region. It was also a means to supply manpower and arms for the effort. In Vietnam, the United States intervened without international support, and when the war soured, there was only one place to lay blame. In the Persian Gulf War of 1991, George H. W. Bush would again seek the support of an international coalition, once again mostly to justify U.S. actions. In many ways it legitimized the war against Iraq just as it had legitimized the war against North Korea and the Chinese armies. George W. Bush's "coalition of the willing" was intended to follow his father's lead in the Middle East. But much of the world was not willing to follow the United States into that war.

So it is today that Korea is the last outpost of the cold war, just as it was the first flare-up in that war of military buildup, misunderstanding, and fear. Only a truce was signed, of course, never a peace treaty, and in what has become almost an anachronistic play, the armies of the ROK look across the ceasefire line at the armies of North Korea. South Korea has become one of the five Asian "Tigers" in the world of economic warfare, while the North continues to languish under socialist stagnation. Both sides still talk of a desire for unification, but the old animosities continue to prevail.

PART II
VIETNAM

5

POSTWAR POLITICS, FOREIGN POLICY, AND THE FRENCH INTERLUDE

In 1972 General Maxwell Taylor, a major participant in both Korea and Vietnam, wrote of the Korean War and the lessons it should have taught the American people but did not:

> The national behavior showed a tendency to premature war-weariness and precipitate disenchantment with a policy which had led to a stalemated war. This experience, if remembered, could have given some warning of dangers ahead to the makers of the subsequent Vietnam policy. Unfortunately, there was no thorough-going analysis ever made of the lessons to be learned from Korea, and later policy makers proceeded to repeat many of the same mistakes.[1]

Almost following the Korean War, Americans began to convince themselves that they had won that war. The road into Vietnam was paved with many of the lessons from Korea, but for most of those making the decisions, the lessons from Korea went unlearned.

In many ways, America's twenty-year involvement in Vietnam grew out of the war in Korea. Many of Washington's policies, directives, and even some of the same people who had conducted the Korean War also played a part in directing the war in Vietnam. And in many ways the situations were the same. Both Korea and Vietnam had been occupied by Japan during World War II, and were then abandoned by the defeated

Japanese army, leaving vast power vacuums on the Asian mainland. Both areas were divided at the end of the war, basically because the Allies were unsure how to handle the situations there; and in both divisions the North (nearest the Chinese border) came to be occupied by Communists, and the South by non-Communists. Moreover, the United States became involved in both wars for many of the same reasons, but most importantly to maintain its role as a world leader, to show the developing world that the United States was the one nation willing and able to stand up to Communism anywhere in the world—even in the hostile jungles and rice paddies of Vietnam. Along with that came the commitment to containment, to halt the expansion of Communism, and to stop Communist aggressions. At the same time, like Korea, Vietnam had little strategic value for U.S. foreign policy, military planning, or its strategy in Asia.

Certainly, the Vietnam War was more devastating to the American psyche than Korea. The United States fought to a standstill in Korea, and was able to come away bloodied but content that its objective of containment had been achieved; the war ended honorably for the United States. But in Vietnam, the United States clearly lost the war. In order to get out of the bog of Vietnam, Washington was forced, by way of negotiations, to leave Vietnam and then stand by helplessly as the North Vietnamese army overran South Vietnam two years later, uniting the nation and finally bringing the war to a close after some thirty years of military conflict. The impact of those events in Vietnam would greatly affect the future conduct of the U.S. military. And of course, probably more significant than anything else is the divisive and lasting effect that the Vietnam War had on the American people.

The Vietnam War was not an aberration in the U.S. foreign policy of the post–World War II period. Intervention against Communist insurgency, as it was called then, had been the dominate characteristic of the U.S. foreign policy since 1945. America's involvement in Vietnam was just one of a number of situations throughout the world that had resulted in U.S. military intervention. Truman, of course, inaugurated this policy and then passed it on to his successors. He supported Jiang and the Chinese Nationalists against Mao and his Communists in the Chinese civil war. He assisted the anti-Communist forces in Greece. He helped put down the Huk insurgency in the Philippines. And he sent advisors to Vietnam and conducted the war in Korea—all in the name of containing Communism. Eisenhower inherited the policy. He assisted in the overthrow of leftist regimes in Iran and Guatemala. He sent Marines to Lebanon. He overthrew an unsympathetic government in Laos. John Kennedy attempted to remove Fidel Castro from Cuba. He used covert forces to aid in the defeat of left-wing guerrillas in Columbia and British Guiana. And he intervened in the Congo to combat leftists there. Lyndon Johnson sent troops to the Dominican Republic to put down a leftist insurgency less than two months after he sent the first ground combat forces into Vietnam. American presidents from Truman to Johnson certainly inherited the mess in Vietnam, but more importantly they also inherited the U.S. cold war foreign policy that virtually demanded U.S. intervention anywhere in the world.

The conflict in Vietnam was a quagmire well before the United States got involved. The Vietnamese people had been in a struggle for their own independence, mostly from China, almost from the beginning of Vietnam's existence. The war in Vietnam, unlike the war in Korea, had no real beginning. It was, in fact, an escalation of fighting that had been going on for centuries. In 1847, it was France, in the vanguard of European imperialism, that moved in to colonize Vietnam and again take away its independence. The French colony of 1847 became Indochina, and included Laos and Cambodia. The French moved quickly to change the local economy to their own advantage, establishing tea, rice, and rubber plantations and importing and selling opium to the Vietnamese people.

In the late 1880s an anticolonial movement emerged in Vietnam, led by a group from the scholar-gentry class. It was a true nationalist movement, but by 1908 the movement was dead, crushed by the French in the tried-and-true colonial manner of imprisoning or murdering the movement's leaders. This Can Vuong nationalist movement greatly influenced a young Vietnamese boy named Nguyen Tat Thanh, who at age fifteen witnessed the brutal repression of the movement. In 1917 he traveled to Paris to lobby the French government for rights for the Vietnamese people, and there he became a prominent leader in his country's longtime independence movement. He changed his name to Nguyen Ai-Quoc, and in 1919 he attended the Versailles Treaty conference in Paris to appeal for equal rights for the Vietnamese people within

The War in Vietnam

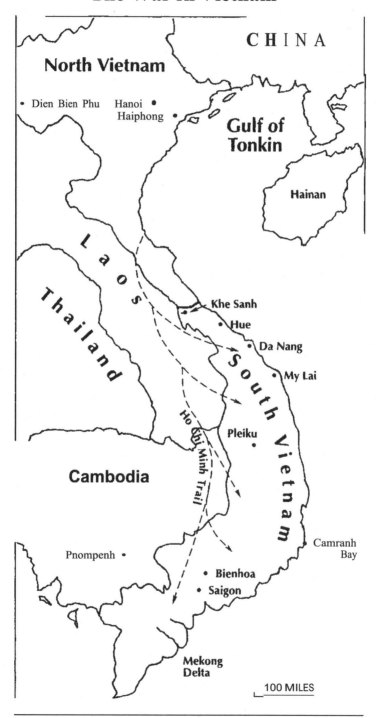

the French government. He asked for Vietnamese representation in the French parliament, freedoms of the press and assembly in Vietnam, and the release of all political prisoners. His demands went unheard.

In 1924 Nguyen Ai-Quoc went to the Soviet Union and openly chastised the Communist government there for not doing more to bring an end to worldwide colonialism. In February, 1930 Nguyen founded the Vietnamese Communist party. Ten years later he again changed his name, this time to Vuong. He joined forces with Pham Van Dong and Vo Nguyen Giap, both history teachers from Hue, the ancient Vietnamese capital in central Vietnam. In 1941 these three men, under Vuong's leadership, founded the League for Vietnamese Independence, or Viet Minh. They considered themselves antifascists, on the side of the Soviets against German and Japanese fascism. The main objectives of the Viet Minh were to achieve independence from France and to establish a new socialist state in Vietnam after the war. They planned to mobilize a peasant force that would create disruption through guerrilla activities against the French. A military school was founded, and the Liberation Army was formed under the leadership of Giap, Chu Van Tan, and Van Tien Dung. In 1942 Vuong changed his name again, this time to Ho Chi Minh, meaning "He Who Enlightens."

The French Vichy regime ceded nearly all its rights to the Indochina colony to the Japanese by agreement on July 29, 1941—an intolerable situation for the Americans who opposed the spread of the Japanese Empire through the western perimeters of the Pacific Rim. To slow the Japanese advance President Roosevelt froze Japanese assets in the United States and placed an embargo on shipments of oil to Japan. The Japanese needed Indonesian oil to maintain their military machine in the Pacific, and on December 7, when negotiations with the United States broke down, the Japanese moved to obtain the oil they needed. To facilitate their attacks south, they bombed the U.S. fleet at Pearl Harbor. On that same day the Japanese army moved into Saigon and took over Vietnam. Ho and the Viet Minh merely shifted their war for independence from the French imperialists to the Japanese imperialists. In 1942, Ho was arrested by the Nationalist armies of Jiang Jieshi. A year later, at the insistence of the American Office of Strategic Services (OSS), he was released to carry on his fight against the Japanese in Vietnam. Thus, like most Communists during World War II, Ho Chi Minh and his supporters fought on the side of the United States and its allies against the forces of fascism. The American leadership maintained its celebrated wartime pragmatism of the enemy of my enemy is my friend.

Throughout the war with Japan, Ho's popularity grew among the people of Vietnam. He became their leader against the forces of imperialism, both the French and the Japanese—and World War II for the Vietnamese became another war for independence. When the war ended, the Vietnamese believed that their nation would be granted its independence and the forces of colonialism in Asia would be laid to rest. After all, the Viet Minh had fought on the winning side and had helped defeat the victor's enemy.

Roosevelt agreed. FDR was an ardent anti-colonialist, and he believed that after the war most of the Asian colonies belonging to England, France, and the Netherlands should receive their independence. The administration of such a plan, he believed, would come from the not-yet-established United Nations through trusteeships. On Vietnam, FDR wrote to his secretary of state, Cordell Hull, in January 1944: "France has had the country—thirty million inhabitants for nearly one hundred years, and the people are worse off now than they were at the beginning." Roosevelt agreed that the colony might remain in French hands, but that it should be administered through an international trusteeship.[2] France, however, made it clear that it intended to reoccupy Indochina after the war, and England supported France against FDR's insistence that colonialism in postwar Asia should come to an end.

In the last year of World War II, the United States and the Viet Minh first made contact as allies against a common enemy. In April 1945, a senior OSS officer named Archimedes Patti went to Hanoi from his base of operations in Kunming, China. His mission was to set up an intelligence operation in Indochina against the Japanese, and to make contact with any Vietnamese contingency that might aid U.S. pilots downed in the area. He found Ho Chi Minh and the Viet Minh willing and able to help. Patti came to know Ho well, and he soon saw that the soldiers of the Viet Minh were a valuable ally in the war against Japan.

Patti knew that Ho was a Communist, but he reported back to his headquarters that Ho was not affiliated with Moscow. "He was more of a nationalist," Patti told an interviewer in the late 1970s, "who was using the Communist techniques and methods to achieve his ends."[3] Ho, Patti recalled, considered himself independent of the Soviets, and he hoped he would receive aid from the United States and even the French after the war, as long as the French did not return to Vietnam as colonizers. According to Patti, Ho also knew that the United States would not aid him in a fight against the French, if, in fact, the postwar era brought a Vietnamese war for independence. He did, however, hope that the United States would lend moral support to the Vietnamese and their independence movement.

When the war ended, the French remained adamant in their intentions to reoccupy Vietnam. French leaders believed that their country would need the money that a colony like Indochina would generate to survive in the postwar period. They also felt that French prestige as a world power had been damaged severely by the French military collapse in 1940, and they hoped to recoup some of that prestige by rebuilding France's nineteenth-century overseas empire. However, in the first months after the war ended, France simply lacked the means to return to Vietnam and take the reins of power there. As the Japanese forces pulled out of Vietnam, a power vacuum resulted, pulling in forces from various areas, all intent on controlling Vietnam, or at least having their power felt there. A Viet Minh force led by Giap, and accompanied by several American advisors, moved south from southern China toward Hanoi. At the same time, Nationalist occupation units from Chongqing in China also moved into Vietnam from the north. The Allies had given them the role of occupying Vietnam north of the 16th parallel after the Japanese moved out. In addition, two Chinese Nationalist-supported Vietnamese groups began moving south from China: the Vietnamese Nationalist party, and the Vietnamese Revolutionary League. The British were assigned the Allied role of occupying southern Vietnam, below the 16th parallel, as the Japanese withdrew from that area. Bao Dai, the Japanese-sponsored Vietnamese emperor, abdicated his throne immediately.

On September 2, 1945, at Hanoi, Ho Chi Minh announced the independence of Vietnam. Patti helped him write the declaration: "All men are created equal," it began. "They are endowed by their Creator with certain unalienable rights, among these are Life, Liberty and the Pursuit of

Happiness. . . . These are undeniable truths." The declaration then concluded: "Vietnam has the right to be a free and independent country; and in fact is so already." It was a declaration of independence from French colonialism; it was John Locke and Thomas Jefferson. The band played "The Star-Spangled Banner." Giap, in his speech, said that the "United States of America paid the greatest contribution" to Vietnamese independence and "against fascist Japan, and so the Great American Republic is our ally." Ho, in his speech, added: "We are convinced that the Allied nations . . . acknowledged the principles of self-determination and equality of nations [and] will not refuse to acknowledge the independence of Viet Nam."[4] During the ceremony a formation of U.S. P-38s flew over the field and dipped down in what appeared to be a salute. According to Patti it "was a quirk of fate . . . one of those things that happens once in a million years."[5] The planes apparently were on a flight path over the area, saw the activity, and flew down to take a look. For those at the ceremony, it all appeared to be an American-sponsored event, an American-sponsored government.

The United States, however, was being pushed to accept French demands for the recolonization of Vietnam. Roosevelt had hoped that one possible solution for a postwar Vietnam might be a trusteeship in Indochina under Jiang's leadership, but at Yalta, Jiang refused to take on that responsibility, although he agreed to accept Japan's surrender in northern Vietnam. Roosevelt needed the consent of the French to set up the trusteeship in Vietnam, but French president Charles DeGaulle would not be deterred from his commitment to return to Indochina as a colonizer. FDR died, however, before he could implement his plan and the entire situation was left to the next administration.

President Harry Truman adopted an immediate cold war stance toward the Soviet Union, and he began to build up U.S. forces in Western Europe in the face of what he and his advisors saw as Communist designs there. That, of course, meant French support for the new U.S. foreign policy in Europe. To gain that support, Truman decided not to push France to give up its Indochina colony, and all U.S. support for Vietnamese independence came to an end—sacrificed for the greater cause of the new cold war.

It was late August 1945, just days before Ho declared the independence of Vietnam, when the first French troops of the postwar era finally arrived in Saigon—with the aid of the British. Along with some French citizens, these French soldiers went on a rampage through the city, killing, raping, and destroying property. On August 24 the Viet Minh, not particularly strong in the South, retaliated against the French attacks. A Viet Minh terrorist squad attacked the Saigon suburb of Cite Herault, killing 150 French civilians. On October 2, a truce was signed between the French and the Viet Minh, but in that same week French reinforcements arrived under General Jacques Philippe Leclerc. With help from the British and a large number of rearmed Japanese soldiers, the French pushed the Viet Minh out of Saigon and into the countryside.

In the North, Ho Chi Minh was powerful and popular. However, around Hanoi, Chinese occupation troops under Jiang Jieshi were in complete control, and they were not willing to give up their position easily. In addition, the Chinese took advantage of the situation by dismantling much of Vietnam's industry in the North and shipping it back to China. France, now well embedded in the South, sat outside this situation in the North. The French could not remove the Chinese and they did not yet have the forces in Vietnam to tangle with the Viet Minh in their northern strongholds. However, it was a French-Viet Minh agreement that would force the Chinese out of Vietnam; Ho had to choose between allying himself with the French or the Chinese, and he finally chose the lesser of the two evils. On March 6, 1946, Ho Chi Minh and the French envoy, Jean Sainteny, came to an agreement that would recognize Vietnam as a free state within the French Union, and the Viet Minh would in turn allow the French to keep 25,000 soldiers in Vietnam for five years. To his critics in Hanoi, Ho argued:

> Don't you realize what it means if the Chinese remain? Don't you remember your history? The last time the Chinese came, they stayed a thousand years. The French are foreigners. They are weak. Colonialism is dying. The white man is finished in Asia. But if the Chinese stay now, they will never go. As for me, I prefer to sniff French shit for five years than eat Chinese shit for the rest of my life.[6]

In June the French violated the March agreement by proclaiming a separate government in the south, now called Cochinchina. By October it appeared that the two sides would not reconcile their differences and would finally fight for control of Vietnam. On November 23, after the French ordered the Viet Minh to evacuate Haiphong, a French cruiser opened fire on the city with heavy guns. The French reported that some 6,000 Vietnamese were killed in the action. Ho responded by urging restraint among his followers. But finally, on December 18, after further outbreaks of fighting and the French occupation of Hanoi itself, Giap reacted by counterattacking against the French troops in and around Hanoi. The French won this battle; it was the official beginning of what has been called the First Indochina War.

Such was the French intervention, designed only as a military action to maintain control of a nineteenth-century colonial empire. The ideological conflict (between Communism and the free world) was of little significance to the French cause in Vietnam. And France, already well past its prime as a world power, had little to lose in Vietnam in the end. U.S. policy makers, however, were playing on a larger world stage, and there was much to be lost by the fall of Vietnam. By the late 1940s, it had become a question of "us" and "them" for the United States, an ideological struggle for world leadership between the forces of freedom and the forces of Communism, between the new perceptions of good and evil. Vietnam by the late 1940s had also become the central focus in Washington of a south Asian defense strategy. France could only lose what it had already lost; the United States could lose its place as the leader of the new world order.

The Viet Minh movement was clearly an independence movement, a fight for freedom from French colonial domination. The suppression of an independence movement, however, did not play well with the French citizenry. So the Paris government moved to set up a common imperialist scenario that would create a situation in Vietnam that would be acceptable for public consumption. France would support one side of a Vietnamese civil war, and then argue that its side was the legitimate political entity. It would then operate the colony through a puppet. The only problem was that Vietnamese nationalism had coalesced around Ho Chi Minh and the Viet Minh in the North; if France wanted to turn the Vietnamese war for independence into a civil war it would have to create an alternative: an anti-Viet Minh, nationalist movement within

Vietnam. And it appeared in the late-1940s that there was no such movement—hence, the birth of the myth (that the United States inherited and perpetuated) that there were two warring courses of nationalism in Vietnam, and that France (and later the United States) supported the legitimate group of nationalists in the South against what was perceived as nothing more than Communist insurgents in the North. So, not only did France (and later the United States) ignore the incredible power of Vietnamese nationalism in the hands of the Viet Minh, it ignored even its existence; it was willing instead to accept the lie that the Vietnamese war for independence was a civil war between the forces of Communism and the forces of freedom.

The necessity of this lie came as a result of the lessons of history. History had taught that a strong nationalist movement could be nearly insurmountable—except by a stronger nationalist movement. It also taught that ideological movements like Communism either failed for lack of support, or they succeeded by force of arms. The French (and the Americans later) came to believe that the government they supported in the South was a nationalist movement and that Ho's government in the North was an ideological movement destined for failure. It was inconceivable to the policy makers in Paris and Washington that the Viet Minh Communist movement in the North could also be a nationalist movement.

The French need for an opposing nationalist movement in Vietnam led to the resurrection of Bao Dai, the abdicated emperor of Vietnam and Japanese wartime collaborator. The French placed him at the head of the new nation of Cochinchina in the South in spring 1949, and around him they tried to build a new Vietnamese nationalism friendly to French colonialism and hostile to the Viet Minh in the North. They also tried to create an army to support this fabricated nationalism; thus, the Vietnamese National Army was born. Understandably, few Vietnamese were willing to fight for the cause of French colonialism, and by the end of 1951 the National Army numbered only about 38,000, about one-third what the French had hoped to raise for their cause.

During this period the Viet Minh were denied any sort of recognition or assistance from the Soviet Union. Stalin was clearly focused on the diplomatic clashes in Europe, and Ho (like Marshal Tito in Yugoslavia) had subordinated Communism to nationalism, a policy that did not fit well into the Kremlin party line. One result of Moscow's disregard for the Viet Minh was that the United States could afford to ignore the situation as well—at least in the first years of the war—allowing the French to deal with their own anachronistic colonial problems. On the other side, the Viet Minh, seemingly neither fish nor fowl, were pretty much left to their own devices by the Communist world. "We apparently stand quite alone," Ho told Patti. "[W]e shall have to depend on ourselves."[7]

However, in the heat of the cold war, Washington never forgot that Ho Chi Minh was a Communist, and (by definition) any nation or group fighting him deserved U.S. support. In 1947, the Truman administration granted financial credits of some $160 million to France to fight the war in Vietnam, and Washington was also willing to look away as Marshall Plan money for French postwar recovery was also used to fight the Vietnamese Communists. Despite this, U.S. interests in Indochina were at best peripheral until about 1950. Aid was indirect, and U.S. support for France was based more on France's role in European affairs than on the future of affairs in Asia.

The French did not fight their war in Vietnam from a position of weakness. They had effective air and naval support, and their ground forces were described over and over as "the crack French forces." There were about 100,000 French soldiers in Vietnam in 1947. Opposing them were some 150,000 Viet Minh troops, but they probably carried less than 1,000 automatic weapons. The Viet Minh also maintained some artillery, probably about fifty pieces, and 150 mortars.

Despite their obvious superiority in men and matériel, the French were at a major disadvantage in Vietnam. There was no front in the jungle war; the Viet Minh occupied certain pockets of strength throughout the countryside, and the French found themselves moving from Viet Minh stronghold to Viet Minh stronghold in an attempt to engage the enemy in a significant battle. They could not establish their control over the peasant-dominated countryside, and it was the peasants in Vietnam who were the true heart of the nation.

The French response to this odd military situation was to build hundreds of small forts throughout the country in an attempt to occupy territory. It became immediately obvious, however, that these forts served more as Viet Minh targets than sources of French strength. The French, as Giap argued in his memoirs, "had to scatter their forces and set up thousands of military posts, big and small, to protect what they had seized. Thus, the war of aggression . . . was a process of constant scattering of [the French] army. And the more it was scattered the better conditions we had to destroy it part by part."[8]

The year 1950 was a turning point in the First Indochina War. By then the French had been defeated in the field; they had lost several major battles, and they had become a drain on American resources (mostly through Marshall Plan funding), and on NATO matériel, believed by most U.S. military experts to be needed in Europe and not fighting colonial wars in Asia. But in that year, North Korea invaded South Korea, Truman signed NSC-68, and Joseph McCarthy told an audience in Wheeling, West Virginia, that Communists in the State Department were directing the nation's foreign policy. Only the year before, Mao had declared the People's Republic of China, and the Soviets had exploded their first atomic bomb. These events changed America's attitude toward the world; and America's attitude changed toward Vietnam as well. In 1950, U.S. aid to France to carry on the war in Vietnam totaled $150 million. The next year it increased to $450 million, which by then was 40 percent of the total French bill for conducting the war. By 1953 the price was up to $785 million. Between 1950 and 1954 the French war in Vietnam was generally being waged by the United States with French troops. The French army had become an instrument of American foreign policy in Vietnam.

In February 1950, NSC-64 laid down an aspect of America's foreign policy that would ring in the ears of U.S. policy makers for the next twenty-five years: The "neighboring countries of Thailand and Burma could be expected to fall under Communist domination if Indochina were controlled by a Communist-dominated government. The balance of Southeast Asia would then be in grave hazard."[9] If it was not the origin of the domino theory, it was nearly so. The idea that all of Southeast Asia would collapse if Vietnam were to fall into Communist hands became a maxim of U.S. foreign policy in Washington. It was believed necessary then, in 1950, to establish a southern Asia defense perimeter of friendly nations surrounding China. And because of the domino theory,

Indochina became the linchpin in a defense line that stretched from India to Japan.

Add to this the growing fear of monolithic Communism, the Soviet bomb, the "loss" of China, the Republican party's continuous charges that Truman and the Democrats were "soft on Communism," and the belligerent attitude that most Americans had been developing toward the Soviets and Communism, and all of a sudden, in 1950, France's war against the Communists in Vietnam became more important. After 1949, the French increasingly warned Washington that direct military aid would be necessary to keep their troops in Vietnam. In February 1950, the National Security Council ordered the Joint Chiefs to "prepare as a matter of priority a program of all practicable measures to protect United States security interests in Indochina."[10] In April, NSC-68 warned that any further "extension of the area under the domination of the Kremlin would raise the possibility that no coalition adequate to confront the Kremlin with greater strength could be assembled."[11] In January 1950, the Soviets recognized the Viet Minh as the sole government of Vietnam, and Acheson responded that Ho Chi Minh had revealed "his true colors as the mortal enemy of native independence in Indochina."[12] The lines were drawn and the stage was set for U.S. intervention—only the French effort had to collapse.

American policy makers in the 1950s missed the mark in analyzing Ho and the situation in Vietnam and the rest of Southeast Asia. The postwar revolutions in that area of the world were viewed as Communist-inspired insurgencies that threatened to engulf all of southern Asia from India to the Philippines, when in fact these movements were almost always nationalist movements that were not at all inspired by either Beijing or Moscow. In fact, the Soviets paid little heed to these movements, probably because they believed they could not affect such strong local nationalism. Although Ho was eventually forced to accept aid from the USSR and China in his fight against France and then the United States, he always refused to subordinate his nationalist movement for independence to the will of the Communist forces in Moscow and Beijing. To Ho, the Soviets were little more than imperialists who wanted to control Vietnam, and the Chinese had been the hated enemy of the Vietnamese people for a thousand years. There was no reason for Ho to trust either Moscow or

Beijing. In addition, the U.S.-inspired domino theory was not based in any clear understanding of Asian history; there was no reason to assume that the rest of southern and Southeast Asia would fall to Communism if Vietnam became Communist. Only in Vietnam was Communism a factor, and even there it took a backseat to nationalism.

There were a number of reasons for the U.S. policy mistakes in gauging these situations in southern Asia. Some analysts of the war have tried to show that the U.S. diplomats assigned to Vietnam were almost always French speakers with no knowledge of Vietnam or the Vietnamese people. Consequently, they spent their time in the controlled environment of Saigon, well away from the life of the peasants and the pulse of the nation. Others believe that the most astute Far Eastern analysts at the State Department were purged by the McCarthyites and then eventually replaced by hard-liners like Dean Rusk and John Foster Dulles, both of whom were added to the Far Eastern branch in 1950 to placate Republicans in Congress. It has also been suggested that the domino theory was based in racism, that Washington policy makers believed that since all Asians looked alike they must somehow think alike as well, and as one went so went the others. Whatever the reason, it is clear now that State Department analysts in the early 1950s misjudged the movement in Vietnam and the other nationalist movements then underway in other parts of southern Asia, and that there was a profound misunderstanding in Washington of Asia and Asians.

In addition, Asian policy makers, particularly those at the State Department, had come under the powerful spell of postwar anti-Communism. As a result of the Korean War, most of these analysts believed in a black-white, good-versus-evil approach to the world order. John Foster Dulles, as Eisenhower's secretary of state, had concluded that the Chinese had allowed the Korean War to end only to redirect their energies toward Southeast Asia. He believed strongly that all Communists and Communist-controlled nations were intrinsically evil, and that the United States, standing in opposition, was on the side of right. But preceding him there were others, such as Dean Acheson, who believed in America's role as the postwar world leader and that only communism stood in the way of that destiny. These men were not prepared to accept a nonaligned world outside the realm of the two superpower systems. Ho

Chi Minh was a Communist. He had said so; he had been to Moscow, and that placed him on the other side, the side of the enemy. There were no gray areas to explore.

Meanwhile, the French effort in Vietnam was on the road to collapse in 1950. France made it clear to Washington that they could not hold on much longer without a massive U.S. intervention of money, matériel, air support, and even ground forces. At Cao Bang, near the Chinese border, the French moved closer to defeat by losing 6,000 men and enough supplies and equipment to make the Viet Minh military effort for the future much easier. In December the flamboyant Jean de Lattre de Tassigny (who had promised to end the war in fifteen months) took over leadership of the French forces. De Lattre seemed to bring France back from collapse with a resurgence of power against Giap's army in the Red River delta in the early days of 1951, but that advance proved only temporary at best. Later that year a French offensive south of Hanoi brought France its worst defeat of the war.

By 1952 it was evident that the French small-fort strategy for fighting in Vietnam was a dismal failure. In that year, the new French commander, General Henri Navarre, consolidated the small forts into larger ones called "hedgehogs." But that plan fared no better. In winter 1953, Navarre decided to build a hedgehog in northwestern Vietnam near the Laotian border at Dien Bien Phu. It was destined to become the site of the end of the French effort in Vietnam.

Although Ho Chi Minh cherished his independence from the Communist superpowers and profoundly distrusted (even hated) the Chinese, he could not stand alone against the growing French-American intervention. In 1949, when Mao concluded his civil war against Jiang and his Nationalists, Ho was able to receive direct aid from the Chinese Communists along his northern border. By 1954 Mao had stationed over 200,000 soldiers along the Vietnamese border and furnished Ho with some 52,000 tons of matériel. But the Chinese wanted the war in Indochina to end; they saw it as a threat to their southern frontier, and in 1954 they began pressuring Ho to come to some sort of truce with the French.

Meanwhile, the French had placed nearly 16,000 soldiers at the Dien Bien Phu hedgehog. On March 13, the Viet Minh had effectively surrounded the fortress and begun shelling it from the nearby mountains. Giap's weapons-of-choice here were several U.S.-made 105-mm howitzers "liberated" by the Chinese from the Americans in North Korea and handed over to the Viet Minh. Navarre, safely tucked away in his headquarters in Saigon, had concluded that the fortress could not be shelled from the mountains because the Viet Minh were incapable of moving their heavy artillery pieces up the steep mountainsides. The Viet Minh, however, had dismantled their artillery pieces, carried them up the mountains, and reassembled them inside nearly impregnable caves overlooking the French fortress. Viet Minh anti-aircraft guns were able to keep the French resupply planes at bay for almost a month, and by mid-April Dien Bien Phu was, to the world, a foregone conclusion. It would fall.

In the first week of April, President Dwight Eisenhower consulted with a few powerful congressmen about the possibility of intervening with American air power to save the French at Dien Bien Phu. The congressmen insisted that if the United States were to intervene in Indochina then a multinational effort—of the type used in Korea—would be necessary for their approval. Britain, of course, would anchor any such UN-type multilateral Allied effort in Vietnam, but the British had just dragged themselves out of the U.S.-sponsored quagmire in Korea and had no interest in following the Americans into another adventure on the Asian mainland. At the end of April, Winston Churchill told Washington that if the United States wanted to intervene to help the French in Indochina, it would have to do it alone.

Eisenhower himself was less than eager to intervene in Vietnam. He had been elected on a platform to end the war in Korea, and with the truce talks all but completed at Panmunjom, he could hardly drag the United States into another Asian war. Also, his "New Look" foreign policy was designed to scale down spending on conventional forces while putting more fiscal effort into atomic research and deployment— the "more bang for the buck" strategy, as it was called at the time. Like Churchill and the British, Eisenhower had little stomach for joining a losing cause in the jungles of Southeast Asia. In February, Ike answered a question about the possibilities of an American intervention: "No one could be more bitterly opposed to ever getting the United States involved in a hot war in that region than I am; consequently, every move that I authorize is calculated, as far as humans can do, to make certain that that does not happen."[13]

General Matthew Ridgway, now the Army chief of staff, also wanted no more Koreas. His attitude was that the United States should never again become involved in a ground war on the Asian mainland. "American intervention in Vietnam might result in local successes," Ridgway theorized, but it would "constitute a dangerous diversion of limited U.S. military capabilities, and would commit our armed forces in a non-decisive theater to the attainment of non-decisive local objectives."[14] Ridgway had experienced one inconclusive war on the Asian mainland; he did not believe the United States should get involved in a second. With the heavyweight military reputations of both Ridgway and Eisenhower standing together in opposition, the Joint Chiefs fell in line. There would be no intervention, no use of ground forces, and no air strikes to save the French cause at Dien Bien Phu. Among the president's inner circle of advisors only Dulles; the chairman of the Joint Chiefs, Admiral Arthur Radford; and Vice President Richard Nixon favored a U.S. intervention in Vietnam in 1954. Dulles argued that if Vietnam fell "it was only a question of time until all of Southeast Asia falls along with Indonesia, thus imperiling our western island defense." But Ridgway saw the situation differently. "When the day comes for me to face my Makers and account for my actions," he wrote in his memoirs, "the thing I would be most humbly proud of was the fact that I fought against, and perhaps contributed to preventing, and carrying out of some harebrained tactical schemes which would have cost the lives of some thousands of men. To this list of tragic accidents that fortunately never happened I would add the Indochina intervention."[15]

The tragedy at Dien Bien Phu was the final nail in the French coffin. They had been fighting for limited colonial supremacy, and losing, in a far-off corner of the world. For France, Vietnam was little more than a way to regain some international prestige following the humiliations of World War II. Paris was no longer a world player. It had very little to lose by cutting its losses and pulling out of Vietnam, and absolutely nothing to gain by staying on. As the situation at Dien Bien Phu unfolded, Paris insisted (over the strong objections of Dulles) that a Vietnam settlement be added to the agenda of a conference about to convene in Geneva, Switzerland. Among other things, the Geneva conference was intended to shape the final political settlement for postwar Korea. Instead, the outcome of the Geneva conference moved the war in Vietnam into another phase. It was as if the Korean War fused into the Vietnam War at Geneva in 1954.

Vietnam reached the top of the Geneva agenda on May 8, the day after Dien Bien Phu collapsed, and the ninth anniversary of V-E Day. By that time the French bargaining position for a settlement in Vietnam barely existed. But with the French hope of American intervention shattered, they approached the conference in Geneva intent on getting an armistice with the Viet Minh and withdrawing their troops under almost any conditions.

China, the Soviet Union, Britain, France, and the United States all sent delegates to Geneva. The Democratic Republic of Vietnam (the Viet Minh) was represented by its prime minister, Pham Van Dong. The French-sponsored Republic of Vietnam was also represented. When Dulles arrived at the head of the American delegation, he announced: "We hope to find that the aggressors come here in a mood to purge themselves of their aggression."[16] Dulles threatened U.S. intervention in Vietnam if France did not receive concessions at Geneva, but if the United States had not intervened to save the French at Dien Bien Phu, the North Vietnamese reasoned, it seemed unlikely that they would intervene to obtain concessions for the French at Geneva. Dulles's threats went unheeded.

The decisions at Geneva set the stage for coming events. The signatories agreed that Laos and Cambodia would retain their independence and sovereignty. They also agreed that elections would be held in 1956 throughout Vietnam to determine which side (the Viet Minh or the Republic of Vietnam in the south) would become the ruling government under a unified nation of Vietnam. Until then there would be a temporary line of demarcation separating the two sides. After some minor haggling, the line was set at the 17th parallel. The Viet Minh protested the line's location, arguing that their victory over the French should give them control of a much greater area, but they relented and allowed the decision to stand because they expected an easy victory in the

1956 elections. In addition, it was agreed that no foreign nation would introduce troops or establish bases in Vietnam.

The French withdrew. Over the eight years of fighting in the First Indochina War, nearly 95,000 French and French colonial troops were killed. Although few knew it, the Second Indochina War had already begun.

6

THE LONG ROAD TO INTERVENTION: VIETNAM POLICY UNDER EISENHOWER AND KENNEDY

In 1954, Ike was still the president of peace, and he intended to stay that way. At the same time, he was haunted by the still-politically volatile "loss" of China by the Democrats, and he was not about to suffer the consequences of losing Vietnam to the Communists. He proposed to do everything possible to avoid a Communist takeover of Vietnam—short of starting a war there. And generally, that would remain the American strategy in Vietnam until 1964.

The lessons of Korea can best be seen in the foreign policy of President Eisenhower. Ike and Dulles had not forgotten Korea or the lesson that intervention in a limited war was largely unwinnable, but that knowledge had not deterred them from using aggression to expand American interests in the world throughout the 1950s. This was done mostly through covert CIA activities. In fact, in order to avoid any Korea-type military interventions, Eisenhower used the CIA as an instrument of his foreign policy to attain what he could not attain through direct intervention of U.S. troops. This policy was born from his New Look foreign policy that called for a decrease in military spending along with a heightened American presence in world affairs. CIA activities were inexpensive compared to direct military involvement, and Ike, willing to save the world on the cheap, relied heavily on the CIA to carry out his policies.

Eisenhower had a number of successes in this area, particularly in Iran, where a CIA-led coup in 1953 (led by Theodore Roosevelt's grandson Kermit and Colonel H. Norman Schwarzkopf, the father of the Desert Storm commander) ousted Mohammed Mossadegh and placed the shah, Mohammed Reza Pahlevi, back in power. It was Schwarzkopf who aided the shah in organizing his secret police, the Savak, his main source of power until he was toppled in 1979. In Guatemala, the CIA overthrew the government of Jacobo Arbenz Guzman. Arbenz's only crime seems to have been that he considered confiscating the banana plantations of United Fruit, a U.S. industry politically connected to the Republican party. And in the Philippines, the U.S.-supported Ramon Magsaysay was finagled into power by CIA involvement. Eisenhower's later covert activities in Cuba, and the U-2 flyovers, were all a part of this new attitude, and a highly classified part of the New Look foreign policy. The cost of these adventures was minimal (the overthrow of Mossadegh had cost the American taxpayer less than $1 million) and they did advance the Eisenhower-Dulles foreign policy objectives. But U.S. prestige in the developing world suffered enormously as a result of these adventures. In addition, a number of these events would come back to haunt the United States in later years.

These successes brought to policy makers in Washington a dangerous attitude of overconfidence toward their ability to alter world events. In addition, America's experience in Korea had reinforced the justification for this new style of international tinkering. The United States could alter world affairs without the pains and costs of direct intervention, without sending in troops, without raising the ire of the American people—indeed, without even telling them. This new attitude was directed at Vietnam after the French withdraw. The lessons of the Korean War dictated that covert-style activity in Vietnam would have to do, at least for a while.

If Eisenhower could not intervene, he could at least threaten military intervention. In Manila, almost before the ink was dry on the Geneva accords, Dulles orchestrated the Southeast Asia Treaty Organization (SEATO), a mutual defense pact supposedly with the character of Europe's NATO. Britain and France, the two major colonial powers of Southeast Asia, signed the treaty, along with Britain's commonwealth nations in the area, Australia and New Zealand. The only three Asian nations that became a part of the pact were Thailand, Pakistan, and the Philippines. Dulles hoped that SEATO would do for the United States in Asia what NATO had done in Europe: give Washington the final say in all diplomatic agreements and military actions in that part of the world. The treaty was a clear threat of a multilateral U.S.-led intervention in the affairs of Southeast Asia. Although Vietnam, Cambodia, and Laos were forbidden by the Geneva accords to sign a mutual defense treaty, a protocol was added to the treaty—signed on the same day, September 8, 1954—extending the protection of the signatories to those countries in the event of an attack. Prince Norodom Sihanouk of Cambodia, hoping to remain neutral in the growing Vietnam conflict, repudiated and denounced the protocol immediately. SEATO ultimately became America's legal justification for intervention in Vietnam.

The French withdrawal left a vacuum in Vietnam that the United States believed it would have to fill—but without committing U.S. forces. One problem was that Bao Dai was an unacceptable representative of American interests in Vietnam, and it was obvious to the world that the anti-Communist nationalist movement was a charade with little popular support. So the United States chose its man to lead what was to be the new nation of the Republic of Vietnam: Ngo Dinh Diem, a nationalist to be sure, but (not unlike Bao Dai) a leader without followers.

Diem was born in Hue in 1901 to an upper-class Catholic family. He had been in and out of government since the early 1930s, and actively opposed the French and Japanese colonial control of his country. Diem's contact with the U.S. government came through one of his brothers, Monsignor Thuc, a Catholic bishop and friend of Cardinal Francis Spellman of New York. Through Spellman, Diem was introduced to such figures in the American government and society as John Kennedy, Senator Mike Mansfield, newspaper publisher Henry Luce, and John Foster Dulles. In summer 1954, when the Eisenhower administration was looking for someone to head the new American-sponsored Saigon government, Diem was the obvious choice.

So the Americans, following in the French footsteps, created their own friendly government in Vietnam in an attempt to invent a contingency in opposition to the Communist enemy. It was another effort to turn Ho Chi Minh's war for independence into a civil war; and like the French before them, the Americans tried to create a side that they could support. There was precious little popular following for Diem in the South, and like the Bao Dai government, the Diem government was largely fiction.

Diem obviously would need a power base to maintain control of the Saigon government, and the United States would create that also. With a very convincing $12 million, the CIA bought off two rival nationalist-religious sects in the South, and Diem was able to consolidate his power and build a small ragtag army from their remnants. The United States then decided to use the Vietnamese Catholics, a national religious minority, to build the new government's political power base. Through a CIA propaganda campaign, Catholics in the North were told to move to the South, that they would be persecuted by the Viet Minh if they remained north of the 17th parallel. Others moved south in response to a CIA-induced fear of a soon-to-come American atomic war on the North. Ships from the 7th Fleet helped to relocate some 860,000 Catholics from the North into central Vietnam, and Washington saw to their well-being with land grants and financial support. By 1960 the Catholic population in the South was about nine percent of the entire Vietnamese population. The United States had managed to make Diem the leader of a Catholic constituency in a predominantly Buddhist nation.

Diem moved quickly to consolidate his power in the South in a way that embarrassed the Americans and seemed to show the world that Vietnam was, at best, not ready for democracy. In an election staged in October 1955, Diem won 98.2 percent of the votes over Bao Dai—even though U.S. advisors suggested that 60 percent would be an adequate majority. In Saigon, Diem won a preposterous 605,000 votes when only 405,000 voters were registered there. Three days later, Diem proclaimed himself president of the new Republic of Vietnam. Like Syngman Rhee before him, Diem had made himself an American-supported dictator.

Not everyone in Washington was happy with Diem or his handling of the new government of South Vietnam. Lawton Collins, Eisenhower's ambassador to South Vietnam, insisted that Diem lacked the capacity necessary to control what promised to be a volatile situation in Vietnam, and he convinced Eisenhower he was correct. Dulles, however, insisted that Diem was the man for the job in Saigon, but the president's reservations forced Dulles to back down. The day before Dulles approved a communique withdrawing U.S. support for Diem, the Binh-Xuyen, a petty organized crime organization, attempted a palace coup against the Diem government. In a surprisingly decisive response, Diem ordered his small army into the streets to confront the enemy, and it quite handily defeated the Binh-Xuyen force with the aid of some CIA leadership. In Washington this act came to be regarded as courageous, and support for Diem grew in Congress. It saved Diem's political career for the moment, but for the United States it brought a great deal of agony until Diem's final removal in 1963. It was a turning point in American policy toward Vietnam. Diem's place was secure, at least for a while.

The United States began sending in advisory groups to South Vietnam as early as October 1954. These first advisors were commanded by Lieutenant General John O'Daniel, a tough Irishman, a veteran of Korea who had developed a reputation for turning raw South Korean draftees into excellent soldiers with the ability to repel the Chinese attacks. He would now try his hand in Vietnam. Under O'Daniel's leadership, the South Vietnamese army grew to over 280,000 within two years. By 1961, U.S. aid to sustain the South Vietnamese government had risen to a lavish $300 million per year with the United States providing an additional $85 million for military equipment ranging from uniforms to tanks. Washington also paid the salaries of the South Vietnamese officers and financed the construction of military installations throughout the South.

Hanoi continued to consolidate its own power in the North during this period. Ho and his advisors fully expected that the elections agreed to in Geneva would give them the mandate they needed to reunite Vietnam under Viet Minh leadership. But overtures to the Diem government from Hanoi to plan for an election were ignored in Saigon at the insistence of Washington, and the deadline for the 1956 elections passed. Considering America's historical position on democracy and free elections, this blatant antidemocratic posture placed the United States in a compromising (even embarrassing) situation as it stood before the world and refused to allow elections in Vietnam. Washington answered the question with double talk arguing only that the Viet Minh had more followers in Vietnam than the Diem government, and therefore the Communists would win the election. That, of course, could not be allowed to happen in the anti-communist 1950s. A State Department research document stated that "almost any type of election that could conceivably be held in Vietnam in 1956 would, on the basis of present trends, give the Communists a very significant if not decisive advantage. . . . Conditions of electoral freedom," it added, "might operate to favor the Communists more than their opponent." Even if a free election were held in the South, the document continued, "maximum conditions of freedom and the maximum degree of international supervision might well operate to Communist advantage and allow considerable Communist strength in the South to manifest itself at the polls." The Diem government, it concluded, should avoid elections at all costs.[1] Publicly, however, Dulles told the doubters that America would certainly be willing to participate in genuinely free elections, but everyone knew, he added, that Communists, by their very nature, did not hold genuinely free elections. So the point was moot.[2] Others believed in the prevailing wisdom of the time that the souls of Asia (and Africa and Latin America as well) were simply not yet prepared to tackle the enormous responsibilities of democratic government. Besides, the Diem government had not been a signatory of the Geneva accords, so why should it be forced to comply?

Hanoi pushed the international community to pressure the United States to force Diem to consent to the elections. Through 1955 and 1956, Ho sent requests to the Soviet Union, Britain, and China—all Geneva signatories—insisting that elections be held. But by then the world was moving toward an East-West detente, and no one wanted to rock the boat over elections in Vietnam. So once again, Ho was left to his own devices. Finally, in December 1957, Khrushchev and Chou Enlai agreed, over violent protests from Hanoi, that both North and South Vietnam should be accepted as independent nations and given seats in the UN. Ho's independence movement had been sacrificed by his own Communist allies to the cause of detente; there would be no elections.

These events pushed Ho and his advisors to abandon all hope of a political solution to the unification of Vietnam, and they again began looking at a military response as the only option available to reunite their country and throw off the imperialist yoke. It had been the Chinese, then the French, then the Japanese, and then the French again. Now it was the Americans who had set up a puppet state on Vietnamese soil, and it was against the American presence that the Viet Minh began rallying their forces in the late 1950s.

In South Vietnam pro-Communist forces developed considerable strength during 1958 and 1959, and they began to demand from Hanoi that they be allowed to take military action against the Diem regime. Many of these soldiers had been left in the South by Ho in the mid-1950s to lead propaganda campaigns against the Diem regime and to plead the Viet Minh cause in the 1956 elections that never came. Other groups, such as the Central Highlands tribesmen, had always been supporters of the Viet Minh. But Hanoi resisted, insisting that they were not yet ready for such action.

In late 1960, the National Liberation Front was established in the South to consolidate all the pro-Viet Minh and anti-Diem factions into a single coordinated effort against the Saigon government. This activity coincided with a tenant-landlord dispute in the South, encouraged by the southern cadre, now known as the Viet Cong. The Diem government aligned itself with the landlords in this dispute and the Viet Cong sided with the tenants. The result was a peasant uprising and increased support for the Viet Cong against the Diem government. The traditional infiltration route south, now named the Ho Chi Minh Trail, was reopened and men and supplies began moving south again. In 1959 Ho finally gave in to demands from the southern cadre and allowed limited armed engagements, which was little more than an acceptance of fact since the Viet Cong had been initiating limited attacks for some time, against the expressed wishes of Hanoi. These limited attacks were manifested mostly in assassinations and other forms of terrorism. By 1961, four thousand South Vietnamese government officials were being assassinated each year by the Viet Cong. Diem responded by cracking down hard in certain parts of the South, and in the process he again alienated large numbers of potential allies. To the peasants in the South, the Diem regime had come to represent the forces of armed imperialism; it was, it seemed, no different than the French.

The National Liberation Front came to be accepted by Washington as Hanoi had originally defined it: a unification of all Communist forces in the North and the South—a unification of the Viet Minh and the Viet Cong. But in fact the two groups often did not work hand-in-hand against Diem's forces, or later against the Americans. The Viet Cong considered themselves to be an independent group. Certainly they were working toward the same objectives as Hanoi, but they were often reluctant to take orders from the North.

John Kennedy came to office in January 1961, a product of U.S. postwar anti-Communism. He espoused containment, the domino theory, and monolithic Communism, the dogma of the U.S. foreign policy religion of the time. He liked journalists' early view of him as "Truman with a Harvard accent." Just after the Cuban missile crisis, Kennedy explained the harrowing events by quoting from the historical record: "The 1930s taught us a clear lesson: aggressive conduct, if allowed to go unchecked and unchallenged, ultimately leads to war."[3] His attitude toward U.S. foreign policy was, in many ways, more aggressive than Eisenhower's. "Vietnam represents the cornerstone of the Free World in Southeast Asia," he told a conference sponsored by the American Friends of Vietnam in 1956. Vietnam is "the keystone in the arch, the finger in the dike," against the "red tide in Asia." He added that Vietnam was not only "a proving ground for democracy in Asia," but a "test of American responsibility and determination."[4] As a senator, Kennedy had been an ardent supporter of U.S. assistance to South Vietnam; and he was a strong supporter of Diem, whom he had met through Cardinal Spellman. In 1960, Kennedy had defeated Richard Nixon by only the slimmest of margins, and throughout the campaign Nixon attacked Kennedy over and over again as "soft on Communism," the Democratic party bugaboo that clearly cost Kennedy votes. The Democrats had "lost" China; Kennedy would not be shackled with losing Vietnam. And his advisors, some of the best minds in America, all saw Vietnam in cold war terms. To them, the Communist activity in Vietnam was a direct challenge to the American mission to lead the free world into the next century.

Among this group of northeastern intellectuals, Harvard professors, and foreign policy experts were several who had served as advisors, policy makers, and insiders during the Korean War; they believed in the containment of Communism, and they were ready to apply what they had learned in Korea to the new situation in Vietnam. Among this group was Dean Rusk, who had been the assistant secretary of state for Far Eastern affairs in the Truman administration. He would serve as secretary of state in both the Kennedy and Johnson administrations, making him one of the chief architects of the Vietnam War. General Maxwell Taylor, Kennedy's personal military advisor, had commanded the 8th Army in Korea. In the Johnson administration he would serve as the U.S. ambassador to South Vietnam. Averell Harriman, who had been Truman's special assistant, now served in Rusk's old job as assistant secretary of state for Far Eastern affairs. In 1968, at age seventy-seven, he would head the United States delegation at the Paris peace talks. At the same time, other important figures from the Korean War years were missing. Dean Acheson, the chief architect of the Korean War, had broken with the Kennedys (more over foreign policy style than content) and was overlooked when the important positions were handed out. However, Acheson's son-in-law William Bundy served in the State Department during the Kennedy administration and then in the all-important position of assistant secretary of state for Far Eastern affairs under LBJ. His brother, McGeorge Bundy, headed the Kennedy National Security Council, and then remained at that job under Johnson. Both men were strongly influenced by Acheson's view that the United States was in a power struggle with Communism and that it must prevail if the United States was to maintain its place as a world power.[5] George Kennan, the father of containment, had become a critic of the foreign policy espoused by the Kennedy family. He had also made it clear that he believed the United States should recognize mainland China, which made him a political liability in 1961. However, like Acheson, Kennan had an advocate in the Kennedy circle: George Ball. Ball served in the State Department and was the first Kennedy insider to oppose the deepening American involvement in Vietnam—much at Kennan's behest.

Other Kennedy operatives included Robert McNamara, the statistics-driven Ford Motor Company executive. He became Kennedy's secretary of defense. Walter Rostow, distinguished professor at MIT, moved into the State Department. Robert Kennedy, of course, served as attorney general. They were America's best and brightest in 1961, the country's best foreign policy minds. They would all be advocates of U.S. intervention and escalation of the war under Kennedy, and then under Johnson. Several would change their minds when the realities of the war came home to haunt the nation. But by then, the depths of American involvement were too great. Like Truman, they got America in, but they could not get the nation out.

The Eisenhower-Dulles New Look foreign policy had relied heavily on what was called "massive retaliation," a strategy designed to curtail defense spending (the major goal of New Look) by threatening the Soviets with nuclear retaliation to achieve foreign policy ends. By 1961, it had become evident to the new Kennedy administration that such a plan left the United States vulnerable in its conventional warfare capabilities, unable to put out the inevitable "brushfires" of Communist insurgencies throughout the world. And it appeared in 1961 that such "brushfires" were being ignited by the Communists in South America, Africa, and of course Asia. The Kennedy strategy to replace massive retaliation was "flexible response," a plan devised by General Taylor to control Communist brushfires throughout the world. It called for the development of a number of options to deal with varied situations, from covert activity to conventional warfare to nuclear retaliation, if necessary. Clearly, flexible response would be expensive, but Kennedy and his advisors agreed that the United States needed such a plan to deal with international Communism. The result was a massive U.S. buildup of its conventional warfare capability—and the eventual use of that capability in Vietnam.

One of the options under flexible response was "counterinsurgency," a fighting style designed to take guerrilla warfare directly to the guerrillas. President Kennedy took a personal interest in this plan of action, and the result was the Green Berets, America's premier counterinsurgency force. These American guerrilla fighters were originally trained specifically to fight Communist guerillas in the jungles of Vietnam, and it seemed that their very existence made for a pressing need to put them into action. As counterinsurgency was perfected as a form of response, the American military became more and more confident of its ability to successfully combat guerrilla warfare.

In his first months in the White House, Kennedy refused to expand the war in Vietnam, but he believed he needed to reassure Diem that the new administration was standing behind him in his fight against Communism. This reassurance would come in the form of an intangible: a visit from the vice president. Lyndon Johnson, in Saigon, would further commit the United States to the Diem government, but more important, he would commit himself to the defense of South Vietnam. Johnson spoke glowingly of Diem, whom he called the Winston Churchill of Southeast Asia. He let Diem and the people of Vietnam know that the United States was firmly behind them. He reported back to the president that "the battle against communism must be joined in Southeast Asia with strength and determination to achieve success here."[6] It was a deeper commitment.

Johnson offered Diem more U.S. advisors. But surprisingly, Diem refused, arguing that a larger American presence would undermine his own power, and that he feared he would become a U.S. puppet. Instead, Diem asked that the United States support an increase of his own forces by 100,000 men, to a total of 270,000. But later that year, after Viet Cong troops inflicted heavy casualties on South Vietnamese forces in Phuoc Thanh and Darlac provinces, Diem decided to accept Washington's offer. In May, Kennedy sent in one hundred more military advisors and four hundred special forces troops. This was in open violation of the Geneva accords, and another turning point in the escalation of the war.

In October, President Kennedy sent General Taylor and Walter Rostow to Vietnam to survey and report on the situation there. At this point, if Kennedy had opposed further intervention (or if he had any doubts about the policy of U.S. intervention at all), he would not have sent Taylor and Rostow. Taylor, the president's chief military advisor, was pushing hard for both his flexible response foreign policy and counterinsurgency; and Rostow was the administration's chief advocate for intervention in Vietnam. Traveling along was Joseph Alsop, one of Washington's most influential columnists. Alsop was a fervent anti-Communist himself, and he spent the entire time with Taylor and Rostow lobbying for a U.S. troop commitment. Not surprisingly, the Taylor-Rostow Report called for a significant expansion of U.S. interests in Vietnam. The report also revealed the serious problems within the Diem administration. The government was unpopular, inefficient, and difficult to deal with. Without the assistance he was getting from the United States, the report warned, Diem would not be able to hang on in Saigon for long. As a solution, Taylor and Rostow called for the introduction of an 8,000-man "logistic task force" that ostensibly would assist in repairing the recently flood-damaged dike system in the Mekong Delta. It would show that the Kennedy administration was serious in its commitment to Diem, and it would help shore up the sagging Saigon government. The Taylor-Rostow Report added that North Vietnam was extremely vulnerable to conventional bombing, "a weakness which should be exploited diplomatically in convincing Hanoi to lay off SVN." They also reported that the United States should not fear a North Vietnamese invasion of the South as long as "our air power is allowed a free hand against logistical targets."[7]

There were objections to the Taylor-Rostow conclusions from within the Kennedy administration's inner circle, particularly from Averell Harriman and Undersecretary of State Chester Bowles. But the rising pitch of the cold war rhetoric drowned out their fears. The administration had suffered a severe foreign policy setback at the Bay of Pigs in Cuba; and in Berlin the Soviets had constructed the Wall in August. Kennedy believed, in his first months in office, that he had to show some strength against Communism. He would show it in Vietnam by increasing the U.S. presence there. In January 1961, when JFK came to office, there were less than 800 advisors in South Vietnam. By December that number had grown to 3,000, including a helicopter unit. A year later there were 11,000 U.S. advisors in South Vietnam, and U.S. pilots were flying sorties out of Bienhoa airbase, providing transport and air cover for the South Vietnamese army. The escalations were small, but they were growing—along with the U.S. commitment.

At the same time, the enemy was matching the U.S. escalations. In 1960 there were probably as few as 7,000 Viet Cong in the South. By 1964 that number had increased to over 140,000. The U.S. escalations were also matched (even exceeded) by Chinese and Soviet assistance to Hanoi. Both Communist bloc nations were eager to see the U.S. military become bogged down in another land war in Asia. It was the Soviets who were the chief suppliers of the North Vietnamese, but the Chinese were also deeply involved, especially in the areas of technical advisory support and training in the use of Soviet- and Chinese-built weapons. The North Vietnamese also escalated the war by dramatically increasing their infiltration of arms and supplies into the South. By 1964 the Ho Chi Minh Trail was a going concern, with the pro-Viet Minh, Pathet Lao, now in control of the main trunk of the trail through eastern Laos. The North's mechanisms of war were beginning to hum.

In an attempt to gain control of the countryside, the Diem government devised the concept of the strategic hamlet. The plan was to move nearly all the South Vietnamese peasant population into barbed-wire camps in an attempt to control the hamlets and thereby deny the Viet Cong one of its main bases of operation. It failed because it unnecessarily disrupted peasant life, and finally the peasants resisted the program. The plan hurt Diem's already-poor standing among the peasants of South Vietnam.

By summer 1963 it began to look more and more as though Diem could not maintain control in Saigon. His government was corrupt, his army had become more of a vehicle to keep him in power than to destroy the enemy, and his power base (weak in the first place) was growing weaker. On June 11 Buddhist monk Thich Quang Duc burned himself to death in protest of the Diem regime. His self-immolation was followed by others. Several were shown on U.S. television news, and for the first time the horrors of the Vietnam War were brought home to America. Large anti-Diem protests in Saigon were also featured on U.S. television. By fall 1963 it was clear to the American people that there was something wrong with the American-backed government in Saigon.

It now seemed that the increased commitment in men, matériel, and money had brought the United States little more than massive problems in Vietnam—and the Kennedy administration had begun to see Diem as the source of those problems. One concern was that U.S. aid to South Vietnam had always been contingent upon reforms, but Diem had usually managed to take the money and avoid implementing the reforms. To bow to such U.S. demands, Diem argued, would make him an American puppet in the eyes of his people. Washington, however, saw this argument as little more than intransigence. By late summer 1963, the Kennedy administration had concluded that the U.S. government would get something for its investment in Vietnam, or Diem would go.

By August a coup was being planned by some of the leading officers of the Army of the Republic of Vietnam (ARVN). The generals planning the coup made their intentions known to the new American ambassador to South Vietnam, Henry Cabot Lodge, in hopes of receiving an assurance that the Kennedy administration would support the new government and not Diem. Kennedy gave Lodge the latitude to communicate to the generals that the United States would support the new government, but there would be no U.S. participation in the coup. Lodge authorized some minor CIA assistance to the conspiring generals, and then on August 28 he cabled the president that the wheels were in motion: "We are launched on a course from which there is no respectable turning back: the overthrow of the Diem government. . . . The chance of bringing off a generals' coup depends on them to some extent: but it depends at least as much on us. We should proceed to make an all-out effort to get the generals to move promptly."[8] In mid-October Kennedy approved a list of aid cuts to the Diem government in hopes of encouraging the coup. On November 1, the ARVN generals assembled their forces around the presidential palace in Saigon and quickly overwhelmed the palace guards. Diem telephoned Lodge, insisting on an opinion from the U.S. government on the events unfolding around him. Lodge's response must have been frightening: "It is 4:30 A.M. in Washington," Lodge told Diem, "and the U.S. government cannot possibly have a view."[9] The next morning, while Diem and his brother Ngo Dinh Nhu were being transported to the coup headquarters, both were shot at close range.

President Kennedy denied U.S. involvement in the murders, and it seems clear that Kennedy, Lodge, and the others involved had not planned that Diem would die in the coup. However, that is quite often the nature of such military takeovers, and for the president not to have considered such a possibility would have been naive. All accounts indicate that JFK was surprised, even depressed, by the murders; and Arthur Schlesinger, Jr., has written that the murders of the Ngo brothers forced Kennedy to realize that Vietnam was the greatest failure of his foreign policy.[10]

The new government that the United States had now wedded itself to, for better or worse, was led by General Duong Van Minh. The day after the coup a CIA operative turned over to General Minh $42,000 to pay his troops, and Lodge assured him that the United States would continue military aid to South Vietnam. Three days later, on November 8, Washington officially recognized the new government in Saigon. What few seemed to realize, however, was that the situation in South Vietnam was in such disarray that new leadership would make little difference. Only a greater U.S. commitment could stop the Saigon government's collapse.

There is some evidence that Kennedy intended to withdraw from Vietnam after the 1964 election and then move toward stronger relations with Beijing. Kennedy told Mike Mansfield early in 1963: "If I tried to pull out completely now, we would have another Joe McCarthy red scare on our hands, but I can do it after I'm re-elected. So we had better make damned sure that I am re elected." He apparently made similar statements to presidential aide Michael Forrestal and to Senator Wayne Morse.[11] That Kennedy made these statements only proves that he had come to see Vietnam as a serious problem for his administration and the nation; it does not prove, however, that he would have withdrawn from Vietnam. While he was making these statements in private, publicly throughout 1963 he continued to insist that the United States should not abandon its commitment to South Vietnam.

Within three weeks of the coup Kennedy himself would be dead, and under Lyndon Johnson's prosecution, the war would move forward with even more vigor than under John Kennedy. Victory over Communist aggression was the only answer to the problems shaping up in Vietnam. U.S. world leadership depended on it. The United States was in; it could not turn back.

7

THE LEGACY PASSES TO JOHNSON

The war that John Kennedy passed to Lyndon Johnson in November 1963 was far expanded beyond the war Kennedy had inherited from Dwight Eisenhower just three years before. Soon after Johnson came to office, it was clear that if the United States did not intervene quickly in Vietnam the South would fall to the Communists; and Johnson, hanging on to the various foreign relations philosophies of the time, was not about to let that happen. "I am not going to lose Vietnam," Johnson said within hours of moving into the Oval Office. "I am not going to be the president who saw Southeast Asia go the way China went."[1] For Lyndon Johnson, Vietnam had become the China of the 1960s, the Communist threat that must be arrested at all costs or he would be the one to suffer the consequences—and many of those consequences would be political. With the most awesome military power in the world in his hands, Johnson would set out on a course that would bring down his own presidency, divide the nation, and ultimately bring a tragic defeat to the United States in Vietnam.

Lyndon Johnson did not come to Washington to deal with foreign affairs, and he did not become president of the United States to get bogged down in a war in Asia. He fully intended to live or die by his domestic policy. He saw himself as a remake of FDR; he would be the man in the White House who would move to solve the nation's mammoth social problems. When Johnson took the oath of office, he probably had little concern for the events in Vietnam. Woodrow Wilson had said when he became president in 1913, "It would be an irony of fate if my administration had to deal chiefly with foreign affairs." Johnson could have said much the same thing in November 1963.

By the early months of 1964 it was clear that the November coup and the new government of Duong Van Minh had not improved the political and military situation in Saigon. By January, Minh was over-thrown by Nguyen Khanh who would not do much more to shore up the sagging South Vietnamese government than his predecessors. Secretary of Defense Robert McNamara, in a memo to the president in March 1964, wrote that South Vietnam was deteriorating quickly, that "the situation has unquestionably been growing worse, at least since September. . . . Large groups of the population are now showing signs of apathy and indifference, and there are some signs of frustration within the U.S. contingent." He added that ARVN "desertion rates . . . are high and increasing. Draft-dodging is high while the Viet Cong are recruiting energetically and effectively. . . . In the last 90 days the weakening of the government's position has been particularly noticeable. . . . The political structure extending from Saigon down into the hamlets disappeared fol-lowing the November coup." McNamara added that the greatest problem that the United States had to face in Vietnam was the uncertainness of the new government, then led by Khanh. The solution to this deterio-rating situation might have been to cut losses and abandon Vietnam, but McNamara concluded instead: "However, the U.S. should continue to reiterate that it will provide all the assistance and advice required to do the job regardless of how long it takes."[2] McNamara seemed to realize how untenable the situation was in Vietnam, that it was collapsing faster than the U.S. government could shore it up. But in these times of cold war, containment, and dominoes, the only answer to the problem was to maintain the commitment—and even escalate America's involvement if necessary. Johnson responded by increasing the number of U.S. advisors in Vietnam from about 16,000 to 23,000 over the next nine months, and by adding $50 million in economic aid. He also appointed General William Westmoreland to the American command in Saigon, and he approved destroyer patrols along the North Vietnam coast.

Westmoreland was a protégé of Maxwell Taylor. He had moved up the ranks with a distinguished career in North Africa and Europe in

World War II, and then as a regimental commander in Korea. He had made his successes through the bureaucracy of the army rather than by any particular brilliance. He took over command of the U.S. contingent of advisors in Vietnam in June 1964, and from that time he worked hard to force Washington to escalate the U.S. commitment. The lessons of the Korean War had fallen deaf on Westmoreland.

Through the summer of 1964 President Johnson hoped to push a resolution through Congress supporting U.S. action in Vietnam. Such a resolution would have given some moral underpinning to the sagging Saigon government of Nguyen Khanh, but it would also have taken some of the wind from the sails of Republican presidential candidate Barry Goldwater. Goldwater had taken a strong hawkish stand on Vietnam, and LBJ wanted badly to score a landslide victory in the November election. Congressional approval for Johnson's Vietnam policy would virtually assure him and the Democrats an impressive victory. However, it was a series of incidents in the Tonkin Gulf in the first week of August that allowed Johnson to secure the congressional mandate that propelled him into the landslide victory he wanted in November. The first incident occurred on the morning of August 1, when the U.S. destroyer *Maddox,* engaged in electronic espionage off the coast of North Vietnam, was attacked by North Vietnamese torpedo boats. The *Maddox* may have sunk one boat in the encounter, and two others were damaged by U.S. planes from the carrier *Ticonderoga.* On the night of August 4, the *Maddox* returned to the area, this time accompanied by the destroyer *Turner Joy.* Both boats claimed to have come under torpedo attack that night, but since then conflicting accounts have raised doubts as to whether an attack occurred at all. The commander on the *Maddox,* Captain John Herrick, radioed to his superiors that an attack may not have occurred and that a complete evaluation of the incident should be made before Washington took any hasty action in response. This Tonkin Gulf Incident was not of the same magnitude as the North Korean invasion of the South in June 1950; however, the response in Washington was to treat the incident in much the same way.

Rusk and McNamara pushed Johnson to retaliate immediately, and the president ordered a retaliatory air attack on North Vietnamese torpedo boat bases and nearby oil tanks. He then spoke to the American people in a televised address explaining his actions. He would, he said, seek a congressional resolution allowing him to "take all necessary measures to repel any armed attacks against the forces of the United States." He received that resolution from Congress with near-unanimous approval. On August 5 the Senate voted ninety-eight to two in favor of the resolution. The only dissenting votes came from Wayne Morse of Oregon and Ernest Gruening of Alaska. Crying from the forest, Morse told his colleagues: "I believe that within a century, future generations will look at dismay and great disappointment upon a Congress which is now about to make such a historic mistake."[3] The House vote the same day was unanimous. Johnson's approval ratings in the polls nearly doubled overnight. It was just three months before the election.

Throughout the campaign, Johnson often promised that he would not send American boys to fight in Vietnam, that it was a war for the boys of Asia to fight, and that he did not seek to widen the war. "What I have been trying to do," Johnson told a New Hampshire audience in September, "was to get the boys in Vietnam to do their own fighting with our advice and with our equipment. . . . We are not going north and drop bombs at this stage of the game and we are not going south and run out and leave it for the Communists to take over."[4] However, just two weeks before he made that New Hampshire campaign speech, Johnson and his staff of advisors (including Rusk, McNamara, Joint Chiefs Chairman General Earl Wheeler, John McCone from the CIA, and General Maxwell Taylor, now ambassador to South Vietnam) had concluded that U.S. involvement in Vietnam would increase immediately after the election, and that increase would include a sustained bombing campaign against the North, and the probable use of U.S. ground troops. The only criterion that needed to be met, the group conceded, was that the political situation in Saigon would have to be stabilized first.

In Saigon, the condition had gone from bad to worse. General Khanh, using the Tonkin Gulf Incident, declared a military emergency on August 6 that, in effect, made him the dictator of South Vietnam. He was almost immediately ousted from power by street mobs. What followed was political chaos. With no central government to lead them, ARVN forces languished in the field while the Viet Cong made significant advances. The first response from Washington was to avoid expanding the war further as long as Saigon was unstable. In addition, Johnson's election campaign, based on a moderate foreign policy, demanded that the bombing of the North begin after the election and not before. Consequently, Washington was forced to stand by as the situation in Saigon worsened through the first week of November.

Johnson's management of the situations in Vietnam, particularly the Tonkin Gulf Incident, catapulted him into a landslide victory in the 1964 election. Clearly, the American people approved of his handling of Vietnam. As the war there turned sour in the late 1960s, and Americans began to look for places to lay blame for the debacle, few looked at the 1964 electorate, those people who made it clear by their votes that Lyndon Johnson was doing what they wanted in Vietnam. The overwhelming congressional mandate on August 5, 1964, and then the additional mandate from the people on November 3, led Johnson to feel he could act further in Vietnam without the consent of Congress and without gauging the opinions of the American people. Those two mandates, coming only three months apart, effectively gave Johnson a blank check to operate in Vietnam as he wished.

It was not Johnson's aggressiveness in dealing with Vietnam that appealed to the American people in 1964, it was his moderation; and that was the image he took into the election. Goldwater had urged an escalation of the war in Vietnam, and he had used the usual "soft on Communism" campaign against Johnson with some success. Johnson had countered by portraying Goldwater as a trigger-happy lunatic. The Tonkin Gulf Incident allowed Johnson to show that he could be tough on the Communists when necessary, but at the same time his actions would be moderate and not hasty. The strategy undermined the Goldwater campaign.[5]

Johnson appeared ready to begin bombing the North immediately after the election, but still the instability of the Saigon government continued to give him pause. Through December, he insisted that Saigon be politically stable before bombing could commence. However, a series of events in the last days of 1964 and in the first months of the new year convinced the president and his advisors that South Vietnam was on the verge of a complete political and military collapse and that ARVN might at any moment fold to Viet Cong pressure if the United States did not, in some manner, come to Saigon's aid quickly. On Christmas Eve a Viet Cong attack at the U.S. Army billet in the center of Saigon added to the president's fears that ARVN was not a force capable of winning the war in Vietnam—or for that matter even protecting American lives in Saigon. Then through January and February, ARVN met a series of disastrous defeats in the field that showed it could not match up to the almost-always outnumbered and outgunned Viet Cong. Also, the new civilian-led government in Saigon began taking an anti-American line that led a few policy makers in Washington to conclude that it might try to come to some sort of bilateral agreement with the Viet Cong. At the same time there were reports from U.S. intelligence sources that large numbers of North Vietnamese regular units were beginning to infiltrate south. By the end of January, it appeared that if Johnson did not act, South Vietnam and its army would finally collapse under its own blundering weight. Johnson and his advisors came to believe that they would have to bomb the North to save the South. The president's stipulation of stability in Saigon would have to wait.

At 2:00 a.m. on February 7, the waiting, the debating, and the compromising all came to an end when Viet Cong soldiers attacked the U.S. base at Pleiku in the Central Highlands, killing eight soldiers and destroying ten U.S. planes. There were ten additional (but less damaging) Viet Cong attacks launched that same day against U.S. and ARVN installations throughout the South. Johnson immediately ordered reprisal strikes against the North. Another attack against Americans at Qui Nhon provoked the president to order additional bombings of the North.

It was just a short step from reprisal bombings to sustained bombings. The argument in the administration to commence with a sustained bombing campaign was led by McGeorge Bundy and General Maxwell Taylor. Within three weeks of the Pleiku attack, Johnson had approved Operation Rolling Thunder, a massive sustained bombing operation against North Vietnam. It was undoubtedly the most significant Rubicon crossing of the war. In 1965 the U.S. Air Force flew 25,000 sorties against the North. A year later the number had grown to 79,000. By the end of 1966 the United States was sending in 12,000 sorties a month.[6]

Rolling Thunder was a massive demonstration of U.S. firepower and military might, but it did little to affect the North Vietnamese prosecution of the war. The flow of men and supplies into the South over the Ho Chi Minh Trail was not curtailed. In fact, in the three years that Rolling Thunder was under way, the North was able to increase dramatically its flood tide of men and supplies south. Rolling Thunder did not succeed because such bombing campaigns are most successful against fixed targets, such as industry. North Vietnam had little war industry (or industry of any sort) to destroy. To bomb them back to the Stone Age, as Air Force General Curtis LeMay had advised, was not to send the North Vietnamese very far back in time. The weapons and matériel used to supply the South were not being manufactured in Hanoi, but in factories in Beijing, Harbin, Chongqing, Moscow, and Stalingrad. And for the United States to attack Soviet or Chinese shipping in Haiphong harbor, or to attack Chinese supply lines into North Vietnam from southern China would, of course, have greatly widened the war. Simply put, there was very little for U.S. bombers to destroy in North Vietnam that would slow the North Vietnamese or the Viet Cong war effort.

Rolling Thunder was not initiated to win the war in Vietnam, or even to force Hanoi to the negotiating table. The objective was to coerce the North into suspending support for the revolution in the South, and in that way the Saigon government could consolidate its power, rebuild its army, and defeat the Viet Cong. And that, Washington believed, would keep American boys out of the fight. Here, in 1965, Johnson would have settled for an independent, secure South Vietnam just as Truman (after the Chinese attacks) would have settled for an independent and secure South Korea. But unlike Korea, the enemy in Vietnam was not simply initiating its own policy of containment; Hanoi had other goals, and they had no intention of negotiating a peace that did not achieve those goals.[7] Rolling Thunder, in the long run, did more to damage the American will to continue the war than it damaged the will of Hanoi.

The significance of massive aerial bombardment has been debated since World War II. The conventional wisdom in the early post–World War II era was that sustained bombing could destroy an enemy's war-making capabilities and force it to the negotiating table, even though it had never happened before. Neither the British nor the Germans in World War II succumbed to such bombing strategy. In fact, large-scale aerial bombardment failed to damage the British morale or move the German populace to turn against their nation's war effort. British war production continued nearly unhampered through 1940, and the Germans increased their war production quotas right up to the war's end. As American B-52s, each carrying nearly 60,000 pounds of ordnance, turned parts of North Vietnam into moonscape from 50,000 feet, the North Vietnamese war effort continued to remain strong. The bombing also apparently had little effect on the morale of the North Vietnamese civilians. Intelligence personnel in the Johnson administration argued often (against the arguments of Rusk, McNamara, Rostow, and others) that such bombing would have little impact on the conduct of the war. In 1968, some nine months before the bombing ended and three years after it had begun, Undersecretary of the Air Force Townsend Hoopes told the incoming Secretary of Defense Clark Clifford: "On balance, NVN is a stronger military power today than when the bombing began."[8] When the war ended, aerial bombardment as a strategy of war came into question. Was it effective? Many concluded that it was not, mostly citing Rolling Thunder as the prime example.

Just as the transition from reprisal bombing to sustained bombing was an easy one to make, so, too, was the step from aerial bombardment to the introduction of ground forces. Airplanes that drop bombs need protection on the ground, and it had become increasingly clear that ARVN units could not effectively protect U.S. airfields in Vietnam. In late February, Johnson moved escalation of the war one step forward by sending (at Westmoreland's urgent request) two Marine landing teams to protect the U.S. air base at Danang. They came ashore on March 8, the first U.S. combat units in Vietnam. It was the beginning of the Americanization of the war.

The escalations were coming quickly now. The United States was on a toboggan ride right into a war that would damage its character and divide its people for decades. Americans in spring and summer 1965 were just becoming aware of Vietnam, although they were largely unaware of the U.S. commitment or the magnitude of the U.S. involvement in that part of the world. In his most famous war speech, Lyndon Johnson, at Johns Hopkins University on April 7, tried to explain to the American people why the United States was becoming so deeply involved in Vietnam. It is a faraway place, he began: "We have no territory there, nor do we seek any. . . . Why must this nation hazard its ease, and its interests, and its power for the sake of a people so far away?" The first reason, Johnson added, is that the North has attacked the South. "Its object is total conquest. . . . Simple farmers are targets of assassination and kidnapping. Women and children are strangled in the night because their men are loyal to their government." But the real crux of the problem was not the North Vietnamese or their brutality against their own people. The real problem, Johnson said, was Communism:

> Over this war—and all Asia—is another reality: the deepening shadow of Communist China. The rulers in Hanoi are urged on by Peking. This is a regime which has destroyed freedom in Tibet, which has attacked India, and has been condemned by the United Nations for aggression in Korea. It is a nation which is helping the forces of violence in almost every continent. The contest in Viet-Nam is part of a wider pattern of aggressive purposes.

Containment was still central to the U.S. foreign policy, and Communism was still the great fear. It was cold war rhetoric reminiscent of Truman, Acheson, and Dulles. "We are there," Johnson continued, "because we have promises to keep. . . . Over many years, we have made a national pledge to help South Viet-Nam defend its independence . . . . We are also there," he added, "to strengthen world order. Around the globe, from Berlin to Thailand, are people whose well-being rests, in part, on the belief that they can count on us if they are attacked. To leave Viet-Nam to its fate would shake the confidence of these people. . . . The result would be increased unrest and instability, and even wider war. . . . Let no one think for a moment that retreat from Viet-Nam would bring an end to the conflict," Johnson went on. "The battle would be renewed in one country and then another. The lesson of our time is that the appetite for aggression is never satisfied. To withdraw from the battlefield only means to prepare for the next. We must say in Southeast Asia—as we did in Europe—in the words of the Bible: 'Hitherto shalt thou come, but no further.'"[9] Johnson had drawn the line in Vietnam just as Truman had drawn it in Korea and in Eastern Europe, and American boys would go to war to defend it. It was the Munich Syndrome, the domino theory, and containment all rolled into one glowing statement. All three of these concepts were by now basic to America's cold war foreign policy, and basic to the reasons and excuses for intervening in Vietnam. All three had been used by Truman to introduce ground troops into Korea in 1950, and all three would be used in George H. W. Bush's argument to initiate the war with Iraq in 1991. At the heart of it all was the challenge of U.S. world leadership.

The need for intervention, in the eyes of LBJ and his advisors in Washington and Saigon, had become more evident in the early months of 1965. By April, Westmoreland, Taylor, and the others had begun to predict the imminent collapse of the Saigon government if the United States did not intervene with ground troops immediately. In addition, the bombing of the North had induced Hanoi to begin moving North Vietnamese regulars into the South to counter the growing U.S. contingent. Hanoi had kept its own regular forces out of the war thus far in an attempt to deter the United States from escalating its influence in the South. But now those restraints had been removed. For Washington this meant that not only was the Saigon government about to collapse, but now there was an increasing threat from the North. By June, reports reached Washington that North Vietnamese regulars were moving along the Ho Chi Minh Trail through Laos and into South Vietnam. At that time there were about 56,000 U.S. military personnel in the South, including 23,000 advisors and 33,000 combat troops.

The only opposition to an increase in U.S. ground forces in this period came from Undersecretary of State George Ball; Vice President Hubert Humphrey (who was expelled from the inner circle for his intransigence, then experienced a change of heart and was allowed to return); Averell Harriman; and the ambassador to the Soviet Union, Llewellyn Thompson. (Distinguished outsiders who opposed the Americanization of the war included George Kennan and J. Kenneth Galbraith.) As the South Vietnamese government continued to teeter, it became increasingly clear to Johnson that bombing the North would not be enough and that unless he sent in ground troops the war would be lost and American prestige as a world leader would be damaged irreparably—along with the prestige of the president and his party.

In Saigon the situation was worsening. The flamboyant Air Vice Marshal Nguyen Cao Ky and General Nguyen Van Thieu had overthrown the civilian government in February, but they hardly seemed a reliable answer to South Vietnam's political and military problems. ARVN desertions were up by about 50 percent, and it seemed certain that the South Vietnamese force would soon topple easily under a full-scale offensive from the North.

On April 2, again at Westmoreland's request, Johnson approved National Security Action Memorandum 328, authorizing the Marine battalions already deployed in South Vietnam to be shifted from a defensive role (unable to respond to the enemy unless attacked) to an active combat role.[10] It was also a logical step on the downhill slide to the Americanization of the war. Westmoreland argued that to remain on the defensive placed American boys in jeopardy, while offensive capability would force the enemy to fall back into a defensive stance, thereby making the American presence less dangerous.

In that same month, at a meeting of the minds in Honolulu, Johnson authorized an increase in the U.S. ground forces to 82,000 in order to protect the growing number of American military facilities in South Vietnam, the logical next step in the slow, plodding escalation of the war. And, again at Westmoreland's urgent request, these troops were to be allowed to carry out offensive operations. In July, Westmoreland again urgently requested more troops: 179,000, to "take the fight to the Vietcong," as he said in his request.[11] At a fateful meeting at Camp David, Johnson mulled over the prospect of such a large U.S. commitment. Clark Clifford argued against the buildup; McNamara argued for it. After a long, lonely drive in his Cadillac convertible around Camp David, Johnson finally decided to authorize the troop buildup. He would send in 50,000 troops, bringing the U.S. force level to 125,000. Such was the growing pattern. Johnson, restrained by the consequences of a ground war in Asia, was seldom willing to authorize everything his hawkish advisors requested. However, he was willing to respond with a compromise. The result, time and again, was less of an escalation than Westmoreland or Rostow might have wanted, but an escalation just the same. Consequently, the United States went into the war little by little and piece by piece over time. Johnson also agreed to add another 50,000 soldiers by the end of the year, and he privately promised Westmoreland that additional troops would be sent as needed. In addition, he told

Westmoreland to commit U.S. troops to combat as he saw fit. It was an open-ended promise of a massive U.S. troop buildup, a blank check for Westmoreland to conduct the war as he wished. Johnson was at war in Vietnam. Getting in was easy; getting out would be more difficult.

Very quickly the war came home. The economy was the first casualty; inflation began to climb in the mid-1960s and would still be a major problem for Jimmy Carter's administration in the late 1970s. As consumer prices rose, and it became apparent that the cause was the war in Vietnam, the American public began to relate the once-obscure war in far-off Asia to their own prosperity at home. It was just one of any number of reasons for many Americans to oppose the war.

Also, the war came home in the form of an antiwar movement that began to raise its head in the mid-1960s and continued to grow almost in direct proportion to the escalation of the conflict in Vietnam. The 1960s' protest movement, however, did not begin with the Vietnam War. The civil rights movement was already well underway by the mid-1960s, and New Left politics were being born in the Berkeley free speech movement and at the first meeting of the Students for a Democratic Society (SDS) at the University of Michigan. But in the Vietnam War, the movement found a cause that brought growth, direction, and finally influence to what quickly became a mass movement of American counterculture. In December 1964, the SDS officially decided that it would protest the war, and its leaders coordinated the first march on Washington in response to America's involvement. On April 17, 1965, nearly 20,000 young people met at the Washington Monument to protest the war in Vietnam. In Congress, the antiwar movement found political leadership in such Democratic senators as Ernst Gruening, George McGovern, Frank Church, Mike Mansfield, and J. William Fulbright, chairman of the Senate Foreign Relations Committee. They pushed Johnson to find a solution to the war, to search for a negotiated settlement with Hanoi. The antiwar coalition was made up of an oddly diverse group of Americans, many of them having little in common with each other beyond their desire to see the war end. Their chief asset was that they were unusually visible and extremely articulate. They would be heard.

The Vietnam War created a favorable climate for radical growth in the 1960s. Through 1965 and 1966 there were sit-ins, teach-ins, campus strikes, and marches throughout the country. The new radicalism of the New Left began to see the government as evil and the establishment liberals as the enemy. The New Left labeled the war an extension of the abuses of American capitalism, and the subjugation of a small peasant nation to further the demonic American system. As the war progressed (and the military draft became a threat to the lifestyles of middle-class American men), the antiwar movement intensified. The masses of marchers in the streets of the nation's cities were mostly young liberals who opposed the war for any number of reasons. They may have seen the war as immoral, particularly the bombings; or they may have believed that America's involvement in the war was counter to the ideals of the United States: that the United States was supporting a corrupt government in opposition to a legitimate independence movement; or they may have seen the war as fruitless and unnecessary in the current climate of the cold war; or that it was simply too expensive when the nation needed fiscal attention in other areas. Young men of draft age often joined the ranks in opposition to the war because they simply did not want to fight in it. African Americans opposed the war for many of the same reasons, but with the added concern that African American soldiers in Vietnam were being killed more often than white soldiers. It may have been the New Left leaders of the movement who received much of the press, men and women like Tom Hayden, Jane Fonda, Joan Baez, Norman Mailer, A.J. Muste, and Dr. Benjamin Spock, but the soldiers of the antiwar movement were simply Americans who often believed in the system, but felt that the current administration had misled them and pushed the nation into a needless and brutal war.

Of all the casualties of the Vietnam War there was probably none so tragic as Johnson himself. Johnson believed he was the American leader who would finally direct the nation's postwar energies and wealth toward bringing an end to poverty and discrimination—and he had the mandate and the resources to accomplish just that goal. Clearly, Johnson's domestic policy, the Great Society, was on the high road in a liberal period in American history when civil rights and antipoverty programs would have undone many of the nation's social wrongs. But Vietnam, "that bitch of a war," as Johnson called it, would destroy "the woman I really love—the Great Society."[12] America could not afford both an expensive social agenda and an overseas war. In his attempt to make both work, both would fail.

The U.S. military strategy in the first years of the Vietnam War can only be described as a strategy of overconfidence, which was in fact no strategy at all. By the mid-1960s the lessons of Korea had been all but forgotten. The civilian and military leaders in Washington and Saigon, and the U.S. soldiers on the ground, all seemed to believe that the mere presence of American might would end the war quickly, that the sight of American ground forces would send the enemy soldiers scurrying home. Consequently, the United States found itself without a viable strategy when the enemy did not scatter at the sight of American strength. When Rolling Thunder was an obvious failure through 1965, the only solution, so Johnson and his advisors saw, was to escalate the bombing. When it became all too apparent that Viet Cong ground forces were a formidable foe, the only answer was to initiate a war of attrition with the sole objective of finding enemy soldiers and killing them—Westmoreland's "search and destroy" strategy of counterinsurgency. The objective in both search and destroy and Rolling Thunder was to kill as many of the enemy as possible in hopes that these losses would force the enemy to the bargaining table. When it became clear that the enemy would not negotiate, the only alternative was again to up the ante. Add to that Washington's perceived need to continue the war to avoid losing its place as the leader of the "free world"—the defender of all those opposing communism—and by 1967 the United States had placed itself in a very difficult situation. It was as George Ball had said in his famous quote: "Once on the Tiger's back we cannot be sure of picking the place to dismount."[13]

The lessons of Korea had taught that China would enter a war in force if its borders were threatened by a hostile army. The China factor, as the problem was called by Johnson and his advisors, plagued the president's decision making throughout the war. Recently, revisionists have argued that the United States was fighting the wrong enemy in Vietnam, that Johnson should have ignored the Viet Cong and taken the ground war to the real enemy in the North. Certainly, an Inchon-type landing somewhere south of Hanoi would have been just as brilliant in Vietnam as it had been in Korea, but of course in Korea, besides putting the United States on the offensive, it also brought the Chinese into the war, causing a mammoth escalation of that conflict. Still-vivid memories of the Chinese intervention in Korea pushed Johnson, McNamara, and most other administration insiders (with the notable exception of Walt Rostow, who lobbied for an invasion of the North) away from any plan to take the war to North Vietnam. When Rostow proposed to the president that an invasion of the North was a viable option, and insisted that China would not intervene, Johnson's reply was "that's what MacArthur thought."[14]

Johnson had good reason to believe that the Chinese would intervene. First of all, and most obviously, it seemed clear that if the Chinese had intervened in Korea when they felt that their border was threatened, then they would do the same in Vietnam fifteen years later under almost the same circumstances. Also, just as the Johnson administration began escalating the war by bombing the North and sending troops into the South in spring 1965, the Chinese began moving support forces into North Vietnam (as many as 50,000 by the spring of 1966) and ground combat troops into Yunnan province just north of the Vietnam border. It was clearly a militant posture, but probably more important, the Chinese made no effort to conceal these troop movements, which were easily detected by U.S. intelligence. It was a widely shared belief in the Johnson administration that these activities were a clear warning that a U.S. invasion of the North would bring China into the war, that China would once again implement its own containment policy against U.S. troops moving toward its frontiers. "I'm not going to spit in China's face" was how Johnson saw the situation in 1965.[15]

In addition, the Chinese army was not the un-mechanized horde it had been in 1950. The Korean War had taught China that massive manpower was not enough to fight the mechanized Western powers, and the People's Liberation Army had responded by mechanizing quickly. In a PLA training manual in the mid-1950s Mao told his soldiers: "The American army is politically a reactionary military organization of the imperialists, and basically a 'paper tiger.' . . . To destroy thoroughly such enemy troops, it is necessary to build up a strong modernised national defense army."[16] After 1955, the Chinese began manufacturing their own version of the Soviet MiG-17 jet fighters (the Chinese version was known as the F-4). By 1965, when the United States moved ground combat forces into South Vietnam, the Chinese had a large modern air force that included Soviet-designed MiG-19s (Chinese F-6s) and MiG-21s (Chinese F-7s). Both jets were generally successful against U.S. fighters in that period. Also, in the mid-1950s China began its own rocket and ballistic-missile programs, and even began moving toward nuclear capability—all under the watchful eye of the Soviets. By the late 1960s, Chinese-built surface-to-air missiles were well on their way to being some of the most feared weapons in the world. And in October 1964, China exploded its first atomic bomb (with no help from the Soviets). Clearly, in 1965, when the Johnson administration was considering the possibility of invading the North, the fear of Chinese intervention was a real one; and the Chinese force that American soldiers and flyers would have encountered in that invasion (and in the war that presumably would have followed) would have been much more formidable than the Chinese "volunteers" who swarmed into Korea fifteen years earlier. Add to this an additional 300,000 well-trained North Vietnamese regulars, and it is not difficult to see that U.S. ground forces might not have fared well in an invasion of North Vietnam.

Then, of course, there was always the additional fear that an escalation in Vietnam might bring on Soviet intervention. Although it now seems that the Soviets had no interest in intervening militarily in Vietnam, they did have a great interest in the war. After Khrushchev was ousted from the Kremlin in 1964, the new regime under Leonid Brezhnev took a stronger interest in the U.S. involvement in Vietnam. The war had reduced the American conventional war-making powers in the rest of the world; in addition, it had lowered America's prestige as a world leader, thus enhancing the place of the Soviet Union. Clearly, the Soviets had a great deal to gain by America's continued involvement in the war. Throughout the 1960s the Soviets quietly escalated their interests in Vietnam, supplying the North Vietnamese with much of what they needed to carry on the fight—from advisors to deadly surface-to-air missiles. As the war progressed, Soviet tanks and Soviet-built MiG jets would show up in the North. However, it was not long before the Soviets and the Chinese came into conflict over their individual roles in the war. This conflict merged with a number of other divisive factors in Sino-Soviet relations in the mid-1960s to cause a split between the two

Communist superpowers, a split that U.S. policy makers knew existed but was unable to turn to U.S. advantage until the United States was nearly out of Vietnam in 1972—when Richard Nixon visited China. By the late 1960s, the Soviets had taken over from the Chinese as the main supplier and director of the Vietnam war against the United States. By that time, the USSR and the PRC had together sent an estimated $2 billion to North Vietnam between 1965 and 1968. The U.S. investment in the war in the same period was about $2 billion per month.

The much-maligned American soldier in Vietnam was not quite as crazed and drug infested as he has been portrayed. However, as the war approached the late 1960s, professional soldiers were being rotated and replaced by conscripts who, in many cases, simply did not want to be in Vietnam. In addition, African American soldiers were often influenced by the Black Nationalist movement, which was gaining strength at home. Add to this no small amount of white racism that permeated the military, and the result was the development of a number of major problems. But for the most part, U.S. soldiers fought well. The conditions for battle were certainly difficult because the enemy, of course, was not drawn up along a front line as in Korea and as they would be in the Gulf War. The Viet Cong, as American soldiers constantly reported, seemed to be everywhere—and in many cases those reports were accurate. When engaged with main Viet Cong units or North Vietnamese regulars, the U.S. soldiers usually won the battles. But that was not the nature of the war; the war was not measured by battles won and lost. Westmoreland did not have a force large enough to occupy land; consequently, as American soldiers moved from one place to another (as the French had discovered over a decade earlier), the land abandoned simply reverted back to enemy hands.

As the war soured, the American soldier was often blamed for the problems in Vietnam. As in Korea, it seemed that the blame had to be placed somewhere, and it was widely believed that the American soldier no longer had what it took to fight; whatever quality had carried the American soldier to that spectacular victory in World War II was gone from the character of the American soldier in the 1960s. As in Korea, the lack of success was blamed on the "new youth," soft and coddled, along with the "new army" and its supposedly less-than-rigorous training programs. Others blamed African Americans, a large and visible minority in the now-integrated armed services, for being less than sufficiently patriotic, and even lazy. Some saw problems in the new liberalism that supposedly reared children without instilling necessary American values and then transferred that deficiency into a poor military attitude. All of this often led to strong feelings of apathy, even animosity toward the homecoming Vietnam soldier, a soldier who had managed somehow to get himself involved in an unpopular war he could not win. Others even insisted on branding returning Vietnam soldiers as criminals, warriors in an immoral war. Some of the same feelings emerged during and after the Korean War, but they were (like many things) exaggerated in Vietnam. America's attitude toward the soldiers who fought in Vietnam was unprecedented in U.S. history.

The main strategic difficulty for American planners in Vietnam was the inability of the United States to isolate the battlefield. This strategic problem was, more than anything else, what separated the military war in Korea from the military war in Vietnam. In Korea the battlefield was isolated naturally. The Korean peninsula *was* the battlefield; the armies could draw up their forces from one end of the peninsula to the other and hold that line, and barring infiltration, they could face the enemy who was also drawn up in force. The situation was much the same in the Gulf War: the lines there were stable, the two armies faced each other, the battlefield was isolated. But in Vietnam, the western and northern borders with Cambodia and Laos were not secure, allowing for infiltration of men and matériel all along the Vietnamese border areas. Even attempts by President Nixon to contain this border by bombing and invading into Cambodia and Laos did little more than force the enemy sanctuaries deeper into Indochina. So, without an isolated battlefield there was no front, there was no central army to fight, and the enemy could be supplied easily.

The enemy in Vietnam learned quickly to fight on their own terms, a fact that gave them a distinct advantage. Because of the nature of the battlefield, they could engage American troops and then disengage almost at will. This allowed the enemy soldiers to choose their place for battle and then retreat into the countryside after inflicting sufficient damage on the American soldiers—or if they believed they were about to be overpowered. They learned to stay away from U.S. helicopter fire by hitting U.S. troops and then melting into the countryside before air support could arrive. Hiding places in local villages allowed the enemy to blend into the landscape, hit, and then be gone. It was definitely a different type of war, fought to the enemy's advantage.

America's conduct of the war provided Hanoi with a propaganda weapon that was more devastating to the United States than any weapon in either nation's arsenal. To most of the world, Rolling Thunder was a brutal act of aggression, an unconscionable unleashing of American might against a small Third World nation fighting for its independence from imperial rule—and it ultimately placed much of the world in opposition to America's prosecution of the war. Secretary General of the UN, U Thant, insisted that the United States work to find a peaceful solution to the war. U.S. allies, particularly Britain, tried to bring Washington and Hanoi to some sort of negotiated settlement. Poland tried to intercede in 1966, and Soviet premier Alexi Kosygin even agreed to be a part of a settlement. But none of these had success. To much of the world it was the United States that was intransigent in this war, not Hanoi. By 1967 McNamara had reached the realization that U.S. status in the world had dropped considerably over the two years of bombing: "The picture of the world's greatest superpower," he said, "killing or injuring 1,000 non-combatants a week, while trying to pound a tiny backward nation into submission on an issue whose merits are hotly disputed, is not a pretty one."[17] Much of the world seemed to agree.

For the first time in U.S. history the American people could watch their nation at war. Into their living rooms, through their television sets, came the reality of Vietnam, of American soldiers being killed and maimed in Southeast Asia. At the same time, the arguments of antiwar activism were reported on television as a sort of counterpoint to U.S. involvement in the war. As a result the American people were generally well informed on the war after about 1965, at least as well informed as Walter Cronkite, David Brinkley, and Harry Reasoner could inform them on the network evening news. Add to that the print media coverage of the events, and the American people came to understand their war in Vietnam. And they began to ask questions: "Why are we there?" "What is the war strategy?" "What is the American plan for withdrawal?"

"When?" "On what conditions?" Often the answers were disconcerting at best.

The role of the American press in the Vietnam War has evoked a great deal of controversy. Certainly, the press brought the war home; it showed the agony and the reality of war for the first time in history. It also exposed what was known as the "credibility gap," the government's reluctance to be entirely honest with the American people on the prosecution of the war. The press exposed that several of the troop escalations of 1965 were not revealed to the American people, that casualty statistics throughout the war were fabricated, that secret wars in Laos and Cambodia raged on without the knowledge of the American people or Congress, and that the rationale for the initial involvement was part fabrication and part overreaction. But the war, in all its reality, existed as the press presented it; the press did not show a war that was not there. And, of course, the misinformation provided by the administration was a reality, perpetuated by the decision makers in Washington, and not fabricated by the press. By simply telling the American people about the realities of the war, the press turned the American populace against it. It was not a pretty war; consequently it did not evoke a pretty image.

Not only was the war reported fairly, it nearly always followed the government line to a fault. For instance, the press throughout the war reported the outrageous casualty figures released by the Defense Department that later turned out to be largely concocted for public consumption. It was not until the *Pentagon Papers* were published that the press began asking questions about such things as the incident in the Tonkin Gulf, the unannounced troop escalations in the mid-1960s, and the secret wars in Laos and Cambodia. In addition, there were numerous attempts by Washington to manipulate the press, and thus manipulate the mind of the American public. Walt Rostow's comment in 1967 that "there are ways of guiding the press to show light at the end of the tunnel" is indicative of the Johnson administration's attitude toward the press during the war.[18] Unfortunately, the myth that the press lost Vietnam was carried forward into the post–Vietnam War period, and finally manifested itself into a strong government censorship of the press in the Gulf War. The press was quieted in the Gulf War because it had asked questions about Vietnam—questions that needed to be asked and answered.

By 1967, U.S. forces in Vietnam had been increased to 500,000, and Westmoreland had asked for an additional 42,000 men by the end of the year. With the increased escalation in troop strength came the inevitable escalation in casualties. Before the fateful decisions of July 1965, the United States had lost 400 soldiers in action in Vietnam. By the end of 1967 more than 16,000 had been killed. With the dramatic rise in casualties came an escalation in the antiwar movement. It seemed that the nation was on a spiral: As more troops were needed, the war escalated, casualties increased, and the antiwar movement intensified.

Toward the end of 1967, Johnson decided that his Vietnam policy needed to be confirmed by the nation's senior foreign policy experts, the old hands and presidential counselors from the 1940s and the 1950s. Attending this November 2 meeting of the "Wise Men," as they were called, were: Truman's secretary of state, Dean Acheson; Clark Clifford, by now LBJ's closest personal advisor; Omar Bradley, chairman of the Joint Chiefs of Staff during the Korean War; George Ball; McGeorge Bundy, now replaced as national security advisor by Walt Rostow; former treasury secretary and the chief armistice negotiator in Korea, Arthur Dean; Supreme Court Justice Abe Fortas; former Undersecretary of State Robert Murphy; Kennedy's ambassador to Vietnam, Henry Cabot Lodge; Averell Harriman; and Maxwell Taylor. This group spoke with one collective voice in late 1967. Even George Ball, the resident "dove" in the group, agreed: "No one in this group thinks we should get out of the war," was Ball's response to LBJ's big question.[19] And Harriman, who had opposed the use of ground forces in Vietnam only two years earlier, sat in silent agreement. This group carried great weight with Johnson, but their opinions would change soon.

The day before the Wise Men met, McNamara sent the president a memo that stated in essence that he had come to the conclusion that the war in Vietnam was unwinnable. It was the beginning of a major policy shift in the administration. "Continuing our present course will not bring us by the end of 1968 enough closer to success, in the eyes of the American public, to prevent the continued erosion of popular support for our involvement in Vietnam." He then went on to suggest that the United States should simply work to keep troops from the North out of the South, halt the bombing, and look for a negotiated peace at all costs.[20]

McNamara's memo was devastating to Johnson mainly because it raised, as Johnson wrote in his memoirs, "fundamental questions of policy with reference to the conduct of the war in Vietnam."[21] McNamara had, more than anyone else, charted the course for U.S. intervention in Vietnam. Now, with no warning, he was the first of the Johnson insiders to see that the war was unwinnable, costly, and destroying the administration and dividing the nation. Johnson appointed McNamara to the presidency of the World Bank and named Clifford his new secretary of defense. On the day Clifford was confirmed by the Senate, the Communists in Vietnam launched the Tet Offensive. Tet was the turning point in the ground war; McNamara's change of heart was the turning point in Washington.

8

JOHNSON'S FALL AND NIXON'S RISE

The spiral of escalation was nearly impossible to stop. Once American troops were introduced into Vietnam, President Johnson found it difficult to deny further requests to send support for those soldiers already in the field. At the same time, U.S. escalations and troop increases were always matched by the enemy, which in turn led to more American casualties and a need for more troops. By 1967 the escalations had achieved nothing; the number crunchers at the Pentagon and the State Department had concluded by then that the war in Vietnam was going nowhere. Escalations, so it seemed, did little more than kill more American soldiers. The war had developed into an unwinnable stalemate with no really honorable way out. "Unless the will of the enemy is broken or unless there is an unraveling of the VC infrastructure," Westmoreland told LBJ in the spring of 1967, "the war could go on for five years."[1] The frustrations mounted.

However, in the last months of 1967 it appeared that the enemy in the South was pulling back, disengaging. That disclosure seemed to balance with the Pentagon's statistics that showed the successes of attrition and a shifting of the balance of power in the countryside toward the American forces. By late 1967 the war managers in Washington began to believe, for the first time, that possibly the war was now moving toward a U.S. victory. "I am very encouraged," Westmoreland told the president in late 1967. "I have never been more encouraged in the four years that I have been in Vietnam. We are making real progress. Everyone is encouraged."[2] The next day he told Congress and the American people that he could bring victory in less than two years. At just that moment of U.S. optimism, the enemy showed how truly powerful they were. The Tet Offensive, launched by the Viet Cong on January 31, 1968, was not a Viet Cong military victory; in fact, it probably did not even achieve its minimum goals. But it turned the direction of the war in Washington; it turned large numbers of Americans against the war, and finally, it brought down Lyndon Johnson's administration.

Before Tet, South Vietnam had settled into a simple balance of power that had marked the war's stalemate. The Americans and ARVN controlled the cities, and the Viet Cong controlled the countryside. Through a process of attrition called "rural pacification," the United States had tried to make headway into the countryside, and in some areas it was successful. The cities were safe havens. The war had become a rural war for control of the countryside. Tet was the Viet Cong's attempt to change that, to take the war to the cities.

Tet was the Vietnamese lunar new year holiday that began on February 1, the most important holiday of the year in Vietnam. The Viet Cong attack that would become the Tet Offensive really began ten days before at Khe Sanh, a battle that Westmoreland, Joint Chiefs chairman General Earl Wheeler, and President Thieu believed was the real objective of Tet.

Khe Sanh was a U.S. Marine base in western Quang Tri province, eight miles east of the Laotian border and eighteen miles south of the Demilitarized Zone (DMZ). The base had been located there to stop North Vietnamese infiltration into the south, and to recruit and train local mountain tribesmen. As early as spring 1967, four divisions of North Vietnamese regulars began digging into the mountains around the base. In October sporadic battles broke out, and in late January the North Vietnamese began laying siege to the base. Westmoreland and Johnson could not shake the comparison between Khe Sanh and Dien Bien Phu, and Johnson became obsessed with the battle at Khe Sanh, where "his Marines," as he called them, were pinned down against a superior enemy force. To quell Johnson's worst fears, Westmoreland kept a contingent of 20,000 soldiers near Khe Sanh in case the situation there got out of hand. In the meantime, the Joint Chiefs assured the president that the 6,000 Marines at Khe Sanh could handle the siege and that the United States was not setting itself up for a defeat like that at Dien Bien Phu.

While the situation at Khe Sanh developed, it became clear to Westmoreland that something else was about to happen in the South. He wired LBJ that "the enemy is presently developing a threatening posture in several areas in order to seek victories essential to achieving prestige and bargaining power. He may exercise initiatives prior to, during, or after Tet." Using this note as evidence, Westmoreland would later claim that he had anticipated Tet, and Johnson would argue in his own memoirs that he had seen Tet coming months earlier.[3] But clearly Tet was a surprise to everyone. Captured documents outlining the offensive were dismissed in Saigon as unbelievable, and Westmoreland himself had begun informing Washington that enemy strength in the South was decreasing considerably. Westmoreland's wire to the president seemingly anticipating Tet was a mere notification that there were some troop movements nearby and not a prediction of an offensive of any magnitude—and that is how Westmoreland's report was received in Washington. Only at the last minute did Westmoreland order all leaves canceled for the Tet holiday in anticipation of increased Viet Cong activity. Even then, no one predicted the size or scope of the Tet Offensive. "I would say that no one really expected the enemy to launch the attack during Tet," Secretary of Defense Clark Clifford wrote in his memoirs. "While we knew something was going to happen, we didn't know exactly when, nor did we know how extensive the attack was going to be."[4] General Bruce Palmer, Westmoreland's deputy, called Tet "an allied intelligence failure ranking with Pearl Harbor in 1941 or the Ardennes Offensive in 1944."[5]

The battle at Khe Sanh, as it turned out, was probably a diversion for the Tet Offensive. The siege at Khe Sanh kept a large number of Westmoreland's best troops occupied (many more than just the 6,000 Marines at Khe Sahn) in the northern reaches of South Vietnam, away from Saigon and the other major cities where the main thrusts of Tet would be. Westmoreland fell for the ruse, maintaining throughout the offensive that the attacks on the cities were intended to relieve the pressure against the North Vietnamese troops at Khe Sanh.

The Tet Offensive began on January 31 when the Viet Cong (few northern regulars were involved) attacked five of the six major cities in the South, thirty-six of the forty-four provincial capitals, and sixty-four district capitals. In addition, munition dumps, airfields, oil storage facilities, and minor U.S. and ARVN strongholds were hit. In the most dramatic (but militarily least significant) of the attacks, nineteen Viet Cong commandos destroyed part of the U.S. Embassy in Saigon and managed to hold the compound for nearly six hours before they were finally killed. Four MPs, a Marine guard, and a South Vietnamese embassy employee were also killed in the attack.

Whether or not Tet was a victory for the Viet Cong is a secondary question. They failed to hold any cities beyond a few days, except Hue, which was finally abandoned after about three weeks of heavy fighting. They lost an estimated 58,000 men, and the attack on the U.S. Embassy was not a success. However, Tet had a profound impact on the war: it caused a major backlash in American public opinion against the war that did not subside until U.S. forces were finally withdrawn. "As a military campaign," wrote Clifford, "the outcome of the Tet Offensive may remain in dispute, but there can be no question that it was a turning point in the war. Its size and scope made mockery of what the American military had told the public about the war, and devastated Administration credibility."[6] It was, General Wheeler later said, "a propaganda victory for the North Vietnamese here in the United States."[7]

The United States lost nearly 4,000 soldiers in eight weeks of fighting; ARVN lost nearly 5,000 men; and some 14,000 noncombatants were killed. At Hue, 500 U.S. and ARVN soldiers were killed in the battle that was partly house-to-house urban fighting. That ancient city was virtually destroyed by U.S. bombing attacks and artillery barrages that left 100,000 civilian refugees in their wake. Some 2,800 Vietnamese civilians were reported executed by Communist troops during the occupation; another 2,800 were declared missing.

Whatever Hanoi's military objective in launching the attack had been, it was not achieved. The countryside did not rise up and support the offensive, ARVN did not collapse, the government in Saigon did not fall to a revolution, and the United States did not find a need to begin negotiations. Also, Khe Sanh was not relieved of any pressure, because Westmoreland insisted until the end that Khe Sanh was the objective, not the South Vietnamese cities, and he continued to maintain troop strengths there. If there was any strategic success at all for the Viet Cong, it was that the United States and ARVN were forced to bring forces in from the countryside to defend the cities, thereby allowing the Viet Cong to regain greater control in the countryside. But even that was short-lived. On February 12 Westmoreland asked for more troops: 205,179 additional troops in three phases on top of the 1968 troop ceiling of 525,000. The Defense Department countered that such an increase would mean more U.S. casualties, a need for a tax increase, probably wage and price controls, an increase in the draft, and possibly a call-up of the reserves.

On March 10 a Gallup poll revealed the political effects of Tet. A whopping 49 percent of the American public believed the United States should never have gotten involved in Vietnam. That was a considerable increase over the pre-Tet polls asking the same question. Only 33 percent believed that the United States was making headway in the war, a drop from 50 percent before Tet. Gallup also polled the self-described "hawks" and "doves." In February, before Tet, the hawks had outnumbered the doves 60 percent to 24 percent. In March they ran about even: 41 percent considered themselves hawks, while 42 percent identified themselves as doves. Also, polls showed LBJ's popularity had dropped after Tet to 35 percent, about the level of Truman's popularity near the end of his second term when the Korean War was quickly becoming unpopular.[8]

The impact of the Tet Offensive was felt again on March 12 when 42 percent of the Democrats in New Hampshire voted for Senator Eugene McCarthy, who was leading a young people's movement to bring an end to the war. This New Hampshire vote was widely perceived as a statement in opposition to the president's Vietnam policies. McCarthy was hardly a political powerhouse in the politics of the late 1960s, and his showing in New Hampshire awakened Robert Kennedy and provoked him to enter the race against Johnson for the Democratic nomination. Kennedy quickly absorbed much of McCarthy's support nationwide and began riding the crest of a movement, already well underway, that was based on getting the nation out of Vietnam. "These are not ordinary times," Kennedy said in announcing his candidacy, "and this is not an ordinary election." Kennedy's successes in the state primaries under-mined Johnson's Vietnam policy.[9]

Disenchantment with the war after Tet also brought down the pil-lars of the American establishment. Walter Cronkite, the much-revered CBS anchorman, announced that he now opposed the war. Johnson was to have said in response: "If I've lost Walter then it's over. I've lost Mr. Average Citizen."[10] Also, *Newsweek,* the *Wall Street Journal,* and NBC News all jumped on the antiwar bandwagon and called for an immediate de-escalation. On March 10, the *New York Times* reported (correctly) that the president was secretly considering a request for 206,000 more troops for the war. The story set off a wave of unrest on the nation's col-lege campuses.

Clark Clifford had entered the Johnson administration on March 1, in the midst of crisis. The national backlash from Tet was just beginning and the secretary of defense was as much a target for that criticism as the president. In addition, the North Koreans had seized the intelligence ship USS *Pueblo,* and that frustrating incident threatened to heat up the war in Korea again. It was a difficult time in Washington for the new secretary of defense. Clifford had always been a hawk. Since 1964 he had been a senior advisor to Johnson, meeting with the president frequently and informally on Vietnam and other issues. He had pushed hard for Operation Rolling Thunder, and had been the primary voice in opposi-tion to plans to stop the bombing. But when Clifford came to the Defense Department, his attitude changed quickly. He found no plans at Defense to conduct the war; he also could find no good reason for increasing the U.S. military presence in Vietnam because Westmoreland and the Joint Chiefs had made it clear several times that the additional 206,000 men they had requested would not bring a U.S. victory. Influenced greatly by his deputy secretary, Paul Nitze, the co-drafter of NSC-68, Clifford quietly changed his position from hawk to dove. And he began to lead others away from the administration's official policy and toward a policy that would stop the bombing, end the war, and bring U.S. forces home. "As time went on," Clifford recalled, "my desire to get out of Vietnam went from opinion, to conviction, to passion. I was afraid that we were never going to get out. We were losing thousands of men and billions of dollars in an endless sinkhole. If I ever knew anything, I knew that: we had to get out."[11] Clifford decided that his job was to try to convince the president.

In the last week of March, the Wise Men, that ad hoc group of esteemed veterans of American foreign policy and politics, met again. This was generally a conservative group, and LBJ expected to receive their support for his policies as he had in the past. Attending the meeting were Acheson, Ball, General Bradley, McGeorge Bundy, Dillon, Fortas, Murphy, General Ridgway, and Cyrus Vance. General Wheeler, Max Taylor, Lodge, and Vice President Humphrey were also there. But the well had been poisoned. The Wise Men had been briefed before the meeting by Philip Habib, who had just returned from a two-year stint in Saigon; also by George Carver, a CIA analyst; and by the former Army chief of operations in Saigon, General W. E. DePuy. All three had laid down a picture of Vietnam for this advisory group that showed that the bombing in the North had not been effective, and that additional troop buildups in the South would have virtually no effect on the outcome of the war. Habib's reply to the question "What should we do in Vietnam?" was "stop the bombing and negotiate."[12] Arthur Goldburg, the ambassador to the UN, attended one of the briefings and asked DePuy how many of the enemy had been killed during Tet. The answer was 80,000. With a ten-to-one ratio of wounded-to-killed, and only 230,000 estimated Viet Cong in the field, Goldburg responded that all the enemy must be either dead or wounded. "Who the hell are we fighting?" he asked.[13] It seemed that what had been confidence and optimism before from the administration was, in fact, little more than deception and misrepresentation.

When the Wise Men met with the president the next day it was clear that they had changed their minds about the war. When General Wheeler admitted that the United States could not achieve a classical military victory in Vietnam, Acheson replied: "Then what in the name of God do we have five hundred thousand troops out there for? Chasing girls?"[14] It was Acheson who led the group, telling Johnson that the era of global containment had ended—Acheson, the figure who more than anyone else had established containment as an American foreign policy. Acheson, the man who had justified and directed U.S. involvement in Korea, and then later advised Truman to cut his losses and negotiate, was now advising Lyndon Johnson to get out of Vietnam.

With what seemed like the world turning against him, LBJ planned to announce that he would not run for president in 1968. With no political pressures of the campaign to weigh him down, he hoped to end the war before he left office: one last grand gesture. In his speech of March 31, Johnson said: "So tonight, in the hopes that this action will lead to early talks, I am taking the first step to de-escalate the conflict." He called a halt to the bombing of the North, except for a small strip along the DMZ, and called on Ho Chi Minh to agree to peace talks. He went on to order the deployment of 13,500 troops over a five-month period, considerably less than the 206,000 soldiers that Westmoreland and Wheeler had requested, and then he surprised the world: "I have concluded that I should not permit the Presidency to become involved in the partisan divisions that are developing in this political year. . . . Accordingly, I shall not seek, and I will not accept, the nomination of my party for another term as your President."[15] Johnson told Clifford afterward, "I never felt so right about any decision in my life."[16]

It was a decision that Johnson had been contemplating for months. He was beleaguered and worn down by Vietnam. He worried about his health. And he saw before him a bitter battle to win another term in the White House with his Vietnam policy at the center of the debate. The United States had gotten deeply involved in a war it could not win, and Johnson was the nation's prime sacrifice to the struggle. It was tragic that he did not want the war. A domestic politician, he had a vision for America that included the elimination of poverty and discrimination against minorities.

Johnson was willing to sacrifice the U.S. effort in Vietnam for the cause of his true love, the social programs of the Great Society. His support in Congress (and for that matter, among the American public) for his social programs was fragile. He feared that a national debate on his Vietnam policies might divide that fragile consensus and wreck the congressional and public support he needed to enact his Great Society programs. Consequently, he refused to open up any cans of worms that might bring his Vietnam policy into question. He escalated slowly; he refused to ask for the tax increases necessary to prosecute the war effectively; he kept many of the problems and horrors of the war away from the American people; and he would not call up the reserves—all for fear of bringing his Vietnam policy into question and dividing congressional and public support for his Great Society. The result was a slowly escalating war in Vietnam that was being prosecuted without the necessary support from Washington, a credibility gap between the president's policies and the portrayal of the war to the public, and a Great Society that generally failed. Senator J. William Fulbright, referring to the Great Society's war on poverty and the war in Vietnam, said, "Each war feeds on the other, and, although the president assures us that we have the resources to win both wars, in fact we are not winning either of them."[17]

Johnson also may have prosecuted the war badly because it was his nature as a politician to compromise—in order to maintain control of the political center. Fearing political reprisals from the Left, he refused to do more than escalate the war slowly, which allowed the enemy to adjust to the escalations over time. There was never a great thrusting attack that might have forced Hanoi into negotiations. At the same time, Johnson feared reprisals from the Right if he did not continue to show success in Vietnam, or if he decided to withdraw altogether. The horror of being the president who "lost" Vietnam haunted Johnson, and it pushed him to grant Westmoreland's requests for more troops and to keep the pressure on Hanoi by escalating the bombing. Consequently, holding the middle of the political road translated into escalation and stalemate in Vietnam.

Johnson tried desperately to bring the war to an end before his term expired in January. But the Paris peace negotiations (accepted by Hanoi after LBJ's March 31 speech) produced little, and in May the Viet Cong launched another offensive, quickly dubbed the "Mini-Tet Offensive" by the press. Hubert Humphrey won the Democratic party's nomination in Chicago in July, but only after antiwar demonstrators disrupted the convention and stole the show from Humphrey and what had become the pro-war faction of the Democratic party. Under pressure from Johnson, Humphrey held the president's line on Vietnam during the campaign, proving to many in the antiwar movement that working within the system to end the war would achieve no significant results. As the election approached, Humphrey tried to distance himself from Johnson and the administration's Vietnam policies, but on November 5, Election Day, that did not prove enough and he lost the election to Richard Nixon.

Meanwhile, negotiations plodded along in Paris. In mid-October, just weeks before the U.S. election, there appeared to be room for a break in the talks. The United States had agreed to halt the bombing; North Vietnam had agreed to stop mortar and rocket attacks on cities in the South. All had agreed that within four days of the ceasefire serious negotiations would begin. But it was the Saigon government that would not agree. Just as Syngman Rhee had been a thorn in the side of UN negotiations in Korea, Thieu moved to sabotage the Paris peace talks. Like Rhee, Thieu feared an American sellout, that political and social pressures from the U.S. home front would finally force a U.S. withdrawal from Vietnam, leaving the situation in the hands of a much-weakened ARVN. But Thieu had other reasons. He knew that a Republican government in Washington would be less likely than the Democrats to make peace with Hanoi, and he was clearly holding up the peace process until after the election in hopes that a Nixon victory would bring more aid to his Saigon government. Even after the election, Thieu continued to sabotage the Paris peace talks with ridiculous demands in order to stall the process until Nixon took office in January. Thieu, of course, achieved his objective, and Nixon continued to prosecute the war for another four years. However, this was probably not a lost chance for peace.[18] Hanoi still maintained its demand for an American pullout from Vietnam, and Lyndon Johnson, despite his desire to end the war before he left office, would not have considered such a demand.

Richard Nixon came to the presidency with a strong anti-Communist background that went back to his early political career in 1946. He could have pulled the United States out of Vietnam without being hurt politically, without having to suffer the stigma of "losing" Vietnam, and without being accused of being soft on Communism. But Nixon was too much of an anti-Communist, too much of an old cold warrior who believed wholeheartedly in the old Dulles maxims of dominoes and containment, to abandon America's role in Vietnam. In 1967, as the realities of the war were beginning to set in on the Johnson administration, Nixon defended U.S. involvement in Vietnam. The war, he said, had contained Chinese expansion and allowed the nations of South and Southeast Asia to become strong enough to ward off future Communist insurgencies. Nixon would not pull out of Vietnam until four years after his inauguration and in that time another 20,000 American soldiers would lose their lives. It was tragic that in the end, Nixon's Vietnam policy gained nothing more than what could have been achieved in 1969 when he took office.

Nixon clearly wanted to end the war quickly; he saw what the war had done to the Johnson administration and to the Democrats at a time when their domestic policies were generally popular. In 1965 Nixon had said, "We must avoid that kind of policy that will make countries in Asia so dependent upon us that we are dragged into conflicts such as the one that we have in Vietnam."[19] In January 1969, just after he took office, Nixon declared to an aide: "I'm not going to end up like LBJ. . . . I'm going to stop that war. Fast."[20] And to reporters after his inauguration, he said: "We have to get rid of the nightmares we inherited. One of the nightmares is a war without end."[21] But Nixon would not end the war by simply pulling out American troops. He had a plan, another plan for prosecution of the war that would not work.

Nixon's plan for "peace with honor," as he called it, was threefold. First, he would continue to pursue peace through the negotiations in Paris that Johnson had opened up in the eleventh hour of his administration. Second, he would move to quell domestic unrest over the war by beginning to withdraw troops from Vietnam. Attached to the withdrawal was a plan for the "Vietnamization" of the war, a strategy designed to tum the war over to ARVN as the U.S. troops withdrew over time. Nixon also hoped to stifle the antiwar movement by ending the current draft system and implementing a lottery system (only those with low lottery numbers would be drafted) that would make the draft more equitable. The third aspect of Nixon's Vietnam policy, however, was secret, kept from Congress and the American people until 1970. While narrowing the war on the ground by bringing troops home, Nixon would actually expand the war by bombing enemy sanctuaries in Cambodia and Laos. This three-part plan was not intended to produce victory, only pull-out—"peace with honor"—by achieving Washington's long-time goal of placing the United States in a favorable negotiating position.

Nixon's plan had no more success than Johnson's, and for many of the same reasons. At the Paris peace talks, the United States insisted on a withdrawal of "all foreign forces from the soil of South Vietnam." This was, in fact, the same demand made by the United States for an independent and non-Communist South Vietnam, a demand placed on the table by the Johnson administration as early as January 1966. The leaders in Hanoi, of course, would never accept it. They countered, as they had always countered, by demanding the reunification of Vietnam under Hanoi's control. For them, it was still an independence movement, not a civil war. And America's involvement in it was little more than age-old western imperialism.

Nixon's plan to defuse the antiwar movement by de-escalating the war and by removing the unfair inequalities of the draft was at least partially successful. Many Americans came to believe that the scale-down meant an eventual end to the war, and those political moderates who had come to oppose the war were satisfied that these measures were making positive progress toward an American withdrawal and the eventual Vietnamization of the war—a very popular notion among moderates. Nixon's plan built a solid coalition of conservatives and moderates who believed the new president would bring an end to the war without subjecting the nation to a humiliating military defeat. This coalition became known as the "Silent Majority," those loyal Americans supposedly standing quietly in opposition to the vocal minority who actively opposed the war. This Silent Majority also wanted the war to end, but they wanted it done "honorably." This became the catchword of Nixon's Vietnam policy during the Nixon years.[22]

The third phase of the Nixon plan was for the secret bombing of Cambodia and Laos, a plan repeatedly called for by the Joint Chiefs, but rejected by Johnson as an expansion of the limited war. Over the next fourteen months, Nixon would authorize 3,600 B-52 sorties that dropped some 110,000 tons of bombs on Cambodia, a nation that had declared its neutrality in the war (but also a nation that could not keep the Viet Cong from establishing base camps on its eastern and southern border). The Cambodian government became an increasing problem to the U.S. action there. The Cambodian leader, Prince Norodom Sihanouk, had tried desperately to keep the war from spreading to his nation, and in the process had refused American aid or support of any kind. When he was overthrown in March 1970 by General Lon Nol, the Nixon administration was delighted to see him go. There is no evidence that the United States had any complicity in the Cambodian coup, although it came at a very convenient time for the Nixon administration, and Lon Nol was a clear U.S. ally who was eager to allow the United States to begin the bombing of Viet Cong bases in his country. Sihanouk took refuge in Beijing, and from there he worked to build a coalition with the Cambodian Left, the Khmer Rouge. The United States bombing campaign forced the Viet Cong deeper into Cambodia, and when the war in Vietnam finally ended, Cambodia was a land devastated and ripe for a postwar holocaust. The Vietnam War now became Richard Nixon's expanded, accelerated Indochina war.

Nixon did have a plan, but it really did not go beyond the basics of America's cold war foreign policy. It was Nixon who had led the Republican right-wing attack on Truman for "losing" China to the Communists in 1949, and he, more than anyone, was responsible for pinning the "soft on Communism" tag on the Democrats in the 1940s and 1950s. Withdrawing in the face of Communist aggression was not in his character. He still saw the mission in Vietnam as containment of Communism, and Communism itself as an evil menace that was trying to take over the world. He also hung on to the premise that the real enemy was in Moscow and Beijing, not in Hanoi. He believed that if the United States capitulated in Vietnam, other nations would fall to Communism, first in other parts of Southeast Asia, then in other parts of the world, and then in America's own backyard. The result of appeasement, he believed, would be more war, not less. He also embraced the most basic of all cold war notions—that the United States must prevail in Vietnam to maintain its place as a world leader; and, at one point, he told a group of congressmen that he was not going to be the first president to lose a war, words Johnson had used. In a speech in November 1969 Nixon evoked all of these basics of U.S. cold war foreign policy, a foreign policy that would not allow the United States to leave Vietnam:

> For the United States this first defeat in our Nation's history would result in a collapse of confidence in American leadership, not only in Asia but throughout the world. . . . Our defeat and humiliation in South Vietnam without question would promote recklessness in the councils of those great powers who have not yet abandoned their goals of world conquest. This would spark violence wherever

our commitments help maintain the peace—in the Middle East, in Berlin, eventually even in the Western Hemisphere. Ultimately this would cost more lives. It would not bring peace; it would bring more war.[23]

So it was, as it had been in Korea, that the United States would negotiate while fighting. And, as in Korea, the war would drag on and on, dividing the nation, consuming American boys, and accomplishing very little. Because of these cold war shackles, Nixon's plan really did not go beyond the plan of those before him, and it would not improve the U.S. position in Vietnam.

To accompany his plan of slow troop withdrawals, Nixon also planned an all-out attack on the New Left, the group that had come to lead the nation's antiwar protest movement. This attack would be conducted in the open by Nixon's vice president, Spiro T. Agnew, and behind the scenes by fellow Communist-hater J. Edgar Hoover and his FBI.

Agnew's attacks have come down as a series of almost-humorous quotes from antagonistic speeches and epithets yelled back at hecklers. He called the antiwar protesters "the enemy in the streets," "small cadres of professional protesters," "nattering nabobs of negativism," and an "effete corps of impudent snobs who characterize themselves as intellectuals." "It is time," he said in 1969, "to discard the fiction that in a country of 200 million people, everyone is qualified to quarterback the government."[24]

Unfortunately for Agnew, who had a fairly remarkable career as a conservative governor of Maryland, history has remembered him for little else than Nixon's "hit man."

On the covert side of this plan, Hoover began compiling his Security Index, a list of suspected subversives to be rounded up in case the president called a "national emergency." The Nixon White House also began compiling its own "enemies list" of subversives. Wiretaps were used, in addition to grand jury investigations and felony prosecutions, to harass the nation's political "enemies" at home. After 1970, the White House initiated the Huston Plan, which authorized intelligence agencies to do everything from opening mail to burglarizing homes and offices in what became a futile effort to connect radical organizations in the United States

with foreign governments. In addition, the press often found itself intimidated if it gave too much coverage to the antiwar movement. All of this,
for the most part, simply added to the growing credibility gap between
the government and the people, and brought a great deal of discredit to
the Nixon administration in later years when it was all uncovered. It also
led to a dirty-tricks mindset that, in turn, led to the Watergate break-ins
in 1972.

Nixon, of course, was not carrying this Vietnam policy alone. At his
side was his national security advisor, Henry Kissinger, a well-respected
Harvard political science professor. Kissinger had found a place in the
Johnson administration by running minor diplomatic errands to Saigon,
but during the 1968 election campaign, he was Nixon's inside man in
the Johnson White House, advising the Republicans on Johnson's plans
to pull off any pre-election surprises in Vietnam that might throw the
election to Humphrey. Initially, Kissinger had voiced reservations about
U.S. involvement in Vietnam; he believed strongly that Vietnam was
little more than a brushfire in world affairs and that the United States
should focus on Europe, where the real foreign policy cards were being
played. However, once the commitment in Vietnam was made, he wrote
in 1969, the United States must sustain that commitment in order to
maintain the world's confidence in American promises.[25]

Meanwhile, the talks in Paris continued to founder. Negotiators
from Hanoi would go no further than to demand a reunification of their
nation under a coalition government, and the removal of all U.S. troops
from the South. Nixon and Kissinger, in response, insisted on an independent non-Communist government in the South—and that anything
else would amount to an American surrender. As the United States began
to withdraw its troops, Hanoi reduced its ground activity in the South
and began a waiting game.

The frustrations continued to mount in Washington as Nixon's plans
and peace offerings all failed. The antiwar movement began to heat up
again with calls for protests and riots throughout the country. Nixon
reacted by directing his National Security Council to draw up plans for
what he called "savage, punishing blows" against North Vietnam and
then deliberately leaking his plans to the press, possibly intending to
imply that tactical nuclear weapons were being considered as an option

against Hanoi's intransigence. But Hanoi held its position. Nixon approached Moscow with promises of better U.S.-Soviet relations if the Soviets would pressure Hanoi to give way at Paris. Failing that, he sought an informal series of peace talks with the North Vietnamese outside the workings of the formal talks in Paris and outside the line of sight of the American press. To that end, Kissinger met with Xuan Thuy at a private residence in Paris on August 4, 1964. But Hanoi again held its ground on the primary issues of a united Vietnam and a U.S. withdrawal. In February 1970, Kissinger met with Le Duc Tho in Paris in the first of a series of secret meetings that went through April and ended with no breakthroughs.

In March, Nixon announced the phased withdrawal of 150,000 U.S. troops over the next year. But on April 30, he also announced to the nation that U.S. and ARVN troops were invading Cambodia to clean out the North Vietnamese and Viet Cong sanctuaries there. "When the chips are down," he told the nation in a belligerent tone, "and the world's most powerful nation acts like a pitiful helpless giant, the forces of totalitarianism and anarchy will threaten free nations and free institutions throughout the world."[26] A combined U.S.-ARVN force of 20,000 combat troops—supported by U.S. helicopters—crossed the border into Cambodia, where they unearthed an amazing series of sprawling complexes used for decades by the Viet Cong to prosecute the war in the South. They had hoped to find the Communist party headquarters for South Vietnam (COSVN, the Central Office for South Vietnam), the elusive Viet Cong command post, but they were not successful. The enemy had evacuated their sanctuaries and moved west, deeper into Cambodia; along the way they armed their Communist allies in Cambodia, the Khmer Rouge. The U.S.-ARVN incursion into Cambodia resulted in the capture of enemy weapons and supplies and certainly it disrupted the ability of the Communists to initiate an offensive strategy from that area, but the damage done by the U.S. and ARVN troops was at best only temporary. And the action did not outweigh the tragedies at home caused by the action.

Meanwhile, Nixon's announcement refueled the antiwar movement, a movement that had been relatively quiet since the 1968 Democratic Convention. Within minutes of the president's announcement, student protests were underway at Oberlin College and Princeton. In a few days, strikes and protests had erupted at campuses throughout the country, and a dozen ROTC buildings were set ablaze. On May 2, four students were shot by Ohio national guardsmen at Kent State University. The horror of the photograph on the cover of *Newsweek* of a young woman screaming for help over a bleeding, crumpled body became an icon of the antiwar movement. By May 10 nearly 450 campuses around the nation were on strike. At Jackson State, a historically black university in Jackson, Mississippi, white policemen, called to protect firemen during an antiwar riot, opened fire into a women's dormitory, killing two and wounding twelve others. By the end of May nearly one-third of the nation's colleges and universities had experienced some sort of upheaval.

Nixon had done little to resolve the nightmare of Vietnam. In fact, his invasion of Cambodia had widened the conflict, and now the U.S. government was responsible for a larger, more expensive, and more complicated war. Washington had to keep the weak government of Lon Nol propped up in Cambodia against the growing Khmer Rouge forces supported by Hanoi and Beijing. In Laos, the Pathet Lao Communists had overrun the country and pushed out U.S.-supported H'mong and Thai forces. At the same time as U.S. troops continued their withdrawal from the South, America's sway over Hanoi diminished considerably. Consequently, Le Duc Tho's position in Paris became even more rigid, concluding that America's only recourse would be eventually to withdraw completely. The North Vietnamese and the Viet Cong boycotted the Paris peace talks and the Kissinger–Le Duc Tho secret talks were interrupted throughout the summer. In late 1970 a National Security Council study concluded that the United States would not be able to force the Communists out of the South. By the end of 1970, the Nixon plan for ending the war was failing miserably.

However, despite the setbacks on the diplomatic front, Vietnamization, Nixon's plan for conducting the war on the ground, seemed to be having some success. The ARVN force had been increased to nearly one million by 1970, while troop training by U.S. specialists had been expanded and intensified. ARVN was also better supplied than ever before. By summer 1970, it looked as though ARVN would be able to do what no one before believed it could: take over the war and allow the United States to withdraw with at least some degree of honor. On April 7, 1971, Nixon proclaimed that the Vietnamization of the war was a success. Kissinger, however, said later that the policy had fallen far short of expectations.

Congress had been left in the dark about the bombing of Cambodia for over a year, and when Nixon moved to widen the ground war in early 1970 without congressional approval, the reaction in Congress was not surprising; Congress had been excluded from a major decision, and again the question of who has the power to make war, the president or Congress, came up for debate. Nixon's opponents in Congress rallied in revolt. In June, the Senate voted overwhelmingly to revoke the Tonkin Gulf Resolution of 1964, and they attached an amendment to the bill that would cut funds for the Cambodian invasion. Additional legislation sponsored by senators George McGovern of South Dakota and Mark Hatfield of Oregon would have forced the United States out of Vietnam by December 31, 1971; the bill was only narrowly defeated. A movement had begun on Capitol Hill to take back the reins of power that had been relinquished to LBJ in the Tonkin Gulf Resolution, and to withhold funds from the president in an effort to halt his prosecution of the war.

To appease his critics, Nixon was forced to accelerate the troop withdrawals throughout 1971. By the end of the year another 100,000 had been brought home, leaving only 175,000 U.S. soldiers in Vietnam. But at the same time, Nixon began heavy bombing attacks against the North and against Viet Cong sanctuaries in Laos and Cambodia. In February, he authorized a major ARVN ground operation into Laos that ended in an ARVN casualty rate of nearly 50 percent. His motive was to disrupt Communist supply lines in the North and along the Ho Chi Minh Trail in Cambodia and Laos in an attempt to buy time for Vietnamization. The plan may have succeeded temporarily, but it was clear that the South Vietnamese forces were still no match for the Viet Cong.

Summer 1971 brought the war home with a vengeance. By then nearly 350,000 U.S. soldiers had been killed or wounded in the decade-old conflict, and Americans were clearly tiring of the war, which was now being delivered up in large graphic doses every evening on the six-o'clock news. That summer Lieutenant William Calley was found guilty of murdering at least twenty-two Vietnamese civilians at My Lai in 1968. The incident sent the American people searching their souls. Besides the all-important question of why were we in Vietnam, it was now often asked: "What have we become?" The trial and investigations that followed seemed to show that My Lai was not an isolated incident—that American soldiers had committed atrocities in Vietnam. News reports at home began to follow up on reports of additional U.S. atrocities, and CBS ran a story about U.S. soldiers' fondness for taking the ears of dead enemy soldiers as souvenirs. Of course, the Viet Cong also committed atrocities, but to the American way of thinking the enemy always committed atrocities—American soldiers did not. To add to the disillusionment, Calley was exonerated for his acts. His term of life-in-prison was reduced to twenty years; the secretary of defense reduced it further to ten years. He was then placed under house arrest and finally pardoned by President Nixon.

Also, in summer 1971 the *Pentagon Papers* were leaked and then published by the *New York Times*. This series of Defense Department documents recounted the U.S. decision-making processes that led to war in the early and mid-1960s, and conclusively showed that the American people were consistently misled about the U.S. involvement in Vietnam during the Kennedy and Johnson years. One particularly damaging aspect of the papers showed that plans for introducing ground troops into Vietnam were being made while LBJ was telling the American people that American boys would not fight in Vietnam. Nixon tried to have the papers censored by securing an injunction to stop their publication, but the Supreme Court overturned the injunction. The papers received even more publicity as a result, assuring an even wider readership.

That summer an organization emerged that again forced Americans to search their souls about Vietnam: the Vietnam Veterans Against the War. These men, honorably discharged veterans of the war and often decorated heroes, seemed to bring home to the American people a sense that there was something drastically wrong over there, that America was involved in something that was more than just an ill-conceived conflict that would not end. In April a group of Veterans Against the War met in Washington and ceremoniously tossed away their medals before a crowd of several thousand. At a Senate hearing investigating the war, John Kerry, representing the group, told of the horrors of the war in graphic detail, chastised the government for supporting "a corrupt dictatorial regime" in Saigon, and spoke of an America that had lost "her sense of morality as she accepted very coolly a My Lai and refused to give up the image of American soldiers who hand out chocolate bars and chewing gum." Kerry concluded, "In our opinion, and from our experience, there is nothing in South Vietnam, nothing which could happen that realistically threatens the United States of America. And to attempt to justify the loss of one American life in Vietnam, Cambodia, or Laos by linking such loss to the preservation of freedom . . . is to us the height of criminal hypocrisy, and it is that kind of hypocrisy which we feel has torn this country apart."[27] If the radical cries of the New Left were not credible to Middle America, here was the credible voice of experience. It was an awful war.

Meanwhile, the polls seemed to show the result of America's growing disenchantment all too well. A Harris poll showed that 71 percent of the American people believed that the United States should not have gotten involved in Vietnam in the first place. Another 58 percent seemed to react to the new information available in the press, concluding that the war was immoral. In response, Nixon took a beating. His approval rating dropped to a dismal 31 percent. He had achieved what Johnson and Truman had also achieved: a high degree of unpopularity in the face of a highly unpopular war.

In this same summer (1971), the world diplomatic structure began to shift when Kissinger made a secret trip to Beijing to arrange for Nixon to visit China that winter. This drastic change of events occurred partly because of a growing discord between the Chinese and the Soviets. In late summer 1968, the Soviets had used tanks to crush a reformist government in Czechoslovakia and then announced that they might do the same to any other Communist country that deviated from the Moscow line. Consequently, Mao and the Chinese began to see themselves as next on the Soviets' list. In 1969 the gap between the Communist giants grew even larger when the two engaged in border clashes along the Ussuri River in northern Manchuria. This was followed by a massive Soviet military buildup on the Chinese border. All of this sent Mao looking for a friend to counter the growing Soviet threat. He found it, surprisingly, in the United States—and Richard Nixon.

This thawing of U.S.-Chinese relations, however, left Hanoi with a problem. Since 1968 Chinese aid had dried up, and now Mao had suggested (at Kissinger's behest) that the unification of Vietnam might take many years. In response, Moscow began to play for U.S. favor in response to the U.S.-Chinese detente, and Hanoi was in danger of being left without an ally in either Beijing or Moscow—and possibly forced to prosecute the war in Vietnam on its own. Nixon's contact with Beijing had done more to disrupt the Communist world and hurt Hanoi than any U.S. military action. It was truly a diplomatic coup that might have pushed the North Vietnamese to bargain. However, both Beijing and Moscow were willing to continue supplying Hanoi, although neither would sacrifice any diplomatic advantage with the United States to do so. Nixon's trip to Beijing in February 1972 changed the face of the U.S. foreign policy in the Far East, but it is usually considered to have had little effect on the conduct of the Vietnam War. However, it may have pushed Hanoi to end the war quickly, fearing what might come out of the growing U.S.-Chinese good will.

Summer 1971 had put great pressure on both sides to end the conflict, and they set their sights on ending the war sometime in 1972. Nixon and Kissinger had spent two-and-one-half years executing their war in Indochina and they had accomplished little. In fact, by removing U.S. ground forces, they had removed what small amount of leverage they held at the bargaining table in Paris. The North Vietnamese correctly assumed that the political climate in the United States would not allow Nixon to reintroduce U.S. forces into South Vietnam. So, with their American enemy before them being rapidly reduced, and with ARVN (they also correctly assumed) unable to carry on the war effectively in place of the Americans, they had no reason to give way in Paris. At the same time Nixon and Kissinger had expanded the war to the rest of Indochina, spreading the chaos, horror, and cost that went with it, mostly for little gain beyond delaying a Communist offensive and buying a little time to shore up ARVN. The Nixon-Kissinger strategy had failed. Like Johnson, they had neither moved aggressively to win the war nor to end it. Their policy had ruined the American position at the bargaining table and ignited additional violence at home, and now, at the beginning of 1972, Nixon had only one action left at his disposal. He would, as others have said, try to bomb his way to victory—or at least bomb his way to a better bargaining position. That, too, would fail.

9

THE LAST ACT

At the end of March 1972, the Communists struck hard at American and ARVN forces throughout South Vietnam. It was their chance to show the world that their fighting ability was still well intact, and to show the American public (by defeating ARVN troops in the field) that the policy of Vietnamization had failed and that the time had come to negotiate seriously for a U.S. withdrawal. Equipped with Soviet-made rockets, artillery, and tanks, the Communist advance defeated ARVN forces in the northern provinces of South Vietnam, overrunning in just two days twelve bases that U.S. Marines had recently turned over to ARVN. With little effort, the Communists took Quangtri province and held it through summer and into fall. In response, ARVN performed poorly in almost every sector of the Communist advance. With only 6,000 U.S. combat troops left in Vietnam, there was little standing in the way of the Communist push. In Washington, Secretary of Defense Melvin Laird declared the South Vietnamese military performance "astonishingly successful."[1]

In May, Kissinger and Le Duc Tho held another secret meeting in Paris. It was becoming a desperate time for Nixon and Kissinger. Congress repeatedly threatened to cut spending for the war and bring an abrupt end to U.S. involvement. Kissinger presented North Vietnam with the most comprehensive plan for peace yet placed on the table: in exchange for U.S. prisoners of war, Kissinger agreed to withdraw all U.S. troops from Vietnam within seven months after the signing of a ceasefire. This simple agreement was an abandonment of the long-standing American demand for a withdrawal of all combat troops from both sides, and for the first time the United States agreed to allow Communist troops to remain in the South after the U.S. withdrawal. This was a major concession, but Le Duc Tho had come to believe that political forces in the United States would soon coerce the Nixon administration into withdrawing unconditionally and he rejected the proposal—demanding that the United States also drop support for the Thieu government. That was unacceptable to Kissinger and Nixon, but Kissinger believed that a deadlock had been broken and that the two sides were on the verge of a settlement. However, the place of the Thieu regime after the U.S. withdrawal brought the talks to a halt—and pushed Nixon to act. He had to implement an end-the-war strategy.

With his leverage against Hanoi quickly evaporating, Nixon, on May 8, ignored the advice of Laird and CIA director Richard Helms and ordered an intensive B-52 bombardment of military targets in North Vietnam, a naval blockade of the North, and the mining of Haiphong harbor, all in hopes of breaking the diplomatic stalemate. He had escalated the war again, but this time it was generally successful. The Communist offensive that began in March was stalled by the U.S. air strikes, and Quangtri province fell back into ARVN's hands in September. From this experience, the success or failure of Vietnamization became perfectly clear: without U.S. air power ARVN was vulnerable—no match for the enemy.

The Democrats in summer 1972 nominated George McGovern, a dove who was prepared to bring an end to the war unconditionally. McGovern, however, was a weak candidate, and most Americans still clung to Nixon's promise of peace with honor—although they wanted it sooner than later. As Nixon continued the troop withdrawals and as the discussions in Paris seemed to proceed, it looked as though the president was headed for a landslide election victory. Of course, Vietnam was not the only issue in 1972; the economy, fueled by the war for nearly a decade, was now weak. The nation was slowly coming out of the recession of 1969–1970 and unemployment and inflation were both high. Nixon responded by freezing wages and prices in hopes of getting the economy under control long enough to pull him through the election. From a political standpoint it worked, but it damaged the economy, and after the election the nation fell into a two-year-long recession. But in fall 1972 Nixon looked as though he would easily be reelected, and the North Vietnamese feared that a reelected Nixon might find in his mandate the incentive he needed to begin a major offensive against the North or to resume a major bombing campaign. For the leaders in Hanoi, a pre-election agreement might be the best agreement they would get. At the same time, McGovern's nomination, although based almost solely on his intention to end the war, did not force Nixon to make concessions in Paris.

As one of America's most uneventful elections unfolded at home, the talks between Kissinger and Le Duc Tho began to make rapid advances in Paris, mostly because Nixon and Kissinger were beginning to make significant concessions to Hanoi. The United States had already agreed to allow North Vietnamese troops to remain in the South, but Hanoi would not agree to a settlement that allowed the Thieu regime to remain in Saigon after the ceasefire. Kissinger tried to solve this problem by suggesting a tripartite electoral commission made up of the Viet Cong, the Thieu government, and a group of neutralists. Le Duc Tho agreed to this, which was a major concession, and for the first time, Le Duc Tho did not insist on Thieu's immediate resignation. But most important, this plan permitted the existence of a postwar South Vietnam, and for the first time, the Vietnam War seemed on the verge of a settlement. On October 26 (just a week before the election) Kissinger announced to the nation that "peace is at hand." The North Vietnamese, believing it was so, told their cadres in the South to occupy as much land as they could in anticipation of a coming agreement that would allow them to remain in control of the territory they possessed at the ceasefire.

This was the best settlement Kissinger could get. The war would undoubtedly go on between the North and the South, and in that war the South would suffer a distinct military disadvantage. But the United States would be out of it, and it would leave behind an independent nation of South Vietnam to fight its own battles. Nixon and Kissinger had avoided their greatest fears: that the United States would be forced to withdraw, leaving behind a united Vietnam under Hanoi's control.

Despite all these drawbacks and reservations, Kissinger was elated at his masterpiece of diplomacy. But there were problems. A major one was the refusal of the Thieu government to accept the agreement.[2] When it became clear that the United States was leaving and that North Vietnamese troops would be allowed to remain in the South after the ceasefire, Thieu tried to sabotage the agreement in hopes that the talks would break down and the war would continue. This scenario was all too familiar. In 1953 Syngman Rhee had tried to scotch the agreements at Panmunjom when he was confronted with the same possibilities. Thieu was demanding a number of changes in the agreements, most of which were aimed at securing a stronger place in the postwar coalition. In an attempt to pacify Thieu, Washington dumped nearly $2 billion worth of military aid on his government in just six weeks. But Thieu refused to budge. He would do everything possible to drive a wedge between Washington and Hanoi.

Nixon refused to force Thieu to accept the agreement, and after the election he sent Kissinger back to Paris with the sixty-nine amendments that Thieu demanded. Nixon and Kissinger both knew that Thieu's demands would not be acceptable to Hanoi, and that the situation could be used as an excuse for the North to bargain for better conditions. At the same time, Congress and the American people were becoming obsessed with the release of U.S. prisoners of war, and as long as Hanoi continued to hold the POWs, a postponement of the settlement was to Hanoi's advantage. Hanoi introduced its own amendments and the talks broke down on December 13. Just before that date, Nixon wrote Thieu: "You have my absolute assurance that if Hanoi fails to abide by the terms of this agreement it is my intention to take swift and severe retaliatory action."[3]

And he did. Nixon responded by ordering "Linebacker II," a massive wave of B-52 bombings against targets in Hanoi and Haiphong. Not knowing the intricacies of the Kissinger–Le Duc Tho talks, the American people were told that the bombings were in response to Hanoi's unwillingness to conclude the agreement. In reality, Nixon was bombing the North to force the Communists to sign an agreement he had agreed to in October. He may also have wanted to damage the North as much as possible before the ceasefire in order to buy the South additional time—to lengthen the time between the U.S. pullout and the inevitable fall of Saigon. For nearly two weeks, B-52s bludgeoned the North with 36,000 tons of bombs, the most intensive and devastating attack of the war. American pilots flew 724 B-52 sorties and about 640 fighter-bomber sorties against the North.

These Christmas Bombings, as Linebacker became known, drew a new wave of rage from Congress and the American people. Few doubted that Congress now had the power to place restraints on Nixon's ability to prosecute the war any further. In addition, much of the world complained bitterly at the unusual brutality of the bombings. Although U.S. pilots were directed to hit only industrial and military targets in the North, credible reports from Hanoi depicted large residential neighborhoods bombed out of existence; Hanoi's largest hospital was hit. The North Vietnamese reported 2,196 deaths and 1,577 wounded, remarkably low figures, owing mostly to the Hanoi government's efficiency in evacuating the city. The Americans lost fifteen B-52s and eleven other aircraft; ninety-two crewmen were killed. The North Vietnamese expended their entire supply of surface-to-air missiles in response to the campaign.

The bombing pushed Hanoi back to the bargaining table. By now both sides needed an agreement. During the bombing a straw poll of congressmen made it plain that when Congress reconvened in January, they would have the votes to legislate the nation out of the war. After the exchange of some un-pleasantries in Paris between Le Duc Tho and Kissinger over the bombings, the two got down to business on January 13. Nixon approved the agreement (which was almost identical to the October agreement) two days later. The next big hurdle was Thieu, whose immediate reaction was that the new agreement was nothing new, and essentially a surrender to the Communists. Nixon promised Thieu that he would push Congress to continue aid to Saigon after the U.S. pullout. Then he told Thieu that the United States would sign the agreement— and added a final ultimatum: if Thieu did not agree there would be "an inevitable and immediate termination of U.S. economic and military assistance."[4] It was a compelling argument, the same one, in fact, that Eisenhower had given Rhee in 1953. And like Rhee, Thieu gave in and did not oppose the agreement.

The agreement called for a ceasefire in place, and a withdrawal of all U.S. troops in exchange for the release of the POWs. It prohibited both the United States and the North Vietnamese from introducing any more troops into the South, and it maintained the demilitarized zone. Two commissions were created to enforce the ceasefire, and another was set up to arrange free elections in the South. The future of Vietnam was placed in the hands of the Vietnamese—and out of the hands of others for the first time in modern history.

The agreement represented little more than what Kissinger called "a decent interval" before the North finally defeated the South, and everyone involved knew it. The agreement allowed the United States to withdraw, and it maintained the Thieu government in Saigon. But all parties involved knew that the ultimate future of Vietnam would be decided by military force. Everyone also knew that the North had the upper hand by far in that regard, and that the United States would not be coming to Saigon's aid. As the treaty was being signed, the North was preparing to get its battle machines underway again—to continue its age-old fight for unification and independence from imperialist domination.

The cost had been high on both sides. For the United States, the war cost somewhere between $112 billion and $155 billion. It also cost the U.S. government much of its national and international credibility, a credibility it had entered the war in Vietnam to maintain. In addition, the U.S. government managed to alienate a major section of its population; the nation had split violently over the war and the government's policies for prosecuting it. The war had become a poison in the American system. On the battlefield, the United States lost 45,943 killed in action, and an additional 10,298 killed in non-combat-related causes; 2,477 were also designated as missing in action and presumed dead. Of the total of 58,718, over 20,000 were killed in the last four years of the war. ARVN lost over 220,000 killed in action, and another 500,000 were wounded. On the other side, it has been estimated that nearly one million enemy soldiers (from the North and the South) were killed in combat. It has never been estimated how many civilians were killed as a result of the war.

Fighting between ARVN and the Viet Cong broke out almost immediately after the truce was signed; the United States responded by distancing itself from the war almost completely. What had been our war, most believed, was now their war, a war fought by Asian boys, as Lyndon Johnson had once said. In March 1973, the POWs were released, but only after the United States threatened to delay troop withdrawals. In that same month the last of the U.S. forces left Vietnam, leaving behind only some 9,000 "civilian advisors," supposedly now employed by the Saigon government. The bombing of Cambodia continued under the guise of support for Lon Nol, but by summer 1973 Congress had had enough of that action and approved an amendment requiring an immediate end to all U.S. military activity in Indochina. In a compromise with Congress, Nixon agreed to end the bombing by August 15.

By that time, Watergate had paralyzed the executive branch of the government, and Nixon had become more and more isolated as supporters found it expedient to abandon his side in the wake of the scandal. In November, Congress passed the War Powers Act over Nixon's veto, a direct response to U.S involvement in Vietnam. It seems axiomatic in the history of U.S. foreign policy that the United States feels a need to take action to avoid the conditions that got the nation into its last war. The War Powers Act requires the president to notify Congress within forty-eight hours of U.S. troop deployments, and forces the withdrawal of those troops within sixty days unless otherwise authorized by Congress. The constitutionality of the War Powers Act would be hotly debated through the 1980s as President Ronald Reagan would seek to have the presidential power of military intervention reinstated into the executive branch. When George H. W. Bush sought to intervene in the Persian Gulf, the question of the executive branch's power to wage war without congressional consent again came into question, with Bush citing Truman's intervention in Korea as precedent, and Congress citing Johnson's intervention in Vietnam as an ominous warning of what might come.

By 1974, South Vietnam was on the verge of internal collapse. Government corruption, a weak economy, a reduction in U.S. aid, and the vulnerability of ARVN forces in the field made a North Vietnamese victory an almost certainty. The only question not answered was when it would occur. In August, the Watergate scandal forced Nixon to resign from office, removing the last possibility of U.S. support for the waning Saigon government; only Nixon would have had a vested interest in saving South Vietnam. In early 1975, Hanoi prepared for the final blow. Military leaders there believed it would take about two years to defeat

ARVN and bring down South Vietnam. But as the Communists moved south, first into the Central Highlands and then through the South Vietnamese coastal cities, ARVN collapsed quickly and fell back on its Saigon defenses. To everyone's surprise, including the North Vietnamese, the drive to Saigon was an amazingly easy one.

Hanoi had correctly concluded that the United States would not again intervene. As North Vietnamese troops closed in on Saigon, Congress rejected President Gerald Ford's request to send military aid. Only $300 million was approved to evacuate Americans from the city. Clearly, the United States had no stomach for further intervention in Vietnam. In April, Thieu resigned, blaming the United States for the debacle. All that remained was for North Vietnamese tanks to enter the newly named Ho Chi Minh City and unite the nation of Vietnam. For America, the nightmare was over.

But on the periphery the war carried on. In December 1975, the Communist Pathet Lao seized power in Laos, and immediately cast their allegiance with Hanoi. In Cambodia, the Khmer Rouge set out to consolidate its power by genocide, killing roughly one-third of the Cambodian population before Vietnam itself invaded Cambodia and finally put an end to the killing. The Khmer Rouge had been supported by China, and within months Vietnam and China were at war on Vietnam's northern border. Thus, the United States found itself in the awkward position of supporting China's containment of Vietnam.

America's second Asian war since World War II had resolved no more than the first. In fact, the Vietnam War was far more devastating, costly, and divisive than the war in Korea had been. The United States had entered both wars for many of the same reasons, and that is clearly the most important factor in comparing the two wars. The point was that Communism had to be stopped, lines had to be drawn. And of course, once those lines were drawn, they had to be defended or they carried no weight. Communism was contained in Korea, but it was not contained in Vietnam. In Korea, the settlement, which achieved no more than the *status quo ante,* was considered a boost for American credibility. The United States had come to the aid of an aggrieved nation that, for the most part, it had no reason to assist. To the world that meant that the United States had taken on the role of international policeman in

opposition to Soviet and Chinese Communist aggression almost anywhere. Those nations of the world that feared the spread of Communism
could now look to the United States for aid and support. The results
of Vietnam proved just the opposite. The Americans no longer had the
stomach for such battles; they had been stung by a small aggressive force;
and the American people, it was now revealed, would not endure the
hardship of war for any length of time. It appeared that the United States
was, as the Communists had always said, a paper tiger. America, so it
seemed, had lost its will.

George H. W. Bush, in the Persian Gulf War, would seek to return
that will to America and its people, and to bring international prestige
back to the United States and its military. But the ghost of Vietnam would
haunt him, although for Bush, Communism was no longer a menace.
The foreign policy philosophies embodied in containment, dominoes,
appeasement, and the Munich Syndrome still played well in Washington
and in the minds of the American people in the weeks before the outbreak
of the Gulf War. As the war in the Gulf got underway, George H. W. Bush
would say: "No more Munichs." He would also say: "No more Vietnams."
He might well have said: "No more Koreas."

PART III
AMERICA IN THE MIDDLE EAST

10

THE FIRST GULF WAR: BACKGROUND FOR CONFLICT

Ten years following the end of the Vietnam War, President Ronald Reagan's defense secretary, Casper Weinberger, looked back and offered a Clausewitzian dictum that reflected the essence of the Vietnam Syndrome. War, he said, should be undertaken only with "clearly definable objectives" and only "with reasonable assurance" that those objectives would enjoy "the support of the American people and their elected representatives in Congress."[1] America's terrible experience in Vietnam had clearly made the nation gun shy—and with good reason. Despite arguments from Presidents Johnson and Nixon to the contrary, the antiwar movement had indeed forced both presidents to come to terms with the war in Vietnam, and to move the nation toward some sort of withdrawal. Faced with the prospect of another backlash against any military action, presidents Gerald Ford, Jimmy Carter, and even the hawkish Ronald Reagan found themselves backing away from military involvement as a means of solving the nation's foreign relations problems. They were not at all eager to see their precious resources (military or political) spent in a war that lacked the support of the American people, had no clear objectives, and offered plenty of jungle and mountain terrain conducive to a long, drawn-out guerrilla campaign. Consequently, the United States committed its military only when it could resolve the problems quickly, before the American people could begin to react against the action; or

Washington chose instead to send vast amounts of money to warring surrogates in hopes that American firepower in the hands of others might advance U.S. interests and policy in a specific region.

In April 1980, President Jimmy Carter staged an abortive mission to rescue American hostages being held in Tehran in the wake of the Islamic fundamentalist revolution there. The dismal failure of that mission seemed to drag the United States even deeper into the doldrums of helplessness that had set in after the fall of Saigon in 1975. The hostage crisis was no small matter in the agonizing death of the Carter administration and the rise of the new Republicanism of Ronald Reagan in 1980. In October 1983, Reagan sought to flex his muscles and reassert the U.S. foreign policy of containment by invading the small Caribbean island of Grenada to halt what was billed as a Cuban Communist insurgency. Despite the rescue of a few U.S. medical students on the island, the U.S. military's massive (and notoriously uncoordinated) attack by 10,000 paratroopers against a few hundred Cuban laborers building an airfield on the vacation island did little to bring back what the nation had lost in Vietnam. In fact, to many Americans the patriotic flag waving that went along with the "invasion" of Grenada appeared exceedingly artificial, even pathetic. Despite the Grenada "victory," America's once-great power seemed even more in retreat. In that same month, 241 marines were killed by a terrorist blast in Lebanon and President Reagan responded by cutting his losses and withdrawing the U.S. peace-keeping forces. The fiasco in Lebanon showed the world that America was still squeamish about the possibility of a prolonged military involvement and would withdraw in haste, it seemed, at the first sign of trouble. America's hurried withdrawal from Lebanon also made it clear to the nations of the Middle East that the United States had a peripheral concern, at best, for the growing problems in that part of the world. Congress, throughout Reagan's intervention in Lebanon, often threatened to invoke the 1973 War Powers Act and force the president to withdraw the troops from Lebanon. In April 1987, in another action, a U.S. attack against the terrorist network of Libyan strongman Moammar Ghadafi was more decisive and more direct, although later evidence proved that the attack was unwarranted.[2] And in Panama, like the other military actions since Vietnam, the U.S. intervention there did little to raise U.S. esteem on the world market, and showed only that the U.S. military could over-whelm a Central American police force with stealth technology, massive firepower, and commando operations.

But the lessons of Vietnam could best be seen in the U.S. operations in Central America during the 1980s. There, an all-too-familiar jungle war had broken out between the pro-Communist Sandinistas of Nicaragua and the Contras, a pseudo-army of American-supported anti-Communists. As in Vietnam, the United States had created a friendly counterforce to combat its pro-Communist enemy. For most Americans the comparisons between U.S. actions in Central America and Southeast Asia were much too great, and the polls made that clear. However, in an attempt to push Americans to accept his actions in Central America, President Reagan announced that the "Vietnam Syndrome" was dead and proclaimed the right of the United States to send troops anywhere in the world to combat Communism. Supporters of U.S. involvement in Central America began to parrot a now-familiar notion: that the hands of the U.S. military had been tied by Congress in Vietnam, that the war could have been won had the military been allowed to fight its fight—a total war. Congress, it was being argued, was again tying the hands of the military—this time in Central America—and the United States should intervene on a large scale and end the Communist infiltration there. In order to maintain the Contras ("freedom fighters," as Reagan called them) the president com-mitted U.S. military advisors and millions of dollars to the anti-Com-munist regime next door in El Salvador. But despite the administration's insistence to the contrary, the specter of Vietnam continued to lurk in the American mind, and Reagan's adventures in Central America never found support from the American people, or Congress, despite the Great Communicator's continued attempts to convince the country that the situation in Nicaragua merited a direct U.S. military response.

In summer 1990, as the crises unfolded that would lead to the Gulf War, the United States was still living in the shadow of Vietnam, still fighting against a popular worldview that the U.S. military was a paper tiger that could not maintain popular support; and that the American soldier was a poor fighter, unwilling to take risks, unwilling to die for his country. Of all the reasons George H. W. Bush had to take the United States into the Gulf War, a resurgence of American self-esteem and military credibility may not have topped his list, but clearly he saw that an American show of effective force in defense of a weak nation overrun by a nefarious villain would increase the stock of the United States and its military. The world would again be able to look to the United States as a world leader, the defender of the weak, a military power that might be called on to halt military aggression. The United States would finally be able to put the ghost of Vietnam behind it. "By God," President Bush told reporters just after the war, "we've kicked the Vietnam syndrome once and for all."[3]

There are a number of important distinctions between the Persian Gulf War of 1991 and America's other wars fought on the Asian continent since 1945. The most important one is the most obvious: that the war in the Persian Gulf played almost no part in the cold war. There was little concern about the disposition of the Soviets or the Chinese as there had been in Korea and Vietnam. China's borders, of course, were not threatened by the U.S. action in Kuwait, and the USSR in 1991 was on the verge of economic and political collapse. For the first time since World War II the United States could initiate a major military intervention outside its own hemisphere without having to fear Communist reprisals, and without the fear that the war might escalate into a nuclear war.

However, the cold war rhetoric was very much a part of the U.S. action in the Gulf. Containment was clearly a motive for American intervention; the U.S. military was deployed to contain an aggressor, a totalitarian tyrant. Also, George H. W. Bush made it clear that he would not be the American president who "lost" Kuwait. The ramifications of such a loss had hurt Truman badly when China fell to the Communists in 1949, and Truman reacted by sending troops to Korea to avoid being shackled with "losing" Korea as well. Johnson did not want to be the president who "lost" Vietnam, and Nixon did not want to be the first American president to lose a war. George Bush inherited these fears in August 1990.

The United States also evoked the domino theory as part of its interventionist policy in the Gulf. Bush told the American people that if Saddam Hussein was allowed to annex Kuwait then the other nations of the Middle East (most significantly Saudi Arabia) might also fall to

Saddam's armies. The result would be a disastrous blow to American interests in the region—both political interests and economic interests.

Probably the most prevalent cold war line that was dredged up to explain and justify American intervention in the Gulf was the Munich Syndrome—the idea that if Saddam were allowed to keep his conquests in Kuwait, if he were simply appeased, he would continue to demand more and more territory. "Some have suggested," wrote Congressman Stephen Solarz in the *New Republic*, "that we offer Bubiyan and Warba, the two Kuwaiti islands that block Saddam's unfettered access to the Persian Gulf, as well as the Rumaila oil fields, just south of the Iraqi border, in exchange for Saddam's withdrawal from the rest of Kuwait." But the United States has "rightly rejected the idea, on the grounds that it would be a reward for aggression and set the stage for additional acts of banditry."[4] The cold war was ending as the war in the Gulf was being fought, but the cold war rhetoric was still alive, as valid, it seemed, against the villainy of Saddam Hussein as against Stalin, Brezhnev, or Mao.

Another concept in the Gulf War that was associated with Munich, appeasement, and the causes of World War II was the phenomenon of the Saddam-Hitler analogy, that Saddam was in many ways like Hitler in his character, demands, and actions. The concept was prevalent in the press, as well as in the administration's foreign policy, and in the propaganda of the war. Interestingly, there is some historical basis for this analogy, a factor that most analysts and columnists missed in their examinations of the Gulf War. The Iraqi Baath party was formed in 1941 by Michel Aflaq and Salah Bitar. Both had lived and studied in Europe during the 1930s, and both were attracted to the fascist movement that was sweeping Europe in that period. It was Nazi Germany that Aflaq hoped to use as a model for a new postwar Iraq, an Iraq that would find a synthesis between nationalism and socialism as Germany had tried to do in the 1930s. Aflaq was, as one observer has noted, "full of enthusiasm for Hitler."[5] Aflaq died in Baghdad in 1989; Saddam was his disciple. In 1941 the most ruthless side of Nazi fascism found a place in Iraq and in the Baath party. In that year, several hundred Iraqi Jews were killed in anti-Semitic riots throughout Iraq. In 1969, Saddam Hussein was responsible for a show trial of spies in Baghdad in which Jews were the primary targets. Several Jewish "spies" were publicly hanged. The link is strong between the antisemitism of Adolf Hitler and the antisemitism of Saddam Hussein.[6]

But to America, the Hitler analogy seemed to take on more than a historical character as the Gulf crisis unfolded. Much of this idea revolved around the consequences of appeasement, but often it went deeper. President Bush was the first to use the analogy in a speech at the Pentagon on August 15: "A half century ago, our nation and the world paid dearly for appeasing an aggressor who should, and could, have been stopped. We are not going to make that mistake again."[7] On August 20, in *US News and World Report,* Mortimer Zuckerman wrote, "We learned something from the '30s, but let us reflect also that Hussein has already gotten away with more than Hitler had before he finally was challenged."[8] On September 3, the cover of the *New Republic* featured Saddam with a Hitleresque mustache. The headline read, "Fuhrer in the Gulf."[9] On August 24, William Safire wrote: "If anyone wondered whether the analogy of Saddam Hussein to . . . Adolf Hitler, might be an exaggeration, all doubt was removed yesterday" when Saddam exhibited to the world on television the women and children he held hostage.[10] Saddam, it seemed, was no less a tyrant, no less a murderer, with many of the same motives and plans for the Middle East that Hitler had had for Europe in the late 1930s. Even his "elite" Republican Guard reminded many of the Waffen SS, Hitler's own elite force. But some observers also seemed to realize that if Saddam were able to subdue Israel, he might try to subject the Jews there to the same atrocities that Hitler had committed against the European Jews in the 1930s and 1940s. We had to stop Saddam now, the nation seemed to be saying, or there would be a larger war later. "No more Munichs," George H. W. Bush declared to the world. The Hitler parallel, however, served to keep the two sides apart in the early negotiations. Simply talking with Saddam (or his foreign minister Tabriq Aziz) conjured up an image of Chamberlain, Hitler, and "peace in our time."

Also linked to appeasement was the fear that if Saddam's war-making powers were not thwarted now there would be a stronger, better equipped, and possibly nuclear-powered Saddam to deal with in the future. Again, Solarz made the point: "If we do not stop him now, we will almost certainly be obligated to confront him later, when he will be chillingly more formidable."[11] This was not a concern in Korea or Vietnam where there was little fear that the enemy might develop a greater war machine over time if the United States did not intervene immediately to destroy their ability to make war.

The origins of the Gulf War, like the origins of the Korean and Vietnam wars, were an outgrowth of the colonial past. In World War I the Ottoman Empire stood on the losing side, and at the Treaty of Versailles its Middle Eastern empire was carved up, mandated between the imperialist powers of Britain and France. Although a Kuwaiti family did exist, the British, in November 1922, drew the boundaries that separated Saudi Arabia, Kuwait, and Iraq. Kuwait was created by the British, at least in part, to deny Iraq an outlet to the Persian Gulf; Baghdad had shown the British enough strength and initiative to dominate the Arab region, and Britain, the consummate imperial power always looking to weaken the colonies, hoped that by cutting off Iraq from the Gulf, it could keep both Iraq and Kuwait dependent on Britain. Saudi Arabia reluctantly recognized the new borders, but Iraq would not. Kuwait became a British protectorate, but throughout the rest of the twentieth century the Iraqis refused to surrender their conviction that Kuwait was a legitimate part of Iraq, taken by an illegitimate imperial power. In 1932 Iraq declared its independence and joined the League of Nations. The Iraqi king Ghazi ibn Faisal immediately proposed a reunification of Iraq and Kuwait, but the Kuwaiti royal family rejected the idea, and their convictions were firmly supported by the British. In 1961, when Kuwait was given its independence by Britain, Iraq tried again to talk Kuwait back into unification, but the plea was again unsuccessful and Iraq prepared to invade Kuwait to unite the two by force. But Britain again intervened to stop the invasion. For two more years, Iraq blocked Kuwait's entrance into the United Nations on the grounds that it was an illegitimate creation of the British Empire and historically a part of Iraq. However, when the Baath party came to power in Baghdad in 1963, Iraq finally seemed to come to terms with Kuwait, but only after Kuwait's ruling Sabah family "loaned" Iraq $85 million, a bribe by any other name and the beginning of Kuwait's long-term practice of paying off Iraq to maintain its northern neighbor's goodwill. Although Iraq said in 1963 that it was willing to accept the independence of Kuwait, it was not willing to recognize the location of the boundary lines between the two nations, and the Iraqis have continued to dispute the frontier.

The Baath Party had its origins in European fascism and Arab nationalism, two movements not at all foreign to one another. Baath is Arabic for "renaissance," a rebirth supposedly of the grandeurs of Nebuchadnezaar's New Babylonian Mesopotamian empire. Bitar and Aflaq received their educations at the Sorbonne in Paris in the late 1920s and early 1930s, and there they fell for the fascist dogma of Benito Mussolini and then Hitler. In 1941 the two formed the Society to Help Iraq, and that organization became the nucleus of what would become the Baath Party of both Syria and Iraq. In 1958 General Abdul Karim Qassim overthrew the Iraqi monarchy in a coup. Three years later Qassim threatened to overrun Kuwait, and in that same year a civil war broke out between the Iraqi government in Baghdad and the Kurds in northern Iraq. That conflict also had its origins in the lines drawn in that area following World War I.

In 1963, the Baathists finally made their move for power in a bloody coup led by Abdul-Salam Arif and the Baathist officers in the Iraqi army. A Baathist party took control of Syria in that same year, although the Syrian Baaths and the Iraqi Baaths have always seen themselves as rivals rather than partners in the Arab world. A young Saddam Hussein worked as a torturer in this period at a Baath interrogation center in Baghdad, a little shop of horrors known as the "Palace of the End."

Nine months after his takeover, Arif turned against the Baathists in his party, purged them from his government, and sought to move closer to Egyptian President Abdul Nassar and his concept of pan-Arabism. In 1966 Arif died in a suspicious helicopter crash and was succeeded by his brother Abdul Rahman Arif. The second Arif made peace with the Baath Party, and the Baathists again began to assert their power in Iraq. Saddam established the Baath party's secret police in this period; it was the beginning of his rise to prominence in the party. In the summer of 1968, the Baath party again rose to power through a coup, naming Ahmad Hassan Bakr as the new president of Iraq. Bakr and the Baath party were supported by the newly organized Republican Guard, an elite military force designed ostensibly to protect the president and thwart coup attempts.

The Baath Party maintained its control in Iraq by brutal force of arms and terror, not by support of the Iraqi people. According to the Baath party's own estimates there were no more than 5,000 party members when the 1968 coup took place. However, their party slogan, "we came to stay," made it clear that they would use force if necessary to maintain power; they would not be ousted as they had been in 1963.[12] The people of Iraq, it seemed, came to accept the oppressions of the Baathists as they have accepted other oppressive rulers of Mesopotamia over the centuries. In his rise to power, Saddam came to control the Jihaz Haneen, the Baath Party's terror and intimidation organization, which at times has had a great deal in common with Hitler's Gestapo. Saddam organized the mass hanging of Jews in 1969; and he terrorized Iraq's political elite, many of whom opposed the Baath regime. By 1973 all of Saddam's rivals had been eliminated, either through murder, purge, or mysterious deaths. Bakr remained the official head of the Iraqi government, but Saddam was in firm control.[13]

In 1972, Iraq signed a pact with the Soviets. The United States responded by aiding the shah of Iran in a large-scale, covert action against the Iraqi Baath regime and by inciting the Iraqi Kurds in northern Iraq. In March 1973 the Kurds went into open revolt against Baghdad, and Saddam responded with a brutal mass bombing of civilian targets in Kurdistan. After two years of fighting, Iran (and the United States) abandoned the Kurds when Saddam sought to make peace by offering the shah of Iran half of the Shatt al-Arab waterway in exchange for withdrawing his support for the Kurds. Without Iranian support, the Kurds were left alone in the conflict, and Saddam moved to crush them. The Kurds felt betrayed by Iran, and ultimately by the United States.

By 1978, Saddam had taken the lead in the Arab world in punishing Egypt for making peace with Israel. Iraq became a sanctuary for the deadliest Palestinian terrorists, and the most boisterous anti-Israeli threats in this period came from Baghdad. It appeared that Iraq was about to become the leader of the Arab world, the position vacated by Anwar Sadat when he signed a peace treaty with Israel at Camp David in 1979.

Through the 1980s the Iraqi-Soviet accord weakened, and the United States began to pull Baghdad closer to Washington as a counterbalance to the radical Shiites who had taken over in in Iran. As the situation in Iran hardened, the United States began to see Iraqi strength as a way to neutralize the anti-American government of the Ayatollah Khomeini. At the same time, Saddam was able to take advantage of the fear that the radical Shiite movement in Iran might spread to the Arab world. By moving to contain the radical Shiites, Saddam hoped to place himself into the role of leader of the Arab world—a position he would continue to seek as a major objective in the Gulf War.

In September 1980, Saddam launched a war against Iran, believing that he could cause the collapse of the Tehran government in a matter of weeks and emerge as the Arab world's savior against the excesses of the Iranian radicals. But the war bogged down for Saddam very quickly as the Iranians seemed to transfer the energy of their revolution to the battle field. Instead of the leader of the Arab world, Saddam found himself standing alone in an expensive, no-win war against the revolutionary armies of radical Islam. Even worse for Saddam, Kuwait refused to cooperate in his war against Tehran, and even Baathist Syrians joined the Iranians by cutting off Iraq's oil pipeline through Syria.

The United States, however, did support Saddam's war against Iran. It was Washington's official policy that Iraq was simply the lesser of the two evils in the war. The term used at the time to describe the U.S. policy was "tilt." The United States was "tilting" toward Iraq. The American people, following the Iranian hostage crisis in the last year of the Carter administration, had come to see Iran as their chief enemy in the Middle East. Still jaded by the failures of Vietnam, Americans had grown tired of watching the Iranians burn the American flag on television, and they were willing to support anyone, it seemed, who was prepared to take on the Iranians. In turn, the Reagan administration saw Iraq as an antidote to the dreaded Ayatollah in Iran, and the U.S. supported Baghdad's objectives through the war, even to the point of sharing sensitive intelligence information with Saddam. After the Iran-Iraq War, which ended in 1988, the United States continued to support Iraq with agricultural credits. Even when Saddam again attacked the Kurds, the Reagan administration and then George H. W. Bush supported Iraq with over $1 billion per year in agricultural product guarantees under the Commodity Credit Corporation's credit-guarantee program. But the relationship soured. In the last years of the Reagan administration it was revealed that the United States had been secretly selling arms to Iran during the Iran-Iraq War and using the profits to support the anti-Sandinista rebels in Nicaragua. This, to Saddam, was a serious betrayal with grave after-effects, and it badly hurt U.S.-Iraqi relations.[14]

Iraq did not do well in its war with Iran. In fact, the Iraqi army found itself on the defensive much of the time. At two different points, Saddam felt his situation was so desperate that he went to his old enemy, Israel, for assistance against the Iranians. By the time the war finally ended in summer 1988, Saddam had come to believe that he had protected the Arab world from the Shiites in Tehran, and he looked to the oil-rich Arab nations to pay the cost of the war, the debt he thought they owed him and the Iraqi people. Saddam had also suffered a military defeat in the war with Iran (or at least he failed to meet his war objectives). And for someone seeking leadership in the Arab world, such a defeat was humiliating. Consequently, he reacted by flexing his muscles against his old enemy in the north, the Kurds, this time with poison gas. On August 25, 1988, Saddam's warplanes and helicopters dropped chemical weapons on several villages throughout Iraqi Kurdistan, killing thousands. Clearly, the attack was intended to send a message to the Arab world as much as it was intended to destroy the Kurdish resistance. Saddam hoped to salvage some prestige by showing the other Arab nations that Iraq had not been weakened by the war with Iran, that Iraq was still a power to be reckoned with in the Middle East. Saddam would try again to regain some of his lost prestige among the Arabs by moving on Kuwait in August 1990 and precipitating another major war.

By the last years of the 1980s, Saddam had been cast as an international pariah. Along with the usual rumors of routine political killings, disappearances, and torture, Saddam Hussein had the distinction of being the only national leader ever to use agents of mass destruction against his own people. He had also executed a British journalist for spying, had begun construction of a supergun (apparently aimed at Tel Aviv), and, most believed, was developing nuclear weapons. The U.S. Senate responded by voting unanimously to impose strict sanctions on Iraq in the wake of the atrocities against the Kurds, but President Reagan reacted with a fierce lobbying campaign that eventually killed the bill. In summer 1989, in the absence of any other

Middle East policy, the Bush administration decided to continue the Reagan policy toward Iraq, including the one billion dollars per year in agricultural credits. Congress, however, continued to debate sanctions against Iraq right up to Saddam's invasion of Kuwait in August 1990.

Between the end of the Iran-Iraq War in August 1988 and Saddam's invasion of Kuwait exactly two years later, a great deal of animosity had developed between Iraq and the other Arab nations. When his war with Iran ended, Saddam began demanding money from the Arab states—states that he had, so he believed, protected from the virulent Islamic fundamentalism of Iran. He made it clear that he expected the Arab nations to launch an Arab "Marshall Plan" to support Iraq's recovery from the war. When the Arab states refused, Saddam conspired to invade Kuwait—to get what he wanted. At a summit of Arab leaders at the Arab Cooperation Council in February 1990, Saddam demanded $30 billion dollars from the Arab nations to rebuild Iraq. "If they don't give it to me," he threatened, "I will know how to take it."[15] His intentions seemed plain enough.

On April 2, 1990, Iraq's National Day, Saddam announced to the world, with a great deal of pride, that Iraqi scientists had developed advanced chemical weapons. He then added: "By God, we will make the fire eat up half of Israel, if it tries to do anything against Iraq." He concluded his speech by making a peaceful gesture toward Iran, possibly to secure his eastern flank for the war he was planning.

Saddam's anti-Israeli comment, uttered in the same breath with the announcement of Iraqi development of advanced chemical weapons, brought even more scorn from the world. A U.S. State Department spokesman called it "inflammatory, outrageous and irresponsible." Ten days after Saddam's speech, five U.S. senators (Robert Dole, Alan Simpson, Howard Metzenbaum, James McClure, and Frank Murkowski) traveled to Mosel in northern Iraq to meet with Saddam. Their plan was to get assurances from Saddam that he would not attack Israel. They also hoped to soothe Israel's fears by confronting Saddam, and to head off those in Congress who wanted to impose sanctions on Iraq by showing that the Bush administration (which opposed sanctions) was coming face to face with the Iraqi leader.

In the Arab world, however, Saddam's "burn Israel" speech was proof that the Iraqi leader had indeed moved into the position of Arab leader. He was the new Nassar, the new Saladin. In May, the Arab League met in Baghdad to praise Saddam for his stance. But the Baghdad meeting went from the praising of Saddam to Saddam's open criticism of the Arab states. He particularly accused Kuwait and the United Arab Emirates (UAE), but the other Gulf states as well, of violating OPEC (Organization of Petroleum Exporting Countries) agreements to their own advantage, of conspiring to keep oil prices low, which in turn kept Iraq poor. It was a theme Saddam would raise again and again as the situation between Iraq and Kuwait escalated during summer 1990.

In June, Saddam demanded $10 billion in aid from Kuwait to make up the difference in what he believed was Kuwaiti intransigence on a number of issues. In his Revolution Day speech of July 17, Saddam again attacked Kuwait and the UAE for overproducing and driving oil prices down. The low oil prices, he said, amounted to a conspiracy to hurt Iraq, "an imperialist-Zionist plot against the Arab nation." It was a "poisoned dagger" in Iraq's back, he added. He then threatened Kuwait and the UAE with military action if they refused to cut production. He also accused Kuwait of placing military posts inside Iraq's borders and stealing more than its share of oil from the jointly operated Rumaila oil field. He demanded another $2.4 billion for the oil. *The Economist* wrote on July 21 that Saddam's speech sounded like a pretext for an invasion. Some Kuwaiti ministers came to believe that Saddam was about to strike their country. Military leaves were cancelled and a general military alert was called.[16]

On July 24, Saddam moved two armored divisions onto Kuwait's border. Within days that force had been increased to about 30,000 soldiers. By then most of the world believed, however, that Saddam's move was little more than blatant extortion and of little real concern. His army would intimidate the Kuwaitis at the bargaining table, but nothing else. Egyptian Prime Minister Hosni Mubarak traveled to Baghdad to mediate this minor Arab-Arab dispute and reported to the world that he had assurances from Saddam that Iraq would not invade Kuwait. However, George H. W. Bush was not convinced, and he sent six naval vessels to the Persian Gulf, ostensibly to engage in joint maneuvers with the

UAE. The situation was escalating, but no one really knew it—with the obvious exception of Saddam Hussein.

In late July, the United States sent several signals to Saddam that seemed to say that the United States was not interested in the area, not interested in the Arab-Arab dispute, and not interested in the survival of Kuwait. All are reminiscent of Secretary of State Dean Acheson's speech before the Washington Press Club in January 1950, which seemed to signal to North Korea that the United States had no interests on the Korean peninsula worth defending. In the last days of July 1990, the House Foreign Affairs Committee questioned John Kelly, the assistant secretary of state for the Middle East, on the developing situation on the Kuwaiti border. "If Iraq, for example, charged into Kuwait for whatever reason," Chairman Lee Hamilton asked, "what would our position be with regard to the use of U.S. forces?" "That, Mr. Chairman, is a hypothetical or a contingency question," Kelly evaded, "the kind I can't get into." "Does the United States have a defense treaty with Kuwait requiring the use of force in this situation?" Hamilton continued. Kelly replied that the United States had no obligation to protect Kuwait if Iraq invaded.[17] On July 24, State Department spokesperson Margaret Tutwiler made it clear to the world that the United States does "not have any defense treaties with Kuwait, and there are no special defense or security commitments to Kuwait." It has been argued that this was a green light for Saddam to trigger his adventure, but in the same address Tutwiler also said that the United States would come to the aid of its friends in the Gulf.[18]

The next day, in what some believe was the final go-ahead signal for Iraq, Saddam spoke with the U.S. ambassador to Iraq, April Glaspie. The Hussein-Glaspie conversation of July 25, 1990, has come under a great deal of scrutiny, and some in the government and the press have charged that Glaspie gave a clear signal to Saddam that the United States was unconcerned with the minor Arab-Arab dispute and would not stand in the way of Saddam's invasion of Kuwait. In a transcript released by Iraq and reported by ABC News, Saddam said: "I say to you clearly that Iraq's rights . . . we will take one by one. That might not happen now or after a month or after one year, but we will take it all. . . . There is no historic right, or legitimacy, or need, for the UAE and Kuwait to deprive us of our rights. If they are needy, we too are needy." To George H. W. Bush, he added, "If you use pressure, we will deploy pressure and force. We know that you can harm us. . . . But we too can harm you. . . . And when we feel that you want to injure our pride and take away the Iraqis' chance of a high standard of living, then we will cease to care and death will be the choice for us." Glaspie responded: "I know you need funds. We understand that and our opinion is that you should have the opportunity to rebuild your country. But we have no opinion on the Arab-Arab conflicts like your border disagreements with Kuwait. . . . The instruction we had . . . was that we should express no opinion on this issue and that the issue is not associated with America." Glaspie continued by trying to show Saddam how the situation appeared to the United States at that time: "Frankly, we can only see that you have deployed massive troops in the South. Normally that would not be any of our business. . . . [But] when we see the Iraqi point of view . . . then it would be reasonable for me to be concerned." She went on to ask Saddam to explain his intentions. What did he plan to do with the 30,000 troops he had amassed on Kuwait's border? Saddam did not answer, but he continued lecturing Glaspie, complaining that "the others [the other Arab states] should value the Iraqi role in their protection." He continued to assure Glaspie that negotiations were under way to solve the dispute between Iraq and Kuwait. "We hope we will reach some result. . . . We hope that the long-term view . . . will overcome Kuwaiti greed. . . . Assure the Kuwaitis," he said at last, "and give them our word that we are not going to do anything until we meet with them."[19]

After the war, Glaspie argued that she believed she had left the meeting with a clear assurance from Saddam that he would not attack Kuwait. In her cable to Washington the day following the meeting, Glaspie wrote that she believed Saddam would not invade Kuwait. However, Glaspie later told the *New York Times* that "I didn't think—and nobody else did—that the Iraqis were going to take all of Kuwait."[20] This seems to imply that she believed an Iraqi invasion was imminent, but that Saddam's objectives were limited to, possibly, the Rumaila oil field or one of the offshore islands, Bubiyan or Warba. Nevertheless, her statements (along with Tutwiler's the day before and Kelly's remarks before Congress) may well have been the green light that Saddam needed to proceed with his invasion; that the United States would not intervene. The day after he met with Glaspie, Saddam moved another 30,000 soldiers into position along his border with Kuwait. By the end of the month his forces in position stood at 100,000, plus 300 tanks. Ambassador Glaspie left for a summer vacation on July 30.

The next day, Saddam kept his promise to talk to the Kuwaitis. At Jidda, the Saudi Arabian summer capital, representatives from Iraq and Kuwait sat down to mediate their differences, with the Saudis playing the role of mediator. The meetings were to continue into August in Baghdad. It was at Jidda that Saddam (represented by the chairman of his Revolutionary Command Council, Izzat Ibrahim) aired his grievances against Kuwait to the Arab world, and it was at Jidda that Saddam first talked openly of war against Kuwait. Saddam felt he needed higher oil prices to rebuild his nation, still in the throes of a severe economic depression following the war with Iran. At Jidda, Iraq again accused the Gulf States, particularly Kuwait and the UAE, of producing beyond their OPEC quotas and forcing oil prices down on the world market. The agreed-upon OPEC price had been $18 per barrel; but the price had been allowed to drop to as low as $7. Saddam claimed that for every dollar drop in the price per barrel, the Iraqi income from oil dropped by $1 billion per year. He called this overproduction "an act of war." Wars, he added in his message, could be waged by "sending armies across frontiers, by acts of sabotage, by killing people and supporting *coups d'etat,* but war can also be waged by economic means and what is happening is war against Iraq. I must frankly tell you," he continued, "that we have reached a stage where we can no longer take any more pressure."[21]

On August 2, the talks at Jidda broke down when the Iraqi delegation stormed out. The Baghdad follow-up meeting was canceled. At 2:00 A.M the next morning, Iraqi T-72 tanks of the Republican Guard blitzed into Kuwait and seized the nation in less than six hours against almost no resistance.

What had Saddam hoped to gain by invading Kuwait? If it was the respect of the other nations of the Middle East, it was a mistake because he was immediately surrounded by hostile nations. Turkey, Iran, Saudi Arabia, even Syria and Jordan, openly opposed his aggressions against Kuwait, and as the opposition to Saddam's invasion developed and coalesced around the United States, none of his neighboring states would come to his aid. Turkey was a member of NATO and deeply indebted to the United States. Its first act was to stop the flow of Iraqi oil through Turkey. The Syrian Baathist regime of Hafez al-Assad had much in common with the Baathists of Baghdad, but their birth had been as rivals for the leadership position in the Arab world, not as allies. During the Iran-Iraq War, Syria had supported Tehran. There was no love lost between Baghdad and Damascus. As the U.S.-organized coalition against Saddam began to develop, Syria would be one of the coalition's most tenuous members, but a member nonetheless. Assad finally sent troops and Soviet-made tanks into the conflict, more to aid Saudi Arabia than to support any U.S. interests. Egypt, the onetime leader of the Arab world and now the Arab nation with an army second in size in the region only to Iraq, fell in with the other Arab states opposing Saddam's move.

Jordan's King Hussein had always been intimidated by Saddam on his border, and of the Arab states Jordan would tilt toward Iraq more than any other. Caught between Saddam and Israel, Jordan might be the battleground for any conflict between the two, and the prospect of such a war frightened King Hussein. Jordan was also home to thousands of Palestinians, most of whom supported Saddam and his move against Kuwait. When the conflict broke out between the U.S.–backed coalition and Iraq, King Hussein found himself in a very bad position. He chose not to antagonize Saddam and refused to support the war against him, but at the same time, he would not support Iraq.

The Saudis, more than any other nation in the Middle East, had the most to lose by Saddam's invasion of Kuwait. With a huge and hostile force now poised on their northern frontier, the Saudis feared that they might be next on Saddam's list. It would be the Kingdom of Saud that would lead the Arab coalition against Saddam and allow their soil to be used for the mammoth military operation against the Iraqis. With a hostile Iran to the east, Saddam found himself, on August 2, 1990, surrounded by enemies: Arabs, Persians, and Turks all opposed his move. By invading Kuwait, Saddam had gone from the new Saladin to an enemy of the people of the Middle East.

But Saddam had a great deal to gain by invading Kuwait—if he could get away with it. Saddam was as much as $80 billion in debt from his devastating war with Iran; and in 1990 he was unable to get loans from most sources because his track record showed clearly that he did not pay back loans. High oil prices could, however, save him from economic disaster. Saddam's advisors pointed out that by combining the OPEC quotas of Iraq and Kuwait and by forcing prices up to $30 a barrel, Iraq could make as much as $60 billion a year. That would double Saddam's development budget and still pay off his war debts in four years. In addition, Iraq would finally have a deep-water port—to be without such a facility was a distinct disadvantage in the oil-producing Middle East.

Kuwait and the UAE, Saddam believed, had overproduced and forced prices down. With his armies in control of Kuwait, and a large force on the Gulf, Saddam hoped to intimidate Saudi Arabia and the other Gulf States into seeing oil prices his way. Essentially, control of Kuwait meant control of the Gulf, control of OPEC, control of oil production, and ultimately control of oil prices. It would not be too much to say that in such a position Saddam Hussein would control the Middle East, and from there build an enormous power structure. George H. W. Bush, however, contrary to the statements of his ambassador to Iraq, was not about to let that happen.

11

"THE LIBERATION OF KUWAIT HAS BEGUN"

On August 2, Saddam Hussein had gambled by moving to take control of the Persian Gulf through an attack on Kuwait. The prize, if his aggression was allowed to stand, was control of the Persian Gulf and its oil production. It would give him the ability to control oil prices, and it would allow him to solve his monumental economic problems resulting from his war with Iran. It would also make him an Arab leader, the strongman in the Middle East. And it would give him the resources necessary to take on Israel—and Iran again, if need be. His enemies would be punished, and he would be a new world giant.

Signals from Washington had told Saddam that the United States might not intervene on Kuwait's behalf, and even if it did, American actions and attitudes since Vietnam had shown clearly that the U.S. military could not stay engaged for long in another devastating land war in Asia, that the American people would not suffer through another long war of attrition. Time was on Saddam's side. He told Ambassador Glaspie: "Yours is a society which cannot accept 10,000 dead in one battle."[1] Of course, he was correct.

In the months between mid-1989 and early 1990, Saddam had stunned the world by first hanging a British journalist for spying, and then trying to smuggle into Iraq components for a supergun and then triggers to detonate nuclear devices. Each incident was carried widely in the international press, and together with stories on his use of chemical weapons against the Kurds, Saddam was depicted as the new personification of evil. The result was that pressure to impose sanctions on Iraq reached a new height in Congress. However, Bush, like Reagan before him, opposed sanctions against Iraq, mainly because a number of large businesses had interests there, and Bush felt compelled to protect the profits of those businesses. In 1990, 486 licenses had been granted to Iraq for shipments of $730 million worth of sensitive technology. Between 1983 and 1989, roughly the dates of the Iran-Iraq War, annual trade between the United States and Iraq had grown from $571 million to $3.6 billion, and the United States had purchased nearly $5.5 billion in Iraqi oil over that same period.[2] However, the Bush administration insisted that the reason for its opposition to sanctions was more that it was necessary to influence Saddam, the strongman in the region with a history of cooperation with the United States, rather than antagonize him and force him outside the U.S. sphere of influence. To carry out this foreign policy, however, the Bush administration had to overlook outrageous human rights violations and other abuses and virtually deal with the devil.

To make that deal, Bush sent Robert Dole and his group to Mosel, Iraq, on April 12. The plan, as discussed in the last chapter, was to show those in Congress supporting sanctions against Iraq that Bush meant business in dealing with this hooligan who would use chemical weapons and threaten Israel. The meeting between Dole's group (including Senators Alan Simpson, Howard Metzenbaum, James McClure, Frank Murkowski, and Ambassador April Glaspie) and Saddam may have sent the correct signals back to Congress, but it was far from threatening to Saddam. At the meeting, Saddam complained that the Western press seemed to be coordinating its efforts in opposition to Iraq. Dole responded that a "Voice of America" announcer who had denounced Iraq had been fired. Simpson added that Saddam's problems were not with the U.S. government but with the U.S. press. "It is a haughty and pampered press," Simpson said. "They all consider themselves political geniuses. . . . [T]hey are very cynical. . . . They live off one another. Everyone takes from another. When there is a major news item on the front page of the *New York Times,* another journalist takes it and publishes it." Dole assured Saddam that President Bush would oppose sanctions, and possibly even veto any bill imposing sanctions on Iraq. Glaspie agreed: "I am certain that this is the policy of the United States."[3] It was hardly a confrontation. It was, in fact, an assurance that George H. W. Bush hoped to work with Saddam Hussein and Iraq in the future.

As soon as Dole and his group returned from Iraq, the administration sent John Kelly, the State Department's undersecretary for Middle Eastern Affairs, into action on Capitol Hill to fight congressional moves to impose economic sanctions on Iraq. According to Kelly, Saddam's actions and statements may have "raised new questions about Iraqi intentions in the region," but sanctions would impair the administration's ability to exert "a restraining influence" on Saddam.[4] Kelly's pro-Iraqi lobbying effort on part of the administration was successful, and it continued until the week before Saddam's invasion of Kuwait.

So it was that as Saddam moved toward war in the Middle East, the Bush administration was working toward a policy of detente with Iraq, assuring Saddam all along that his problems with America and the West were not with the Bush administration, but with a "haughty and pampered press," and that the president would work to quell any anti-Iraqi sentiment in Congress. It was a pact that certainly sent Saddam another wrong signal: that the Bush administration was working in Iraq's favor. Add to this the statements by Margaret Tutwiler and John Kelly, and the statements made by Ambassador Glaspie to Saddam several days before the invasion that the United States had no interest in the Iraq-Kuwait border dispute, and it might be easy to see that Washington might not contest Saddam's invasion of Kuwait.

Saddam's troop movements (together with all his bluster against Kuwait, the UAE, and Israel) did not turn on any warning lights in Washington. On July 21, the CIA reported to General Colin Powell, chairman of the Joint Chiefs of Staff, that spy satellite reconnaissance had picked up significant Iraqi troop movements and increased logistics trains to the south. That, however, was probably only an indication that Saddam was rattling his saber to intimidate Kuwait into cutting oil production and force up the price of oil. At worst, it seemed, Saddam might take the Rumaila oil field. The United States responded to the troop movements by sending six combat vessels into the Gulf, ostensibly to join in maneuvers with the UAE. The U.S. press barely covered the developments. On the last day in July, three days before Saddam's attack on Kuwait, a Defense Intelligence Agency analyst sent a top secret electronic mail message to Powell: "Saddam Hussein," the analyst wrote, "has moved a force disproportionate to the task at hand, if it is to bluff. Then there is only one answer: he intends to use it."[5] Powell did not act on the message because it was not based on any new information. However, two days later a CIA assessment of the situation came up with many of the same conclusions: that an invasion was at least "probable." "They're ready," the assessment concluded, "they'll go."[6] On that same day, August 1, General Norman Schwarzkopf was brought in to brief the Joint Chiefs and Secretary of Defense Richard Cheney. Saddam had placed 100,000 troops and 300 tanks on the Kuwaiti border, and although all agreed that the Iraqi troop deployment might be intended only to intimidate the Kuwaitis, they also agreed that Saddam had placed himself in a position to invade Kuwait if it was his plan. Their decision was to notify the president. From there the action died. Possibly the White House was making decisions based on reports from Glaspie and Mubarak, both of whom had discussed the situation with Saddam only days before and had been promised that he would not invade Kuwait; or possibly the administration believed that if Saddam moved it would only be against the Rumaila oil field and the Gulf islands of Warba and Bubiyan, a situation that would most likely be mediated among Arabs or in the United Nations. Whatever the reasons, the White House did not move on the information it received from Powell and Cheney.

The next day, on August 2, Saddam made good on all his threats and promises that no one seemed to hear and invaded Kuwait. His troops surrounded Kuwait City, scattered the hapless Kuwaiti army, and then engulfed the capital. The Republican Guard was sent in first to destroy any resistance put up by the Kuwaiti army. They were followed by the People's Army, mostly peasants, conscripts, and cannon fodder— Saddam's human waves used so successfully against Iran. Behind them came the Muk Habarat, Saddam's secret police. They would supervise Kuwait (under Iraqi rule) through murder, torture, and general terror.

The one-thousand-member Sabah ruling family of Kuwait barely escaped the onslaught. As close to the situation as they were (being the recipient of Saddam's threats for over a year and witnessing the angry Iraqi walkout at the meeting in Jidda only forty-eight hours before) they still did not believe that Saddam would invade. The Kuwaiti cabinet had agreed to cancel military leaves and call an alert, but few believed that Saddam would move to capture all of Kuwait. The emir and a number of other figures escaped in a private helicopter only minutes before Iraqi rockets hit the Dasman Palace. Other members of the Sabah family escaped across the desert to Saudi Arabia in a stream of Mercedes limousines.

The Kuwaiti air force put up a good fight, flying two successful missions against the Iraqi ground forces before their two airfields were overrun. The pilots escaped to Saudi Arabia with their planes; they would fight again. The Kuwaiti army disintegrated quickly, but an effective resistance movement did develop in Kuwait City that continued to harass the Iraqi army through the occupation period.

Iraq announced immediately that the new government of Kuwait would be headed by a Kuwaiti national, Colonel Ala Hussein Ali. But on August 8, less than a week after the invasion, Saddam proclaimed the annexation of Kuwait. On August 28 Kuwait was designated as Iraq's nineteenth province. The new governor was to be Ali Hassan al-Majid, Saddam's cousin and the man responsible for "law and order" in the Kurdish provinces in 1987 and 1988 when the Kurdish villages were gassed. Saddam immediately terrified the world by detaining several hundred Western nationals, calling them "guests" of the Iraqi government, and he proceeded to place them in militarily strategic sites around Baghdad. Apparently, to show he meant these people no harm, Saddam appeared on Iraqi television with several of his "guests," but the incident was a testimony to Saddam's insensitivity and the hostages' obvious terror at being held by the Iraqis. The entire affair played badly for Saddam in the international press, and on December 6, possibly in hopes of winning back some respect, he announced that all detained Western nationals would be released, and that potentially dangerous situation came to an end.

George H. W. Bush first received word of the invasion from his National Security Advisor, Brent Scowcroft, at about 8 p.m. on August 2. That was followed by a series of crisis meetings at the White House. The next morning, Bush signed executive orders freezing all Iraqi and Kuwaiti assets in the United States. A few hours later he met with reporters and said that he would not send troops to the Middle East, that the situation there could be handled through other means. Later that day, however, Bush joined Margaret Thatcher in Aspen, Colorado, for a previously scheduled meeting. On Air Force One on his way west, Bush spoke by telephone with King Fahd of Saudi Arabia and Hosni Mubarak of Egypt. Both were hoping for an Arab solution to the crisis, and neither asked for U.S. troops. In Aspen, Thatcher spoke with Bush for over two hours. She apparently convinced him that Saddam had to be stopped, and that a deployment of U.S. troops was the only logical response to the aggressions. The prevailing wisdom by then was that Saudi Arabia might be Saddam's next target—that aggression unchallenged would lead to further aggression. When the president returned to Washington he was prepared to take action; his attitude toward the situation had changed. "It was not that some magical, restorative medicine was applied that day to the president's rubber spine," recalled a senior British aide who was present at the Bush-Thatcher discussions in Aspen. "But the Rubicon between what happened and a much weaker response was crossed that afternoon."[7]

In the next three days, President Bush held a series of emergency meetings with his chief advisors at Camp David and at the White House. Present at most of these meetings was a group of advisors that Bush would keep near his side for most of the next seven months; they included Powell and Cheney, Secretary of State James Baker, National Security Advisor Brent Scowcroft, and White House Chief of Staff John Sununu. The opinions of others were occasionally sought by this tightly knit circle of decision makers, such as Scowcroft' s deputy Robert Gates; Lucius Battle, the former president of the Middle East Institute; Fouad Ajami, the well-respected professor of Middle Eastern foreign policy at Johns Hopkins University; and Vice President Dan Quayle. But for the most part this inner circle of advisors was insulated, making the decisions and establishing the policy.

Among this group, Dick Cheney emerged as an urbane, intelligent, and impressive figure, adept at briefing the press and fending off inappropriate questions at news conferences. Vice President under George W. Bush, and (by most accounts) the chief architect of the Persian Gulf

War against Saddam's forces in 2002, Cheney became the leader of Gulf War operations in Washington in 1991. Cheney was a hawk from the beginning, lobbying the president hard for a flexing of American muscle. When Bush decided that the United States must go on the offensive against Saddam and remove him by force from Kuwait, the military was reluctant. The horrible sounds of the Vietnam War still rang in their ears, and by 1990 the belief that the United States should never again get involved in a ground war in Asia had nearly become established military policy. Cheney, however, had taken a strong hand on the reins of control at the Pentagon, and he was able to convince the reluctant generals that an offensive operation against Iraq was both necessary and possible.

Scowcroft, a former Air Force general, came across in the press as a quiet, behind-the-scenes figure, but in reality he was probably George Bush's closest advisor, the coordinator of the day-to-day policies. Of those on the inside, Scowcroft was the most hawkish, clearly believing war to be an instrument of foreign policy. While the Pentagon and the White House were putting together their plans for defensive action in the Middle East, Scowcroft (supported by Cheney) pushed hard for an offensive strategy as an alternative. Bush and Scowcroft seemed to think alike; it was Scowcroft more than anyone who finally pushed Bush over to the offensive strategy when that decision finally came.

More than any other, it was Colin Powell who was the reluctant warrior, the soldier who believed that Saddam Hussein could be dealt with through means other than war.[8] Powell had been a protégé of Casper Weinberger and Frank Carlucci in the 1980s, and had come to believe, as had most military men at the time, that America's experience in Vietnam was a tough lesson for the future, and that U.S. military action should only be launched under certain circumstances. Powell had served two tours in Vietnam, where he earned a Purple Heart, a Bronze Star, and the Soldier's Medal for Valor. To him, war was young men being killed and maimed in battle; it was a situation to be avoided. But if war is necessary, began Powell's own Clausewitzian dictum, "strike suddenly, decisively and in sufficient force to resolve the matter. Do it quickly, and do it with a minimum loss of life."[9] Such cautious pronouncements had become basic to the Pentagon's way of thinking as a result of the lessons learned in Vietnam. As the war in the Gulf developed, it became clear that other military figures shared Powell's apprehensions. Past Joint Chiefs Chairmen Admiral William Crowe and General David Jones, both Powell's predecessors in the office, became the most visible spokesmen for the continuation of sanctions in the months before the war began. So Powell's reservations can hardly be considered unusual for a military man in the post-Vietnam era. Powell was willing to accept war as an instrument of foreign policy, as were Scowcroft and others, but he wanted it used only as a last resort, after all other alternatives had been explored thoroughly. He also believed that overwhelming support from Congress was a political necessity before the United States should consider large troop deployments and offensive actions.

As options in the Gulf were being considered, Powell urged Bush: "There is a case here for the containment or strangulation policy. This is an option that has merit. It may take a year, it may take two years, but it will work someday." But Bush responded from another side of the government: "I don't think there's time politically for that strategy."[10] It was here that the political and the military sides of the Vietnam Syndrome came into conflict for the first time. Powell feared the military repercussions of another land war in Asia, while Bush obviously feared the political backlash that a long, drawn-out, and slowly escalating American involvement might bring on. In the end, however, when the decision was finally made to go on the offensive, Colin Powell was very much on the Bush team and a part of the inner circle. When war became the stated objective, Colin Powell was no reluctant warrior.

Secretary of State James Baker played the cool diplomat in the Gulf War. He traveled to Baghdad to tell the Iraqi foreign minister, Tariq Aziz, what was about to be unleashed on his nation if Saddam did not atone, and to the world capitals to piece together the fragile military coalition against Iraq. But Baker, probably more than anyone in Bush's inner circle of advisors, believed that the conflict over Kuwait could be settled at the conference table instead of on the battlefield. Clearly, Baker wanted more maneuvering room to find a diplomatic settlement than the White House was willing to give. And in January, as the UN deadline approached and Baker's peace missions failed, the secretary was pushed into the background among the president's inner circle of advisors.

The silent voice of the inner circle was Chief of Staff John Sununu. Conservative, aggressive, and clearly having the president's ear on most important matters, it can only be assumed that Sununu's voice was heard in the policy-making sessions that determined the nature and direction of the war. Postwar reports stated that Sununu spent most of his time weighing the political consequences of a war in the Gulf.

This group of five Washington insiders ran the war from the Oval Office, with little input from Congress, Middle East experts, academics, cabinet members, or even the Joint Chiefs. They insulated themselves, and they made policy alone. Possibly, Bush believed that too many policy makers, too much input from others, would spoil the pot. He may have recalled Lyndon Johnson's policy-making procedures: calling on literally dozens of advisors from all branches of the administration and private life. Smothered with opinions, Johnson (Bush may have felt), made the wrong decisions in Vietnam. At the same time there were no dissenters in the Bush inner circle. Clearly, Bush's plan of action was a pattern for disaster. Had the war turned into another quagmire or a stalemate, finger pointers certainly would have directed their attention to the isolated nature of the White House insiders.

Back in the Middle East, the Saudi royal family was arguing over the wisdom of asking for U.S. military support. Prince Bandar bin Sultan, the Saudi ambassador to the United States, told Cheney in Washington two days after the invasion that he doubted that the United States had the mettle to drive Saddam out of Kuwait by force. He reminded the Defense Secretary of Jimmy Carter's limp response to Saudi Arabia's defensive needs in a Middle East flare-up in the late 1970s: a dozen unarmed F-15 fighters, and of Reagan's pullout in Lebanon in February 1984 when the going got tough there. Saudi Arabia would not request U.S. troops, Bandar said, if Washington only planned to send a token force. Cheney promised that he would push the president for at least two and one-third U.S. divisions, an air wing, and a carrier task force. Bandar's attitude changed. On August 5, Cheney left for Saudi Arabia to get permission to deploy U.S. troops on Saudi soil. But King Fahd remained shaky. Bush told Fahd in a telephone conversation on August 5 that the United States was firmly committed to defending Saudi Arabia and that the United States did not want permanent military bases in the Middle East. The

U.S. forces, he said, would be completely withdrawn from Saudi soil when the job was done. By then, most policy makers in Washington had come to believe that Saddam was gearing up to move into the eastern oil fields of Saudi Arabia. The Saudis, of course, had no ability to stop him. The royal family remained reluctant, but they finally decided to welcome American troops. Their only demand was that if there was a fight, as Fahd told Cheney, that Saddam would "not get up again."[11]

On Sunday, August 5, the situation in the Gulf escalated a bit more. After returning from Camp David (and having just watched King Hussein of Jordan denounce U.S. intentions on the television news program *60 Minutes*) Bush emerged from his helicopter in an angry mood that some recall was not quite characteristic of the president. "This will not stand," he growled at reporters. "This will not stand—this aggression against Kuwait." It was a statement that surprised many, even those in the inner-circle. Clearly the president had moved beyond his most important advisors, none of whom had, as yet, seen a need for an offensive strategy. Colin Powell was stunned. He was prepared to use all the power necessary to stop Saddam from invading Saudi Arabia, but the president's words had the sound of offensive action, of removing Saddam from Kuwait by force. He was "popping off," Powell told Bob Woodward: "It was almost as if the president had six-shooters in both hands and he was blazing away."[12]

On August 8, Bush spoke to the American people from the Oval Office. He called the invasion an "outrageous and brutal act of aggression." He demanded an immediate withdrawal of Iraqi troops from Kuwait and the restoration of the legitimate government. He talked of a need for security in the Gulf region. He told the American people of the embargo, sanctions, and frozen Iraqi assets. He added that the 100,000-man Iraqi army, "the fourth-largest military in the world," was threatening Saudi Arabia. "To assume that Iraq will not attack again would be unwise and unrealistic." He then said that the Saudis had requested aid and that he was sending it, a force to "enhance the overall capability of Saudi armed forces to defend the kingdom. America," he concluded, "does not seek conflict." After his speech, a reporter asked Bush about the possibility of using the troops to force Saddam out of Kuwait. "It is not the mission to drive the Iraqis out of Kuwait," Bush answered. "We have economic sanctions that I hope will be effective to that end."[13] Bush and the nation, it seemed at this point, would take the defensive road. The President would move to contain further Iraqi aggressions by helping the Saudis defend themselves, and use sanctions to strangle Saddam economically and force him out of Kuwait. But other forces were beginning to enter the equation.

Bush was quickly coming to realize that a mere defensive stand would not be enough. Saddam was a threat to the entire Middle East, and unless the United States did something to reduce or remove that threat, Iraq would continue to be a destabilizing factor in the region. This quickly became more important than any other factor. It was always clear that the United States would not allow Saddam to remain in Kuwait. An aggressive military state standing astride the Persian Gulf oil reserves was something the United States and the West could not allow. So, the objective of removing Saddam was in place from the moment the first Iraqi soldier set foot in Kuwait. But now Bush and his advisors began to see the real danger of Saddam Hussein, and Washington's goals and objectives began to turn toward neutralizing Iraq, removing the threat, removing his weaponry and his power to make war. Simply to defend Saudi Arabia with U.S. troops and then to force Saddam out of Kuwait through economic sanctions would do little more than reproduce the situation before August 2: a strong Saddam, growing stronger, and threatening the region with chemical and possibly even nuclear weapons. That was not an acceptable situation, and thus sanctions became an unacceptable solution.

Of those in the inner-circle, it was Scowcroft who argued most often that a military answer was the only way to rid the world of the forces of Saddam Hussein, and on *Meet the Press*, a week before Saddam's invasion of Kuwait, Scowcroft made that point clear. Cheney also believed that it was necessary to present the president with a military option, and he pushed Powell hard to produce one. But Bush himself probably needed no pushing. Very early, the president became convinced that sanctions would not work, based on the conclusion that sanctions could only remove Iraq from Kuwait; sanctions did not have the power to destroy the Iraqi war machine. On August 19, Henry Kissinger spouted what must have been by then the prevailing wisdom inside the inner circle at the White House: even if the sanctions work and Saddam leaves Kuwait, Kissinger told the *Washington Post,* it would "provide only a breathing space if Saddam Hussein remains in office and Iraq continues to build up its nuclear and chemical weapons potential."[14] Other world leaders began to see that a peaceful solution to the crisis (one that would leave Saddam in power and his arsenal intact) was no solution at all. Hosni Mubarak of Egypt abandoned all hopes of an all-Arab solution to the problem and began pushing Bush for an offensive military response to the invasion that would ultimately neutralize Saddam. Israel argued long and hard that a neutralized Iraq would bring stability to the region.

Consequently, the inner circle began moving the wheels of the military option very quickly. Plans for a ground force invasion of Kuwait were being demanded by the White House as early as mid-August. General Norman Schwarzkopf, commander in charge of what was now being called Operation Desert Shield, presented his first offensive battle plan in October. Schwarzkopf had begun his career as a tank commander, and his plan reflected a tank commander's strategy. His proposal was little more than an elaborate lunge into Iraqi defensive positions—positions that were quickly becoming stronger. Army Chief of Staff Carl Vuono, along with Cheney and Powell, suggested something a bit more luminous, like an end run to the north following a feint from the south. Schwarzkopf also insisted that the process of placing enough force in the Middle East to push Saddam out of Kuwait would take most of a year. Such a delay was unacceptable, and the White House insisted on a quicker deployment. Under duress, Schwarzkopf agreed he could make use of an all-purpose deployment plan maintained by the Pentagon for emergency situations anywhere in the world (known as Central Command Operations Plan 90–1002) and have the force in place in seventeen short weeks. In the end, Schwarzkopf would be the man to do the job in Kuwait, but in late summer 1990 it did not appear that way. By late August, all other options and objectives were being rejected quickly, and the inner circle had begun to conclude that there would be only one way to defuse the Iraqi war machine. By the middle of January, Schwarzkopf would be ready to fight.

However, while the U.S. military continued its buildup in Saudi Arabia, the sanctions against Iraq were allowed to work. In mid-October,

Baker told a Senate panel that "sanctions are beginning to have an impact. We believe that the sanctions on imports have been particularly successful. There is no oil getting out."[15] The sanctions had nearly stopped both Iraq's imports and exports, bringing about a drop in the nation's GNP by as much as 50 percent. The CIA reported that within nine months the Iraqi air force would be crippled and their ground forces would not be able to mount a serious campaign. There were strong voices in Washington for the sanctions, including the two former chairmen of the Joint Chiefs, Admiral Crowe and General Jones.

But by then the inner circle had concluded that the Iraqi military had to be destroyed; there were pressures from the leaders in the Middle East to remove Saddam from their midst; the U.S. troops, now on their way to Saudi Arabia, would have to be rotated in six months; the Iraqi army was in the process of raping Kuwait, killing, looting, and removing to Baghdad anything of value. Saddam was beginning to move troops toward the Saudi Arabian border with what seemed to be a clear intent on either invasion or intimidation; and there was a national election approaching. George H. W. Bush-the-candidate was not about to campaign for a second term with 200,000 American men and women rotting in the deserts of Saudi Arabia. In addition, thoughts of Vietnam lurked. There was no time to languish and escalate slowly. For the inner circle, time was the enemy, and the sanctions alternative gave nothing to George Bush except more time.

At some point between August 2 (when Saddam invaded Kuwait) and November 8 (when Bush announced his plan for offensive action), the president and his advisors made the decision to remove Saddam from Kuwait and destroy his war-making powers. This decision evolved over time and seems to have solidified sometime in early October. By then the argument for containment and sanctions had been pushed aside by the president. On October 30, the inner circle met to consider a second phase of the buildup suggested by Schwarzkopf that included an additional 100,000 troops. The next day, Bush approved Schwarzkopf's "enhanced option," as it was being called. It moved the United States from defense to offense. On November 8, two days after the midterm elections, the president announced his plan to the American people. He would increase the size of the force in the Middle East "to insure that the coalition has an adequate offensive military option should that be necessary to achieve our common goals."[16] The increase in size was to double the existing force from about 100,000 to about 200,000. For the American people, the mode changed on November 8, but for the inner circle this was merely an announcement of their long-term planning.

On November 29, the United Nations, in its twelfth resolution condemning Iraq's invasion of Kuwait, gave its full support to the Bush administration's initiative. The Security Council set a January 15, 1991, deadline for Iraq to withdraw, and authorized the member states "to use all necessary means to . . . restore international peace and security in the area."[17] Add to that an almost international outcry condemning Saddam and in support of U.S. actions and George H. W. Bush entered the new year with a mandate that seemed to include everyone except the United States Congress, the representatives of the American people. Getting that mandate would be a sensitive maneuver that would drag out the skeletons of Vietnam once more.

On November 30, Bush announced that he would send Baker to Baghdad and invite the Iraqi foreign minister, Tariq Aziz, to Washington in an attempt to settle the dispute before the deadline. He was "going the extra mile for a peaceful settlement," he said. This brought a glimmer of hope to a quickly deteriorating situation, and much of the world applauded Bush's initiative for peace. However, by this time the inner circle had focused on what they considered the only remaining alternative. Only Baker and Powell continued to hope for some sort of diplomatic settlement, and the November 30 peace initiative may have been to appease Baker—to give him the chance he wanted to use diplomacy to head off a war.

The peace initiative bogged down immediately when the two sides began to argue over a date for the meeting. Bush had offered, almost casually, any time before the UN deadline of January 15. When Saddam chose January 12, Bush said the date was too close to the deadline. After much bantering, Baker and Aziz met in Geneva on January 9. Unfortunately for the prospects of a peaceful settlement, neither man was given enough rein to settle the issue. "Aziz and Baker both went to Geneva determined not to give an inch," *Newsweek* reported. "They both succeeded."[18] Bush had little regard for Aziz, and he believed that Aziz, in fact, might not tell Saddam what Baker had to say. To make sure there were no misunderstandings, Bush wrote Saddam a letter and instructed Baker to present it to Aziz personally. It was little more than a strongly worded ultimatum, and Aziz elected not to present it to Saddam, citing the letter's irreverent tone. "When a head of state writes to another head of state a letter," Aziz said in his statement following the January 9 meeting, "and if he really intends to make peace with that head of state or reach genuine understanding, he should use a polite language."[19] The rebuff simply placed more ammunition in Bush's pocket. The president had, as he said, gone the extra mile for peace, and the other side had refused to listen. Following the meeting, Aziz invited Baker to Baghdad to resume the talks. Baker, following orders from the president, declined. In a television interview the next weekend, Secretary Baker expressed his disappointment over the president's decision to call off the follow-up summit in Baghdad. Baker clearly wanted a diplomatic settlement to the issue, and his push in the administration for that end placed him on the outside of the inner circle as the deadline approached. Baker remained the president's closest friend, but whatever influence he had with Bush on this issue seemed to pass over to Cheney and Scowcroft.

Following the Geneva meeting, Aziz dropped a hint of what was to come. He said that if war came between Iraq and the Allies, Iraq would attack Israel. Such a situation would not only widen the limited war, but it might well destroy the fragile Arab coalition then in place against Saddam. It was clearly part of Saddam's overall plan: if Israel could be forced to join the war against Iraq, Saddam believed, the Arab coalition would be forced to switch sides rather than fight on the side of Israel against another Arab nation. Israel immediately went on alert and began preparing for the worst. Assistant Secretary of State Lawrence Eagleburger was dispatched to Tel Aviv to assure the Israelis that the United States would protect Israel from attack. It was the touchiest diplomatic situation of the war. Israel would have to restrain itself and stay out of the conflict.

The new Iraqi position at the negotiations in Geneva became known as "linkage," the idea that any settlement involving Kuwait would necessarily be linked to the Palestinian question in Israel. It would be an exchange: the Iraqis would leave Kuwait and the Israelis would leave the

Palestinian strongholds of the West Bank and the Gaza Strip. The White House considered linkage a last-ditch distraction by Baghdad, and Bush remained adamant that he would not consider linking the two issues, stating simply that they were not connected and that Saddam did not invade Kuwait in the first place to aid the plight of the Palestinians in Israel.

Bush later called the Baker-Aziz meeting in Geneva "a total stiff-arm . . . a total rebuff."[20] But Scowcroft informed Saudi Prince Bandar that the meeting was, in fact, "all exercise," that the war plans were going forward, and that Bush simply wanted to show the world that he was a man of peace and that the choice for war was now Saddam's.[21] In his speech following the Baker-Aziz summit, Bush told America that "Secretary Baker made it clear that he discerned no evidence whatsoever that Iraq was willing to comply with the international community's demand to withdraw from Kuwait and comply with the United Nations resolutions. . . . Saddam Hussein continues to reject a diplomatic solution." But now," Bush concluded, "as before . . . the choice of peace or war is really Saddam Hussein's to make."[22]

The president and Congress have been at odds over presidential war-making powers since the end of World War II. The Constitution states explicitly that Congress controls the nation's power to make war. But the limited wars of the post–World War II era have not seen a war declaration, and much of the power has slipped (in many ways by default) into the hands of the executive branch. In Korea, Truman simply bypassed Congress by declaring the conflict a police action and working within the framework of the United Nations. At the time Congress protested little, and few realized the precedents that were being set there. In Vietnam, gradual escalation without congressional approval had dragged the nation so deeply into the conflict by 1964 that congressional approval for further escalations seemed like a rubber stamp of Johnson's policies. Nevertheless, the Tonkin Gulf Resolution, and the misleading character of the incidents that brought it on, made many congressmen leery of supporting George H. W. Bush's hawkish initiatives in the Gulf crisis. As the situation unfolded in the Persian Gulf in the last months of 1990, many congressmen began to demand the constitutional right of Congress to make war. Both Capitol Hill and the White House knew that the vote would be close. Clearly, a vote from Congress against his policies in the Gulf would virtually bring an end to the entire operation, or worse, send the nation to war against the wishes of Congress. And even a close vote might damage the president's leverage with Saddam.

Many congressmen, particularly on the Democratic side of the aisle, faced a difficult dilemma in the Gulf crisis. Congressmen who had voted for the Tonkin Gulf Resolution in 1964 had found themselves with a great deal to explain to their constituents through the next four years as the war soured and casualties mounted. Now, in 1991, the specter of having to share responsibility for another long, nasty war of attrition was a fearsome thought. At the same time, being perceived as undermining the president's diplomatic efforts just prior to a popular war was no less fearsome. Standing on the wrong side of history in this case could end a political career quickly.

Democrats, who found themselves uncertain about the impending events, discovered a place to hide early. Senator Sam Nunn, the chairman of the Senate Armed Services Committee, was a prominent Democrat and a strong supporter of the military. But as the events unfolded in late 1990, Nunn made it clear that he believed sanctions, and not war, would be the answer to the escalating Gulf crisis. Nunn went on *Face the Nation* and paraphrased George Marshall's famous statement about U.S. involvement in Korea. It was, Nunn said, the wrong strategy in the wrong place at the wrong time. To support the military, as Nunn did, but not the war became a conviction of those who rallied around Nunn. Nunn ordered public hearings on the buildup in the Gulf that kindled a public debate on the crisis. Certainly, the final vote in the Senate was much closer than it would have been had Nunn fallen in behind the president's initiatives.

In October and November, the White House (through the efforts of Saudi Prince Bandar) set up the Committee for Peace and Security in the Gulf, an organization to lobby Congress in favor of the president's initiatives in the crisis. Despite its White House leadership, the organization picked up support from several prominent Democrats, giving it the appealing air of bipartisanship. Among those Democrats who joined was Representative Stephen Solarz of New York. Solarz was a senior Democrat on the House Foreign Affairs Committee and a co-sponsor of the use-of-force resolution in the House. He had also opposed the war in Vietnam. His arguments against sanctions on the floor of the House, and then published in the *New Republic* during the debates in Congress, swayed many Democrats to the president's side.[23]

Finally, after the New Year, Congress decided that a close vote was a better accounting of itself than no vote at all. Urged on by the president, who had concluded that he had the votes he needed to win approval for his actions against Iraq, Capitol Hill sat down to debate the issue. Congressmen had clearly hoped that the situation would resolve itself through a diplomatic peace settlement and they would not be forced to commit themselves to this potentially career-destroying issue. But the delay had destroyed any real hope that Congress could stop the war if it were so determined. A defeat in Congress for the president's initiatives in the Gulf within days of the UN deadline would have had devastating consequences not only for U.S. policy in the Gulf, but also for the international coalition that Bush and Baker had been building against Saddam. Although many in Congress opposed the idea of going to war, no one wanted to contemplate the constitutional issue of a president going to war against the expressed wishes of Congress.

The bill giving Bush the power to go to war against Iraq was, as *Newsweek* called it, a de facto declaration of war.[24] It passed the House easily, by sixty-seven votes, but it stumbled in the Senate, where Sam Nunn led powerful Democrats in favor of continued sanctions. Nunn had made it clear, in a statement aimed at Saddam, that the divisiveness in Congress was not a sign of U.S. weakness in the face of war, and that Saddam could not depend on a Vietnam-like division in Congress to aid his initiatives: "These are the voices of democracy. Don't misread this debate. If war occurs, the constitutional and policy debates will be suspended, and Congress will provide the American troops whatever they need to prevail. There will be no cutoff of funds for our troops while they engage your forces on the field of battle."[25] On the day of the debate, Baker quietly announced that if Saddam did not withdraw, the United States would go to war shortly after the UN deadline date of January 15.

Eleventh-hour attempts to find a peaceful settlement came from several directions: from UN Secretary General Perez de Cuellar, France, Libya, Yemen, and Algeria. But all failed. On the afternoon of January

15 the world seemed to sit and wait. Many expected Saddam to attempt to muddy the diplomatic waters by slowly withdrawing his troops as the deadline approached. But he did not. And on January 16, a massive Allied air war against Iraq was launched. Bush and his inner circle clearly acted sooner than later after the deadline to avoid being preempted by an eleventh-hour withdrawal or a last-grasp at a diplomatic stall by Iraq. In a paraphrase from Eisenhower's D-Day statement of June 1944, Bush's spokesman, Marlin Fitzwater, told an American television audience at 7:00 p.m. Wednesday Washington time (3:00 a.m. Thursday in Baghdad): "The liberation of Kuwait has begun." In a televised address from the Oval Office, Bush told America that after months of fruitless diplomatic overtures, the United States and its allies "have no choice but to force Saddam from Kuwait. . . . We will not fail." He added that it was not his goal to conquer Iraq, only to liberate Kuwait. He also stated for the first time his goals of destroying Saddam's nuclear and chemical weapons potential. And of course, there were the ghosts of Vietnam: "Our troops will have the best possible support in the entire world," he added, "and they will not be asked to fight with one hand tied behind their back."[26]

12

DESERT STORM: THE AIR WAR

Desert Storm, the new code name—now changed from Desert Shield—was appropriate considering the force of the U.S. air attack. This amazing techno-war was seen live by millions of Americans on their televisions. Vietnam, it is always said, was the first war fought on American television, in American living rooms. But the Gulf War was the first live war, bringing amazing footage of weapons doing their jobs with a precision that few Americans could conceive. Americans knew of these weapons from the congressional debates in which they were often maligned as inaccurate, dangerous, and outrageously expensive toys. But in the Gulf they were almost hauntingly flawless in achieving their missions. The Navy, for instance, launched 150 Tomahawk Cruise missiles on the first day of the attack, the first Tomahawks ever used in battle; over 85 percent, the navy reported, hit their targets. U.S. bombs and air-launched missiles, guided by laser beams, infrared images, and television pictures, slammed into target after target. The Air Force F-117A, the secretive Stealth fighter-bomber, did its job with pinpoint accuracy. As one flier reported to *Newsweek,* "You pick precisely which target you want . . . the men's room or the ladies' room."[1] Americans watched with amazement at a video from an F-117A Stealth fighter-bomber as the pilot honed in on what the viewer was told was a communications complex in Baghdad, and almost gently placed a 2,000-pound spider bomb in a vent stack of the building. War, it seemed to Americans, had become a video game. British and Italian Tornadoes, Apache helicopters, F-4G Wild

Weasels, F-14 Tomcats, and F-15 Eagles: their successes became familiar to American television viewers—and certainly to Iraqi anti-aircraft gun operators who tried, mostly in vain, to shoot them down. While all this technological wizardry worked its deadly magic, the ponderous B-52s pulverized Republican Guard positions in southern Iraq with a carpet-bombing campaign that was boring but devastating.

This massive aerial armada of nearly 2,000 Allied planes flew 1,800 sorties each day against Iraqi forces from six U.S. aircraft carriers and nearly thirty bases in Saudi Arabia, Egypt, Turkey, and Cyprus. This was essentially the same air force that NATO had been building since the early 1950s to challenge the Warsaw Pact forces in Central Europe. The key to the success of that force was to maintain a technological superiority over the Soviet Union. The results for the desert war of 1991 were a spectacular advantage for the Americans and their allies. When the ground war was finally launched in the last week in February, Allied superiority would become even more apparent as U.S.-NATO technology was overwhelming in that phase of the war as well.

Presidents Truman and Johnson went to war in 1950 and in 1964 with the support of the American people. But in January 1991 George H. W. Bush did not go to war with similar support. The reason, of course, was, as *Newsweek* reported in the first days of the war, that "there was a foreboding . . . an intuition that this war, like Vietnam, would sooner or later go horribly wrong."[2] A *New York Times* poll, published on August 12, before the air war began, showed that over 40 percent of Americans thought Bush was "too quick" to send troops.[3] That figure held up until the air war began and Allied successes finally pushed up the nation's support for the war.

The early fears that the war in the Gulf would develop into another Vietnam brought out a fairly broad-based antiwar protest movement that took off with a tremendous thunder and reached its peak in the very early days of the war. In contrast, the 1960s antiwar movement began slowly and escalated (like the war itself) over time until it peaked some three or four years after the conflict began. The antiwar rhetoric in 1991 was not particularly offensive or insulting to most Americans, at least partly because of the Vietnam experience. Consequently, the movement was tolerated and seen as legitimate, even a necessary part of the conflict.

Not surprisingly, some of the same figures from the past again emerged as local leaders of various antiwar movements, including Daniel Ellsberg, Ron Kovic, and Dick Gregory.

Gulf War protesters, however, clearly harbored no animosity toward American soldiers, as the antiwar protesters had in the 1960s. Those opposed to the war tended to see the soldiers as victims. A common aphorism was "I support the soldiers, but not the war." One peace activist told *Newsweek:* "You won't see protesters spitting on soldiers as they come off the plane."[4] In the 1960s many American protesters believed that the U.S. involvement in Vietnam was so heinous that they found solace in a North Vietnamese victory, and it was not unusual to spot North Vietnamese flags among crowds of antiwar protesters. Among the 1991 protesters there was no comparable support for Saddam Hussein or an Iraqi victory, and there were no reports of burning American flags. "No one is going to carry the Iraqi flag," Todd Gitlin, a 1960s New Left leader, told *Newsweek.* "It's not hate-America time."[5]

American protesters opposed the war because they saw the United States becoming involved in another Vietnam, a war that would last a long time and kill American men and women—a war that possibly the United States could not win. The *q* word, "quagmire," was dragged out again and dusted off by politicians and the press. Many Americans, protesting in the streets or not, clearly harbored this fear of another Vietnam-type disaster. A *CBS-New York Times* poll in mid-January reported that "many Americans . . . [feared] that war in the gulf could bring about a repetition of the United States' bitter experience in Vietnam."[6] And the fears were not only coming from the Left, the traditional haven of antiwar activism, but from the Right as well. H. Ross Perot and John Connally both expressed opposition to the war, and Pat Buchanan, the darling of the neoconservative movement, wrote in August: "The war for which the neocons pant has quagmire written all over it. . . . America could find herself in a Korean-style meat grinder."[7]

Another common saying associated with the antiwar movement of 1991 was "No blood for oil." The protesters believed that the war was being fought to maintain U.S. control of the Persian Gulf and its oil reserves, and they did not feel that protecting that material interest was worth American lives. America, it seemed, was sending its best men and women to defend the oil companies: "Hell, no, we won't go," they yelled again, but this time they added, "we won't kill for Texaco."

African Americans supported the war less than any other major national group. Only 55 percent of blacks supported the war, as opposed to 85 percent of the majority population. Many observers found this surprising considering the role of Colin Powell as the primary U.S. military figure in the war, but African Americans seemed to recall the horrors of Vietnam and their place in that war. For most African Americans, Vietnam was a war fought by blacks for white interests. African Americans were drafted in greater numbers than whites, placed into combat in greater numbers than whites, and consequently a greater proportion of African Americans died in Vietnam than whites. In addition, African Americans got very little out of the war. Their social status did not improve, and most black soldiers returned from Vietnam to an inner-city ghetto or housing project that offered very little. In the Gulf, the old patterns seemed to be in place again. Over one-third of the American soldiers in the Middle East were African American, but only seven percent of the commissioned officers there were African American. Of course, much of this had to do with the nature of post–Vietnam era society in which it was more economically advantageous for African Americans to enter the military than whites, but to African Americans, poised to fight another far-off war, it seemed that the system was again being set up for African American men to die unnecessarily in a white man's war.

The "can-do" spirit that got Americans into so much trouble in Vietnam was back and soaring during the Gulf War, particularly among American pilots, who succeeded in showing a skeptical world that American air power was, in fact, devastating. But from the very beginning, the old Vietnam question was raised again: can air power break the enemy's will to fight and force a surrender without the introduction of ground troops? The answer, certainly from the Army, had always been "no," but in the Gulf in 1991, American air power shut down the Iraqi military machine to the point that the ground war was a quick four-day rout of the enemy. By the time the ground assault began, Saddam was cut off from his troops, the Iraqi air force was gone, Iraqi concrete defensive positions in Kuwait and southern Iraq were nearly destroyed, Baghdad was without power or water, all major infrastructure links had been cut, and the Allies controlled

the skies over the battlefield. In Vietnam, air power against an un-mechanized force was generally a useless waste of power and technology. But
against Saddam's mechanized army, stuck out in open desert terrain, the
U.S. and Allied air forces hit hard and easily, severely damaging the Iraqi
military—and its will to resist the ground assault. Unlike Vietnam, the
U.S. air war against Iraq was a rousing success.

However, despite the successes, as the air war progressed into its second
week, some old horrors from Vietnam resurfaced. Seven Allied POWs, all
airmen, were paraded through Baghdad and then exhibited on Iraqi television. The incident seemed to show America that it would be a long and dirty
war with all the agony and brutality of the other wars that the United States
had fought since World War II. The airmen (three Americans, two British,
one Italian, and one Kuwaiti) appeared to be badly beaten and dazed. The
battered and swollen face of a twenty-eight-year-old Navy lieutenant named
Jeffery Zaun seemed to be on the front page of every news publication in the
country. Each of the prisoners was forced to make an anti-American statement before cameras: "Our leaders and our people have wrongly attacked
the peaceful people of Iraq," Zaun said in a heavy voice, clearly under
severe duress. As Zaun spoke, he occasionally winced at an unseen action
taking place just off the screen to his right, and most Americans came to
believe that he was watching the torture of a comrade while he spoke. The
Pentagon refused to speculate on whether the POWs had been tortured,
but the prevailing view was that the men had been beaten into denouncing
the war. "In staging the performance," *Newsweek* charged, "Saddam added
Iraq's name to a tradition of dishonor that snakes from the Third Reich's
Stalag 17 and Japan's Bilibid Prison to the POW pens of North Korea and
the Hanoi Hilton in Vietnam."[8] Washington charged Saddam with a breach
of the Geneva Convention and threatened to put him on trial when the war
ended. The horrors of Korea and Vietnam returned to the American psyche.

On another front, the members of the American press in the Middle
East found that they were also mired in the memory of the Vietnam War.
The Grenada and Panama invasions foreshadowed what was to come in the
Gulf when the press in those actions was told to stay back while the U.S.
military did its work. The usually aggressive American press elected to complain little about these restrictions, and in the Gulf War they paid dearly for
their earlier passivity. Clearly, those running the war, from the Pentagon to

the White House, had come to believe the old Vietnam myth that it was an unsympathetic press (along with a small but vocal anti-American protest faction) that forced the United States to pull out of Vietnam before the job could be done. In the Gulf, the plan was clear: the press would be restricted and censored. The news coming home from the war zone would be good news. Military personnel escorted "pools" of reporters to sites designated as newsworthy. All film footage and stories were then subject to review and censorship by military personnel. Any reporters who ventured out on their own had their credentials revoked and were subject to being shipped back to the United States. According to one reporter, as many as twenty-four journalists had been detained and reprimanded by the military by the middle of February, less than one month after the air war began.[9] The American people, in turn, appeared to applaud the military's quarantine of the press. A *Newsweek* poll showed that only thirty-two percent of Americans believed that the Gulf War coverage was too controlled by the Pentagon.[10] From that, one can only conclude that the public had also come to accept the old myth that the American press contributed to the United States defeat in Vietnam.

When it became clear in the nation's major press headquarters that those reporters in the field were simply regurgitating the military's sanitized version of the war, the nation's top correspondents were called home, leaving in the press room at Riyadh some less-than-experienced reporters to send back the information being doled out by the military. "I know about half the people in [the Riyadh press room]," one senior member of the media mused, "and they couldn't cover a fire."[11] The result was the ascension of a dark cloud of inexperience and stupid questions that came across American television sets at least once a day. In the end, the American press was probably the most important casualty of the Gulf war. "The flower children," said a Republican congressman after the war, "were relegated to the middle rows of the Pentagon briefing room."[12]

Although the news from the war was censored, the American people at home were bombarded with information about the war. Live coverage from Riyadh, Dhahran, and several cities in Israel showed reporters, with the fear of death in their eyes, literally ducking incoming Iraqi missiles. Watching reporters as they mumbled their stories through the muzzle of an atrocious-looking gas mask became a national pastime. New heroes (and some villains) emerged among the press corps: Bernard Shaw of Cable

News Network (CNN) reported under fire from a bunker in Baghdad the night the air war began; Peter Arnett (also of CNN) filed censored reports daily from Baghdad while being denounced by the American Right as a tool of Saddam; CBS correspondent Bob Simon, who was captured by Iraqis and held near the Kuwaiti border for the duration of the war while trying to get a story outside the military's pool system; Arthur Kent from NBC, whose good looks brought him the unwanted signature of "the SCUD Stud." Wolf Blitzer, Fouad Ajami, and a bevy of retired military officers nightly gave their impressions of the war, each armed with a pointer and a large map of the Middle East. Add the drama of the war itself, the remarkable films of "kills" released by the Pentagon, virtually no blood to muddy the waters, a minimum of U.S. casualties, and the result was a war that verged on entertainment for many Americans.

Of the many news teams in the Gulf, CNN seemed to stand above the rest. Broadcasting twenty-four hours a day, CNN scooped the "big three" networks on the first night of the war and quickly became a clearing house for much of the news coming out of Baghdad, Dhahran, Tel Aviv, and Washington. When Tom Brokaw of NBC interviewed CNN's Bernard Shaw from Shaw's own hotel room in Baghdad, something seemed to snap in the long, fifty-year dominance of network news. At one point, CNN seemed to be directing the war when U.S. Marines were deployed in response to a CNN report of an Iraqi attack on Khafji. Also, it was widely known that Saddam, with no satellite surveillance available, received most of his intelligence information from CNN. U.S. television news was now so up-to-date, so immediate, that its information was valuable to the nation's enemy in time of war.

On the night of January 18, the face of the Gulf War changed when Saddam launched SCUD missiles into Israel. These old-style, Soviet-built SS-1s had been pumped up by Iraq to make the longer-than-designed flight to Israel from western Iraq. Highly inaccurate, they were tactically worthless, little more than terrorist weapons. But Iraqi missiles striking Israeli cities caused a more immediate problem. A retaliation from Israel might cause the anti-Iraq coalition to break down, clearly the exact reaction that Saddam wanted. At the same time, U.S. officials feared that Israel might respond with nuclear weapons if hit with chemical weapons from Iraq. Following the first SCUD strikes, the verbal responses from Israel were aimed at an immediate retaliation. "We're not going to allow Israel to be in a position where every night or every day its citizens are threatened with gas attacks by this savage, brutal dictator," said Israeli Deputy Foreign Minister Benjamin Netanyahu on CNN. Israeli army Chief of Staff General Dan Shornron warned that "such an incident requires a response." And Defense Minister Moshe Arens promised that Israel would respond.[13] But Bush appealed personally to the Israelis for restraint. He also promised to step up searches for Iraqi SCUD launchers in western Iraq in what he called the "darndest search and destroy mission ever undertaken."[14] The United States also supplied Israel with two Patriot missile launchers, the anti-SCUD weapon that had achieved some success in shooting down SCUDs over Saudi Arabia.

The American people were told that this plan to protect Israel had worked, that the Patriots had protected Israel from SCUD attacks, and that the launchers were destroyed. A postwar assessment, however, showed that the Patriots had intercepted no SCUDs over Israel and only twelve of Iraq's thirty fixed launchers were knocked out, and no Iraqi mobile SCUD launchers were ever destroyed.[15]

The attack on Israel did show that U.S. intelligence had vastly underestimated the number and power of Saddam's missiles—and his ability to attack Israel. Intelligence sources had reported that when the war began, Saddam had about thirty-five SCUD launchers; he had, in fact, nearly two hundred. Before the war ended, Saddam was able to fire eighty-one SCUDs. Few did any harm, but one SCUD killed twenty-eight American soldiers when it hit (or exploded over) a barracks in Dhahran. The Allied forces spent a great deal of time and effort searching in vain for Saddam's mobile SCUD launchers. The search mission pushed the date for the ground invasion back at least a week.

Another aspect of the war was what the press called "ecoterror"— Saddam's intentional dumping of crude oil into the Persian Gulf in an attempt to hamper an Allied amphibious landing. In the last week of January, Saddam opened the oil pumps at Sea Island Terminal, a supertanker loading dock ten miles off the Kuwaiti coast, and pumped over ten thousand barrels of crude oil a day into the Gulf. The Iraqis also emptied five Kuwaiti tankers into the Gulf, releasing an additional three million gallons of oil. Before the war was over, Saddam's retreating army would blow up nearly 750 of Kuwait's one thousand oil wells. The northern Persian Gulf was covered in 1.5 million barrels of oil, causing a slick that easily surpassed the Alaskan *Valdez* spill (which was about 260,000 barrels). Oil wells in Kuwait burned until November, when the last ones were finally extinguished and capped.

In mid-February, a last-minute peace initiative came from the Soviet president, Mikhail Gorbachev. The Soviets were absorbed at that moment in the collapse of their entire political and economic structure and elected to declare neutrality in the conflict. But with the United States poised to dominate the region just south of the Soviet border, Gorbachev moved to negotiate a peace before the ground war could begin. For Bush, however, Gorbachev's peace initiatives presented a problem. The U.S. had not deployed over 500,000 soldiers to the Saudi Arabian desert and conducted a month-long air campaign against Iraq, only to withdraw its forces, leaving Saddam strong enough to threaten the region again on another day. At the same time, Bush could not appear to deflect peace proposals, even those in the eleventh hour, for fear of appearing warmongering and callous. He also could not get bogged down in endless negotiations while his soldiers sat waiting in the desert and the world judged his sincerity. The objective of the inner circle became clear: get Gorbachev and his peace proposal out of the picture so they could get on with the war.

The Soviet interference had begun as early as February 15 when Gorbachev asked Bush to delay the ground war until the talks in Moscow between the Soviets and Iraqi Foreign Minister Aziz were completed. But in these talks Gorbachev was playing a role greater than a simple intermediary; he was making behind-the-scenes unilateral promises to Aziz. If Iraq withdrew its forces from Kuwait and averted a war, Gorbachev promised, the Soviets would arrange for the Palestinian question to be addressed immediately. Gorbachev also agreed to protect Iraq's territorial integrity and to ensure Saddam's personal safety after the war. A time frame for an Iraqi troop withdrawal was not specified in the proposal, and the Soviets promised that all UN sanctions would be lifted when Saddam pulled back two-thirds of his force. It was an end game that could have stalled the entire forward motion of Desert Storm, to say nothing of leaving Saddam in the position of *status quo ante* and still with strength enough to threaten the region in the future.

Many believed that Saddam would use Gorbachev's proposal to begin a face-saving withdrawal from Kuwait, and it appeared that peace might break out, but in a telephone conversation, Bush told Gorbachev that the Soviet peace plan was far from acceptable and that Soviet interference at this late date was generally unwelcomed. As the pressure for peace mounted through the middle of the week, it was Saddam, however, and not Bush, who finally took the air out of the peace initiative. In one of his characteristically rambling radio speeches, Saddam said on Thursday, February 21: "Note how those who feared a ground battle have now avoided the showdown for over a month. . . . They are doing this . . . to cover up their inability to confront our land forces. . . . Iraq," he added, "does not seek a temporary truce or capitulation which the failures and shameful people want or have illusions about the possibility of achieving."[16] To the Bush inner circle, this was a clear rejection of Gorbachev's peace proposal. In fact, it was an invitation to attack.

Gorbachev, however, did not give up. On the same day as Saddam's speech, he presented Aziz with another proposal that eliminated many of the concessions of the original plan. But on the telephone, Bush complained to Gorbachev that the new proposal allowed Saddam to withdraw slowly, keeping his army and munitions intact as he left Kuwait—and that the United States was not about to let that happen. On Friday, Gorbachev tried again with another proposal, again tougher on Saddam, in hopes that Bush would relent. But that morning, Bush countered with a cowboy's ultimatum. Saddam, he said, would have "until noon Saturday to do what he must do: begin his immediate and unconditional withdrawal from Kuwait."[17] Bush also insisted that Saddam comply with all twelve UN resolutions. There was a flurry of negotiations. Aziz accepted the Soviet plan: "Iraq agrees to comply with [United Nations] Resolution 660 and therefore will withdraw immediately and unconditionally all its forces in Kuwait."[18] But there was no mention of the other eleven resolutions and Saddam's army continued to remain poised. He had let the deadline pass. Gorbachev and Bush again talked on the telephone. Gorbachev asked for a two-day delay. Bush responded that the decisions had been made and would not now be called back. The next morning at 4:00 a.m. the coalition ground forces blitzed into Kuwait. The ground war had begun. It would last just one hundred hours.

13

DESERT STORM: THE GROUND WAR AND THE TRIUMPH OF LESSONS LEARNED

Schwarzkopf hoped that the air war had reduced the enemy's numbers by half by the time his ground forces engaged the Iraqi troops. The five weeks' work had probably achieved that goal, but the CIA would only estimate that Saddam's force had been depleted by one-third. After the Vietnam War, the Defense Department was criticized severely for "cooking the numbers," for underestimating enemy troop strength and then overestimating the enemy body count in an attempt to make the U.S. position appear stronger and more successful than it actually was. Undoubtedly, the CIA (in charge of the numbers for the Gulf War) found itself overcompensating and underestimating the United States successes to avoid any such post–Gulf War criticism. Probably for the same reason, the CIA vastly overestimated the projected Allied battlefield casualties (set at nearly 40,000), and then overestimated the size of the enemy force—at one time thought by the CIA to be well over 500,000, but was probably considerably less.[1]

These projections and estimations, along with the CIA's estimates of Saddam's remaining troop strength following the air war, pushed several of the Allies' top generals to argue for a delay in the ground assault. Some wanted to continue the job of softening the Iraqis from the air, and others even argued that a few more days of pounding might force the Iraqi soldiers into a mass surrender, ending any need for a ground assault at all, and reducing casualty rates significantly. But such a plan did not sit well with the Army and the Marines, who still believed in the military maxim that wars had to be won on the ground. At the same time, Bush and the inner circle also wanted to get the ground war off as quickly as possible for fear that a new round of Soviet-sponsored negotiations would force Washington to halt the war while Saddam regrouped; or worse, force a long negotiation process that would allow him to retreat with his forces intact.

There was also a fear in Washington that if the ground war were delayed for any reason, the prolonged bombing campaign would turn American public opinion against the war. The message from Vietnam on this point had been very clear: devastating bombing campaigns like Rolling Thunder and Linebacker II were considered gratuitously violent by a large segment of the American population, and the longer the bombing continued, the more public opinion tilted against the war. For George H. W. Bush, in February 1991, delay was the enemy.

Saddam also seemed to realize the negative effect that the U.S. bombing of civilian targets in Baghdad might have on the American will to continue the fight. On February 13, a U.S. Stealth fighter-bomber dropped two 2,000-pound penetration bombs on a concrete building in a residential neighborhood of Baghdad. The report from Iraq was that the structure was an air raid shelter full of hundreds of innocent civilians. Four hundred civilians, said the Iraqis, were killed in the blast, and photos of badly burned corpses and weeping survivors were provided to U.S. television. U.S. officials insisted the structure was an Iraqi command and control center, and then accused Saddam of converting the building to military use and placing civilians there because it was a likely target of a U.S. air attack. Whether or not Saddam intentionally placed civilians in that situation is not clear, but he was certainly prepared to exploit the incident as much as possible for the benefit of the American public, whom he believed would force the U.S. government to withdraw its troops quickly if the war became too messy. Saddam claimed several times to be a student of the U.S. character and of the U.S. involvement in Vietnam, and he had come to believe that the U.S. population simply could not stand to be an accessory to the horrors of war.

The U.S. battle plan was what Schwarzkopf called his "Hail Mary pass," and what the press later dubbed his "left hook"—a plan that would culminate in a massive pincer movement to trap the Iraqi Republican Guard. In just ten days, Schwarzkopf had successfully deployed some 200,000 troops of the XVIII Airborne Corps (including 1,200 tanks) and the VII Corps (including the French 6th Light Armored Daguet Division, plus a brigade of the 82nd Airborne) some three hundred miles to the west of the Kuwait border and without Saddam knowing it. Add to that 4,500 trucks full of supplies and matériel for the attack, and it was no less than a massive logistical undertaking that went virtually unnoticed in Baghdad. With the exception of the coalition forces involved, only the Soviets, through satellite reconnaissance, were aware of this massive maneuver. The big question in the Pentagon was "Would the Soviets share the information with Saddam?" Most, including President Bush, believed they did not. But others were skeptical—and still are. However, if the Soviets did pass the information on to Baghdad, it was done too late to allow Saddam to counter the U.S. troop movement.

Saddam massed his troops south of Basra and to the north of Kuwait City, obviously expecting a Marine-led amphibious landing to come out of the Gulf—a classic American-style attack. More than once Schwarzkopf spoke in press conferences of the quality and readiness of U.S. amphibious forces. "We have very large amphibious forces," he said on January 30, "and they are continually training and ready to do the job when called upon to do so."[2] Saddam, of course, was watching CNN.

Schwarzkopf had in the Kuwaiti theater about 530,000 U.S. soldiers, plus an additional 200,000 from other Allied countries. The Allies commanded about 3,500 tanks. CIA estimates at the time placed Iraqi forces at about 540,000 soldiers supported by about 4,700 battle tanks (including numerous Soviet-built T-72s), but again that number may have been considerably less. Iraqi artillery support was estimated to be superior (at least in number) to U.S. artillery. The enemy was supposedly battle hardened and confident from the eight long years of war against Iran; they were dug in to a strong defensive position, and they were renowned for their tenacity in defensive warfare. The simplest of military doctrines (which states that an attacking force should have a three-to-one advantage against a well-entrenched enemy) would have placed Schwarzkopf in a very poor position, but he knew he could count on two factors to give him preeminence on the battlefield: uncontested air superiority and vastly superior communications. He would find later that he also had better soldiers and better weapons; the combination would make for an Allied attack that would overwhelm and then rout the enemy. But in mid-February, Schwarzkopf was not as confident as he might have been; he estimated that it would take between ten and fourteen weeks to defeat Saddam.

When the Allied forces crashed across the Iraqi border at 4:00 a.m. on February 24, the war was essentially over. To the south, the 1st and 2nd Marine divisions (flanked by Arab forces and supported by the U.S. Army Tiger Brigade of the 2nd Armored Division) raced for Kuwait City in what Saddam must have believed was the main Allied thrust. From the west, the XVIII Airborne, under the command of Lieutenant General Gary Luck, initiated a rapid flanking drive over the open desert toward Republican Guard units entrenched (and by now nearly blinded by a lack of communications) south of Basra. The VII Corps, with its four heavy divisions of over 1,200 tanks, provided the real muscle of Schwarzkopf's assault. Heading first north into Iraq then swinging east, the VII Corps hit the real enemy targets: the Tawakalna and Medina divisions of the Republican Guard. The faked amphibious landing off Kuwait City in the Gulf caught the Iraqis looking the other way. Saddam was taken completely by surprise.

Just as in the air war, which had begun just over one month before, the ground war had its "tools," as Colin Powell called his new miraculous weapons of war. Chief among them was not, however, the American soldier. American soldiers were certainly trained properly and were well prepared for combat, and they did their jobs admirably in the Gulf. But the human toll in Vietnam, the Pentagon believed, had been a major factor in the public's insistence that the Vietnam War end. Consequently, the Pentagon worked diligently after Vietnam to make use of America's technological superiority to develop weapons that would keep U.S. soldiers out of harm's way, and alive to return home to their mothers and wives. The Vietnam War had taught that the fewer American lives lost in battle, the less public agitation there would be against the war. In fact, a popular series of Vietnam War statistics has shown a direct correlation between

The War in the Gulf

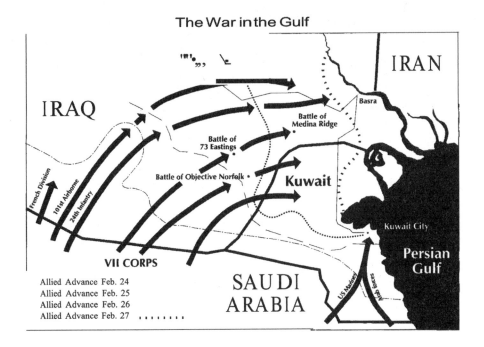

IRAN

IRAQ

Basra

Battle of
Medina Ridge

Battle of
73 Eastings

Battle of Objective Norfolk

Kuwait

Kuwait City

Persian
Gulf

VII CORPS

Allied Advance Feb. 24
Allied Advance Feb. 25
Allied Advance Feb. 26
Allied Advance Feb. 27 ⋅ ⋅ ⋅ ⋅ ⋅ ⋅ ⋅ ⋅

SAUDI
ARABIA

French Division
101st Airborne
24th Infantry
US Marines
Arab forces

deaths in battle in both Korea and Vietnam and growing antiwar activity and opinion in both wars. Prudent nations have, through history, tried to protect their own soldiers while inflicting as much damage as possible on the enemy's army. The strategy was simple: the larger the army, the better chance for victory. But the lessons learned in Vietnam (and to some extent in Korea) showed that there was more to modern warfare than simply controlling the battlefield. Loss of life now translated into a corresponding loss of confidence at home that could quickly turn the nation against the war and force a withdrawal. To save lives on the battlefield, the United States used its technological superiority to virtually remove the American soldier from battle. The air war alone, with its technological marvels of destruction, reduced the need for a major army-to-army shootout in the desert. The United States also developed ground vehicles and weapons that kept American soldiers out of battle for as long as possible, and inflicted damage on the enemy without exposing American soldiers to enemy fire. Chief among these life-saving devices were the Bradley Fighting Vehicle and the Marine Corps' Light Armored Vehicle (LAV-25). Both were designed to give American soldiers protection behind armor plate and a tactical advantage on the battlefield.

They also protected U.S. troops from small-arms ambushes, the scourge of every American soldier in Vietnam. These and other devices were designed to do the jobs that combat soldiers once did, all with the objective of saving American lives. And fewer casualties meant less antiwar agitation at home. All this was clearly a success. In the Gulf War only 148 Americans died in battle.[3]

So, the workhorse of the U.S. battlefield is no longer the American foot soldier. It is instead the "tools" of Colin Powell's trade. In the Gulf these tools included the M-1A1 Abrams tank, the world's premier battle tank. It was supposedly a risk because it guzzled too much fuel, had delicate electronics, and could not keep its air filters clear in the desert dust. But of the 2,000 that operated in the Gulf only nine were lost to enemy fire. The tank performed well and moved across the desert terrain so fast that support field artillery and fuel trucks could not keep up. The TOW Missile, the army's main portable anti-tank missile system, was devastating against Iraqi armor. Air support for the ground war was also effective, with the most accolades going to the A-10 "Warthog." This anti-tank jet fighter had amazing success in destroying Iraqi tanks. Of the 1,000 Allied fighters in the war, only 140 were A-10s, but they were responsible for knocking out over half the Iraqi tanks. Iraqi POWs confirmed that the A-10 was the most fearsome thing in the Allied skies over Iraq. And the F-117A Stealth fighter certainly silenced its critics. All this mobility and firepower was tied together with sophisticated communications networks such as AWACS (Airborne Warning and Control System) and J-STARS (Joint Surveillance Target Track Radar System) that located enemy movements on the ground and in the air, and directed fire against a highly mechanized and vulnerable enemy.

Of some questionable success was the Patriot Missile, the much-touted anti-SCUD missile used in Dhahran, Riyadh, and several locations in Israel to intercept incoming Iraqi SCUD missiles. Once this untested missile system (supposedly a triumph of Star Wars technology) was deployed in the Gulf, Americans seemed to believe that the threat of SCUD attacks was over. President Bush called the Patriot's success nearly perfect, and just days before the ground assault began he traveled to Andover, Massachusetts, where the system is made (and where Bush went to prep school) to praise the workers. But of the eighty-six SCUDs launched, only about thirty-seven were intercepted by Patriots—and even that figure has come under question since the war. Israeli defense officials Moshe Arens and General Dan Shomron both complained that at best the U.S. Patriots knocked out only one SCUD over Israel, and possibly none. The U.S. Army continues to insist that the Patriot had a forty-percent success rate over Israel during Desert Storm.[4]

The Patriots' problems may have revolved around extensive use of the system's radar, which placed undue stress on the Patriots' batteries that in turn may have compromised the system's accuracy. In the single most devastating attack of the war, twenty-eight U.S. soldiers were killed when an Iraqi SCUD collapsed the roof of the barracks of 14th Quartermaster Detachment in Dhahran on February 25. The Patriot radar system had not picked up the incoming missile and had not fired.[5]

Directly south of Kuwait City, the 1st and 2nd Marine Corps divisions (flanked by Arab forces) crossed the Kuwait-Saudi border at 4 a.m. on Sunday, February 24 in A-60 tanks, armored troop carriers, and supported by AH-1 Cobra helicopter gunships. They easily breached the Iraqi minefields along the border and moved slowly against little resistance toward Kuwait City, their objective. The Iraqi soldiers they encountered were Saddam's B team, his conscripts, mostly poorly equipped and poorly trained soldiers who generally did not want to fight. Either they surrendered by the thousands, or they headed overland toward Baghdad and Basra.

The next day (Monday, February 25), as the Marines and their allies continued to make their way toward Kuwait City from the south, U.S. intelligence detected a massive retreat out of Kuwait of trucks, buses, and cars, all headed along Highway 6 north toward Basra. The Iraqi army was trying to get out of Kuwait before the advancing Allied troops entered Kuwait City. It was a big mistake. They only presented themselves as armed targets. Schwarzkopf allowed the convoy to escape Kuwait City into the open well north of Mutlah Pass, and then he ordered an air attack. Navy fighter-bombers involved in the search for mobile SCUD launchers were diverted to Highway 6 to stop the convoy, but low clouds hampered their attack. F-15Es, however, were successful in flying below the clouds, and by the next morning (Tuesday, February 26) they had trapped the convoy by turning the lead vehicles into a barrier of rubble. The weather cleared on Tuesday, and U.S. fighter bombers and tanks from the U.S. 2nd Armored Division bombed and pounded the retreating convoy into a mass of twisted metal, burned-out cars, trucks, and buses, and dead bodies. The military called it a "target-rich environment"; the press called it the "Highway of Death." Over 1,000 vehicles were destroyed in the attack. No one knows how many Iraqis died, but postwar analysts assumed that most Iraqi soldiers had enough time to abandon their vehicles and get out of the area on foot before the U.S. air strikes began. On Tuesday, a second convoy was detected along the Bubiyan Highway, again trying to make a break for Basra. Navy jets were scrambled from the carrier USS *Ranger*, and that convoy was also destroyed. Reports of the bloodshed along Highway 6 and the Bubiyan Highway were both probably exaggerated, but they would push Powell and Bush to call an end to the war before the U.S. military's objectives were achieved—before the Iraqi army was encircled and destroyed.

Schwarzkopf's flanking blitz took the Republican Guard completely by surprise. The large sweep of the XVIII Corps' 24th Infantry Division headed north toward Highway 8, and from there the 24th Infantry penetrated farther into Iraqi lines than any other part of the Allied force. They reached Highway 8 at 6 p.m., Tuesday, February 26. That sweep, called "an unbelievable move" by Schwarzkopf, was that. But the 24th's dramatic sweep was designed mostly to protect the left flank of the VII Corps, the main punch of the Allied attack, as it hit directly into the center of the Republican Guard units just south of Basra along the Iraq-Kuwait border.

In the early morning hours of Tuesday, February 26, after two days of a generally unopposed advance across the Iraqi desert in their M-lAl Abrams tanks and Bradley Fighting Vehicles, portions of the VII Corps wheeled to the east and finally came into contact with the Soviet T-72 tanks of the Tawakalna Division of the Republican Guard. In a blinding sandstorm following a night of heavy rains, the 2nd Armored Cavalry Division and the 3rd Armored Division of the VII Corps destroyed as many as twenty-one T-72s in the battle of 73 Eastings. Just after nightfall that same day, portions of the 3rd Armored Division encountered another wing of the Tawakalna Division and were forced to withdraw under heavy fire after a seventy-five-minute battle between the light U.S.

Bradleys and the more heavily armored Iraqi T-72s. In response, U.S. artillery and air strikes from A- 10s and Apache helicopters were called in, and they destroyed the T-72s from the air. On the morning of the next day, February 27, the United States 1st Infantry Division attacked the center of the Tawakalna Division, and in a four-hour battle in the middle of the night they defeated the Iraqi tanks and breached their defenses. The battle, Objective Norfolk, sent most of the Republican Guard units into retreat.

The largest battle of the war took place near Basra on the afternoon of Wednesday, February 27, the war's fourth day. By then most of the Tawakalna Division had broken up and was in full retreat to the east toward Basra. In the Battle of Medina Ridge, a brigade of the 1st Armored Division destroyed a major portion of the Republican Guard's Medina Luminous Division and sent it into a disorganized and rapid retreat. The Iraqi Adnan and Hammurabi divisions followed suit and headed for Basra. With the main body of the Iraqi forces quickly falling back on the Euphrates River in the direction of Basra, U.S. and British armored divisions under VII Corps Commander Frederick Franks moved rapidly toward Basra to envelop the Republican Guard and to bring the war (along with Saddam's fighting ability) to an end.

To the south, U.S. Marines captured Kuwait International Airport just before 7 a.m. on Wednesday. Their only real problem was that some 23,000 Iraqi soldiers now blocked the highways attempting to surrender. Later that day, as the Marines approached Kuwait City, they pulled to the side of the roadway to let Kuwaiti and other Arab soldiers pass. The plan had always been to allow them to be the first Allied troops to enter the capital.

After the first day of fighting, Powell had predicted that the war would be over by week's end. By Tuesday, the third day of the ground war, several members of the inner circle were prepared to call off the attacks, clearly fearing a backlash if the war turned into a mass slaughter. Powell briefed the group that day, arguing that the Allied forces would achieve the goal of removing the Iraqi army from Kuwait within twenty-four hours. He went on to add that the retreating Iraqis were no longer a fighting force, and to pursue them further "would be un-American and unchivalrous." "Do you want another day?" the president asked.

"No," replied Powell, "by tonight there really won't be an enemy there. If you go another day you're basically fighting stragglers."[6] Everyone in the room agreed, except Vice President Dan Quayle, who questioned Powell that the job might not be completed, that the Iraqi army might not yet be destroyed. His objections were overruled by Powell and Cheney, both of whom insisted that the military objectives had been accomplished and that there was basically no longer an enemy to fight. There was also pressure on the president from the Arab coalition to end the war quickly, before the coalition broke down, before Israel decided to retaliate against Iraq, and before the Arab people turned against the war. The pressure was greatest from King Fahd of Saudi Arabia and Hosni Mubarak, then the president of Egypt. Both feared a disintegrating Iraq, a Middle East power vacuum that might become dominated by radical Shiites and allied with Iran. Nothing would be more destabilizing in that region of the world. Both Fahd and Mubarak were, however, willing to live with a weakened, disarmed Saddam. Bush and Scowcroft had come to accept this philosophy, but everyone in the White House inner circle agreed that if Schwarzkopf wanted more time to finish the job, he would get it. On Wednesday evening, Washington suggested a ceasefire to begin at 8 a.m. Thursday (midnight Washington time). With no hesitation, Schwarzkopf agreed.

On Wednesday evening, a triumphant George H. W. Bush went on national television and announced: "Kuwait is liberated. Iraq's army is defeated. Our military objectives are met." He went on: "Seven months ago, America and the world drew a line in the sand. We declared that the aggression against Kuwait would not stand, and tonight America and the world have kept their word."[7] At midnight the war ended. One hundred hours had passed since the ground war began. *Newsweek* declared: "For the first time since World War II, triumphant Americans liberated an occupied nation like swashbuckling storybook heroes—and the United States rejoiced in its military might."[8]

The ceasefire was signed just before noon on March 3 at an airfield somewhere in southern Iraq. Schwarzkopf and the Saudi Commander, Lieutenant General Khalid ibn Sultan, dictated terms of the ceasefire to Iraqi Lieutenant General Sultan Hashim Ahmad. The event was only of minor significance. Allied POWs were released immediately, and the

American soldiers packed up and went home. With the exception of an incident in which an American female helicopter pilot was apparently brutally beaten and raped by Iraqi soldiers, the POWs received reasonable treatment. By summer, most of the nation's major cities were launching parades to welcome home the new heroes. And President Bush, perceived as something of a hero himself, received a whopping eighty-percent approval rating in a *USA Today* poll.[9] Speaking off-the-cuff after a speech in the Rose Garden, Bush said, "By God, we've kicked the Vietnam syndrome once and for all."[10] He spoke vaguely of a new world order and peace in the Middle East. In summer 1991 the United States was victorious, standing astride the world for the first time since World War II. But by August, *Time* magazine was asking on its cover: "Was it worth it?"[11] What had gone wrong?

One immediate problem was that Bush and his advisors, in their apparent desire to shake off the Vietnam nemesis and fearing a backlash against the administration's policies, may have ended the war too quickly, or at least many thought so. It seemed that the loose ends had not quite been tied up. A *Newsweek* poll, in May, showed that as many as 55 percent of the American people believed the war was not a victory because Saddam remained in power after the U.S. pullout.[12] In addition, Powell's analysis of the battlefield situation on February 25 may have produced a hasty decision. The midnight ceasefire left U.S. troops of the VII Corps just short of encircling the retreating Iraqi army. Although a large part of Saddam's forty-one divisions was destroyed or surrendered, as many as 110,000 Iraqi soldiers (over four Republican Guard divisions) escaped through Basra, carrying with them a fleet of helicopters and as many as 700 tanks. On March 3, when he surrendered to the Allies in the Iraqi desert, Saddam still maintained as many as 300,000 effective soldiers in uniform, 1,200 artillery pieces, 2,000 armored personnel carriers, 2,100 tanks, and possibly as many as 150 SCUDs.[13] Clearly, their escape route could have easily been blocked and the hardware destroyed. Was it a case of unfinished business? Evidence now seems to indicate that Powell recommended an end to the war based on reports from the attacks on Highway 6 and the Bubiyan Highway, and failed to realize that armored Iraqi divisions were making their way to a safe haven through Basra. Schwarzkopf, on the other hand, apparently believed that he needed another twenty-four hours to complete his task, but failed to make that fact known to the president.

Within hours of the March 3 ceasefire, Iraqi Shiites in Basra rose up against Saddam. In northern Iraq, Kurds took the signal that Saddam was weak and they, too, broke into revolt. Saddam used his escaped Republican Guard divisions to crush both rebellions. The Iraqi divisions that escaped not only allowed Saddam to retain his place as ruler of Iraq, but they also gave him the power to continue his ways of wreaking havoc on the less powerful. Considering it was a main U.S. objective to destroy Saddam's ability to make war on his neighbors, this revelation brought with it a sense of failure to the American people. By the summer, the Kuwaitis were again trembling in fear: "Saddam is still thinking and planning further operations aimed at destroying Kuwait," said Kuwaiti Prime Minister Saad al-Abdullah al Sabah on June 19.[14] And in early 1992 the Pentagon drew up a plan to remove Saddam again from Kuwait and Saudi Arabia sometime in the late 1990s.

One question seems to remain: why did George H. W. Bush leave Saddam in power in Baghdad? He may have believed that an Iraq without Saddam would result in a dangerous power vacuum that would have to be filled, and the options to fill that vacuum were clearly not too appetizing. The U.S. Army could occupy Iraq, but that would have placed the United States in the unacceptable position of occupier and imperialist. The United States suffers greatly from a perception throughout the world that it is economically and culturally imperialistic, and its track record in Vietnam has made it hard to argue that the purpose of a U.S. military force stationed on foreign soil is to maintain stability. To have occupied Iraq after the war would have placed the United States in a very unfavorable position in the world. At the same time, a second option of setting up a puppet-like U.S.-backed government in Baghdad would have evoked many of the same anti-U.S. sentiments. And again, the American experience in Vietnam had added to the worldwide perception of the United States as an imperialistic power. Both of these options, of course, pointed to a long-term Vietnam-style U.S. involvement, something that no one wanted.

Another option might have been to support the Kurds in a takeover, but the Kurds were a long way from being a reliable and stable political force in the Middle East, and an independent Kurdistan in present-day northern Iraq would have been unacceptable to Turkey, an American ally and NATO member. Bush and the inner circle may also have feared that an Iraq without Saddam might lead to an invasion of Iraq by Iran—and a Shiite-led Iraq would surely have caused additional problems in the future. Bush's only real option was to encourage moderates to overthrow Saddam. But when that failed, the president could only defeat Saddam's army quickly and decisively, leave him in power as a weak but stable force, and withdraw. No quagmire, no muddle, just clean, quick, and sharp. But the plan also called for the destruction of Saddam's ability to fight again, and that was not done.

Another disappointment came in postwar Kuwait. Immediately after the war, the emir retracted all his earlier promises of democratic reforms, and his nation reverted to its feudal society, which had always been anti-American and anti-Western. For those Americans who want to believe that the United States fights wars to maintain freedom, liberty, and democracy, the lack of those basics in Kuwait after the war brought on further disenchantment and questions about the motives for U.S. involvement in the first place.

But it was America's long postwar involvement in Iraq that seemed to show that there was really no such thing in the post–World War II era as a clean, uncomplicated war. When Saddam used what remained of his military power to crush the Kurd and Shiite rebellions, the U.S. military was drawn into an internal Iraqi civil war, mostly to protect the aggrieved Kurds in the north. Washington felt responsible for the anti-Saddam refugees that the war had created, and the United States moved in troops and food to protect and aid the Kurds as they fled into the mountains along the Turkish border ahead of Saddam's advancing army. As the situation worsened, and as the frightened faces of blue-eyed Kurdish children hit the covers of *Time* and *Newsweek,* Bush responded by creating a safe zone for the Kurds in northern Iraq that the press persisted in calling "Bushistan." It was a big step into a quagmire, and Bush realized it. He turned the situation over to the UN, declared a U.S.-guaranteed "no-flight zone" north of the 36th parallel and withdrew as quickly as possible. He would not allow his quick and decisive victory to turn into a long and drawn-out Vietnam-like mess. A conspicuous

American presence continued on in Iraq, and confrontations seemed to make it clear that Saddam was not going away, that he would not, as one administration official put it, "stay in his box."

The first of a series of incidents occurred in late June 1991 when Iraqi guards prevented UN inspectors from checking an Iraqi nuclear facility. Bush threatened reprisals. In late September, UN inspectors were detained for four days after they discovered documents linking the Iraqi government to nuclear weapons development. They were finally released, but only after they provided an inventory of the documents they took. In late February 1992, Iraq refused to allow a UN team to dismantle a SCUD missile production plant. Finally, following a month's standoff, the Iraqis relented, but only after the UN threatened military action. In July, the same UN inspectors were barred from searching the Iraqi Agricultural Ministry. During the month-long standoff Iraqi police allowed the UN inspectors to be harassed by violent Iraqi protesters outside the ministry. The inspectors finally left Baghdad, but when they returned a week later to complete their mission, they found nothing. The incident clearly humiliated the Bush administration, and the president vowed that he would not again be humiliated by Saddam.[15]

A second hot war seemed to be in the making when in late August 1992, Bush declared (with the support of Great Britain and France) a second no-fly zone in Iraq, this one in the south (south of the 32nd parallel) in an effort to protect the Shiite Muslims who were still receiving a pounding from Saddam as a result of their post–Gulf War uprising. During the first week in January 1993, Iraq moved surface-to-air missiles into the southern zone, and then at almost the same moment Iraqi soldiers crossed the border into Kuwait in an attempt to seize UN-guarded Chinese Silkworm surface-to-air missiles left over from the war. These challenges by Saddam, coming in George H. W. Bush's last days in office before Bill Clinton's inauguration on January 20, were a clear attempt to do little more than humiliate the outgoing president. Saddam seemed to be saying to the world that he remained firmly in power while Bush had been rejected by his people. The result of these incidents was a series of attacks by the UN (with the approval of the incoming administration) against Iraqi missile sites in the southern no-fly zone. Then, following

Clinton's inauguration, Saddam made a number of conciliatory remarks toward the United States, and immediately UN inspection teams were welcomed back into Iraq.

But the detente was short-lived. On April 13, two years after the Gulf War ended, a dozen Iraqis and Kuwaitis were arrested in a plot to assassinate George H. W. Bush, who was scheduled to visit Kuwait the next day. On June 26, after the FBI concluded that the Iraqi government had originated the plot, President Clinton launched a Cruise missile attack on Baghdad in retaliation.[16] A defiant Saddam responded in a speech over Iraqi television: "Another battle has started. Another holy war ordained by God, so that we can attain another great victory for you, the Iraqi people."[17] And in another speech, he claimed to abrogate the March 1991 ceasefire that ended the Gulf War. "We accepted a ceasefire," he said, "but we never signed a surrender document with anybody. What we accepted at the end of the fighting we refused to accept a year later. What we accepted a year later we do not accept now, and what we are accepting now we will refuse a year from now."[18] But despite all the bluster, the incident died down in late February—and Saddam returned quietly to his box.

Surprisingly, the American people forgot about the Gulf War almost as quickly as it occurred. George H. W. Bush rode an amazing eighty-percent popularity rating in July after the war ended, but his numbers dropped quickly to below 50 percent by Christmas. In November 1992, Bush was defeated by Bill Clinton in the midst of a recession. Like Churchill in 1945, Bush had won the war but lost the peace. The image of Saddam Hussein was reduced to that of a cheap thug.

The Gulf War brought a new patriotism to America of the type that goes with winning a war against a palpable evil. There was a feeling immediately after the war that America had regained something it had lost in the years between Vietnam and the Gulf War, that the United States had a new power, a new life, that it was uncontestedly the most powerful nation in the world for the first time since the Soviets got the bomb in 1949. Much of this may have had to do with the simultaneous collapse of the Soviet Union and the end of the cold war, but the victory in the Gulf brought a new confidence in America—and in Americans, that they were somehow again on the right side of history.

One of the big winners in the Gulf War was the American soldier. Derided in Korea for not quite measuring up to those who won the good victory in World War II, accused of being soft and poorly trained, and of committing atrocities and fighting and losing the wrong war in Vietnam, the American soldier after the Gulf War was raised to the status of the new American hero. The war placed the American soldier again on the level of the mythical John Wayne–type World War II soldier: tough, well trained, and able to complete his job. The American soldier was no longer the backbone of the U.S. military, superseded by technological might, but in the eyes of the American people he was again worthy of the uniform and worthy of praise and respect.

There are a number of comparisons to be made between the war in Vietnam and the war in the Gulf—comparisons that say a lot about the mind of post-Vietnam leadership in America. During the Gulf War, George H. W. Bush and his inner circle seemed to act on the assumption that everything Lyndon Johnson did in conducting the Vietnam War was wrong, and that the opposite reaction in the Gulf War would produce an opposite result. It was Johnson, of course, who insisted on choosing the North Vietnamese targets to be bombed during Operation Rolling Thunder, at one time drawling: "They can't even bomb an out house without my approval."[19] But more importantly, Johnson (possibly looking at Truman's troubles with MacArthur in Korea) decided to run the war himself from the Oval Office. For the most part, Bush handed the conduct of the war over to Powell and Schwarzkopf, setting only a few ground rules, such as banning the use of nuclear weapons and insisting that nonmilitary targets, particularly mosques, be avoided. A direct-line telephone from the Oval Office to Schwarzkopf's field command office in Saudi Arabia was barely used. And when the Pentagon's war plan was finally presented, the president made no changes.

The ghost of Vietnam can best be seen in the Gulf War by the size of the force Washington sent. In the first days after Iraq's invasion a number of options surfaced that sounded all too familiar. One was for surgical air strikes against Iraq; another was the use of a small rapid-deployment team to guard against an Iraqi attack on Saudi Arabia. Powell, particularly, cringed at the thought of a slow escalation that could give Saddam time to cement his actions and fortify his positions. Again, if the United

States was going in, Powell believed, then it should be quickly and with a force strong enough to do the job. Early on, that job was to repel an attack from Iraq if one came. Later, after November, the job description changed to one of evicting Saddam from Kuwait and destroying his ability to threaten the region again. Powell immediately requested a force of over 100,000 soldiers, including reserves. By the January 15 deadline, the deployment had grown to over 500,000 soldiers, a massive buildup that included professional soldiers, enlistees, and reserves from all branches of the service—but it did not include draftees, another Vietnam ghost that had to be exorcised in the Gulf War. To Powell, Bush, and the inner circle, there was only one way to fight the Gulf War, and that was opposite from the way Johnson had fought Vietnam, with a massive stroke that would hit the enemy hard and destroy it quickly. Such a plan would make the best use of American technological superiority and result in the fewest battlefield casualties.

Interestingly, George H. W. Bush fought the Gulf War the way Truman intended to fight the Korean War: with a quick and easy removal of an aggressor from an aggrieved nation. Truman, like Bush, was decisive and did not commit the United States slowly or cautiously. Truman, of course, would have succeeded in Korea as George H. W. Bush succeeded in the Gulf had he not listened to MacArthur and pushed on to the Yalu, bringing the Chinese into the conflict and adding nearly three years of stalemate to the war. But George Bush's aggressiveness and decisiveness in the Gulf must be seen as a reaction to America's slow and indecisive buildup in Vietnam. The Vietnam tactic failed, so a massive quick buildup must succeed.

In the Gulf War, the military and civilian concepts of the Vietnam Syndrome came into conflict for the first time. Colin Powell, the career soldier and Vietnam veteran, had come to see warfare since Vietnam in much the same light as the rest of the nation's military establishment: it was messy, lethal, and in the post–World War II nuclear world, it was generally unwinnable. Powell's first response to the Gulf situation was to allow the sanctions to work; use war only as a last resort. But Bush, faced with the political repercussions of a long, drawn-out, Vietnam-like escalation, could see only one answer to the situation: hit the Iraqis hard, obtain the objective, and withdraw immediately before the American public could grow restive of the involvement. Sanctions, he told Powell, would work too slowly. As Truman and MacArthur argued over the nature of warfare in the 1950s, so did Bush and Powell argue over the nature of warfare in the 1990s.

In South Korea and South Vietnam the United States had set up friendly governments and then moved in to defend them against what was termed a Communist incursion. To maintain some degree of respect in the world and to fend off the accusation that Syngman Rhee in Korea and Ngo Dinh Diem and later Nguyen Van Thieu in Vietnam were merely American puppets, the United States allowed these men to maintain a large degree of control in their governments. Rhee became one of the biggest stumbling blocks to the U.S.-Chinese peace initiatives in the Korean ceasefire talks, and the Thieu government sabotaged LBJ's eleventh-hour attempts at peace in 1968. With one eye looking to the past, George H. W. Bush made no attempt to deal with either the Kuwaitis or the Saudis in that way. The United States had gained nothing by appearing to deal with Rhee, Diem, and Thieu as equals, and giving them the power, as leaders of their countries, to sabotage U.S. intentions. The Saudi government was only consulted to seek permission to deploy foreign troops on its soil. The Kuwaiti government-in-exile was not given any power to force the United States to conduct the war on its behalf. George H. W. Bush fought the war with a free hand.

It has always been deemed a mistake that Lyndon Johnson fought the war in Vietnam nearly alone, with no significant coalition to support American action. The Korean War had been, at least ostensibly, a war of the UN powers against an aggressor nation, and that seemed to bring to the United States a degree of worldwide support for conducting the war with the approval of at least some of the nations of the world. Johnson, on the other hand, inherited a unilateral commitment in Vietnam and chose to go it mostly alone, without UN support. The U.S. unilateral strategy in Vietnam paved the way for an international outcry against the United States, which was using its technological superiority in a vain attempt to bludgeon a small Asian nation. Here again, Bush was not going to get caught in that trap. The nations of the world, even the Arab world, would help in the fight against Saddam, and the United States would emerge, not as a bully or a policeman, but at the head of a new world order of nations. The coalition also helped pay for the endeavor, which was no small factor.

It may have been for George H. W. Bush and the Republicans, "no more Vietnams," as they entered feet first into the Gulf War, but it was the ghosts of Vietnam and Korea that followed George Bush and his advisors through the Gulf War and into the period after it. Clearly, when it came to the grand strategy, the lessons of Vietnam were in the cards. George H. W. Bush pronounced the Vietnam Syndrome dead at the end of the Gulf War, but the way in which he conducted the war itself shows that he and his inner circle of advisors spent most of the war looking over their shoulders at the Vietnam War and its many failures.

There is yet another aspect of the Vietnam Syndrome: the United States, because of the Vietnam debacle, is still somewhat reluctant to engage in overseas military operations. That is the aspect of Vietnam Syndrome that Bush had in mind when he announced its death. Certainly, as a result of the Gulf War victory, the United States has pushed behind it some of those fears that any limited war will turn into a long, drawn-out war of attrition. But the Gulf War was an unusual example of a military conflict in the post–World War II era. It was what one military figure has called, "the mother of all military anomalies."[20] Saddam was a Hitleresque villain. His act was a brutal attack on a small defenseless nation. He chose to fight rather than negotiate. His army was mechanized and vulnerable to American air power. And, amazingly, he gave the United States six months to build up its strength. With the lessons of Vietnam in hand, George H. W. Bush was able to destroy the Iraqi military with little difficulty. Does that remove the fear of Vietnam from the American psyche? Certainly not. The United States continues to be fearful of becoming entangled in wars of nationalism. Also, the United States will continue to be reluctant to fight in areas of the world where its technological superiority will not be decisive. And the U.S. military will even be reluctant to fight in the jungles of the world against guerrilla armies. The Vietnam Syndrome is not dead. The way the Gulf War was fought, with Vietnam in place as the anti-plan, is the best evidence of that. In the Iraq War, which began in 2003, the United States again made an attempt at state-building, an attempt at turning a conquered Iraq into an American-style democracy—and this time with some success. In addition, the United

States policy makers (possibly again looking to Vietnam) saw, in 2003, that a prolonged war against an irregular force might not sit well with the American people. Thus, the war in Iraq (the 2003 war) was fought by an all-volunteer force (unlike in Vietnam), and the war was fought as part of a coalition against the evils of Saddam Hussein.

14

AFGHANISTAN AND IRAQ, POST 9/11

The Gulf War was over by the spring of 1991. Between 1981 and 1993, the United States became involved in a series of minor skirmishes throughout the globe: in Lebanon, Libya, Grenada, and Panama, all at minimal cost to blood and treasure. In addition, the United States sent both military and economic aid to a number of UN operations, including floods in Bangladesh, and damage caused by volcanic eruptions in the Philippines and Italy. Much of this attitude toward military intervention (or missions) had to do with George H. W. Bush's own illusion of "a new world order," which focused on the reduction of NATO forces and nuclear arsenals through treaty negotiations. These negotiations led to a goal of reducing warheads to about 3,000 each for the old Soviet Union and the United States. The Strategic Arms Reduction Treaty of 1992 disarmed the one-time Soviet regions (and now new nations) of Belarus, Ukraine, and Kazakhstan. There was also a significant downsizing of the American military in this period, with a plan to be both smaller and more mobile. That strategy included a focus on advanced technological innovations, mostly as a result of the Gulf War successes. Much of that focus was directed at precision-guided weapons, designed to be under the care and direction of long-term professionals. The successes of American weaponry during the Gulf War also led to the continued a belief that the United States was more advanced technologically than most other nations.

This American drawdown worried a number of world leaders, many of whom feared that the United States would no longer be able to police world problems. From that, there was also a prediction of the rise of rogue nations, significant nuclear proliferation, and a growing number of civil wars. There was also a specific need to deal with genocide in central Africa, southern Sudan, and even in parts of southern Europe. There was piracy off the Horn of Africa, and growing drug cartels in Columbia and Mexico. The point was clear: who would put out these brushfires? The United States, the United Nations, a coalition of nations?

Bill Clinton was elected to the presidency in November 1992, and he took the oath as president of the United States in January of the next year. He served as president until January 2001. By that time, the nation's political candidates were speaking often of a "peace dividend," cash given to the American individuals to defray the costs of the nation's military during a time of peace. It was during this period that the U.S. government spoke of keeping Saddam "in his box," mostly through a no-fly zone over parts of Iraq.

During Clinton's two terms in the White House, the United States became involved in several military events that defined the nation as it passed into the twenty-first century. But Clinton was not a foreign policy president. Like most American presidents, he was elected to office on domestic issues—on his abilities to deal with domestic problems. And, of course, governors-as-presidents (Clinton had been the governor of Arkansas) often find foreign policy challenging. It became clear early that he had a short attention span when it came to international issues. After Clinton spoke at the United Nations in October 1993, *The Economist* noted, "[S]omehow the fire is not in Mr. Clinton's belly when he speaks on foreign policy."[1]

At the same time, Republicans mostly ignored foreign policy issues as well, pushing the age-old go-it-alone foreign policy view of America's role in the world. They criticized America's foreign aid programs and denounced the United Nations. North Carolina Senator Jesse Helms, the chairman of the Senate Foreign Relations Committee, condemned the UN's initiatives, particularly its environmental programs and its peacemaking efforts. Congressional Republicans also withheld UN dues, amounting to over $1 billion. Despite Clinton's lack of interest and the Republicans' disdain for foreign entanglements, the United States would

Somalia

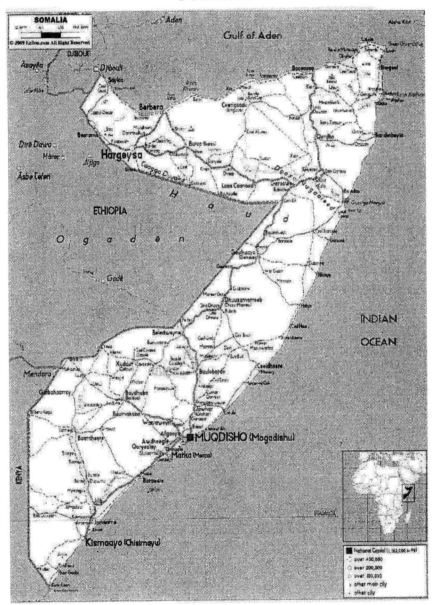

find (as it had found through most of the twentieth century) that it could not turn its back on the world.

One such case was Somalia, a lawless and mostly failed nation located on the Horn of Africa. During the cold war, Somalia received a consistent flow of Soviet weapons and aid, and it was vital to controlling the western Indian Ocean and the southern passages to the Middle East. But in the 1990s, with the end of the cold war and the collapse of the Soviet Union, its strategic significance became minimal and, without some sort of aid, it fell into a labyrinth of ethnic and religious hatred. Clinton inherited the mess in Somalia from the Bush administration, and he followed Bush's lead by sending in some twenty-five thousand peace-keeping troops in an attempt to deal with the widening civil war and poor harvests that had left thousands dead and starving—many of them children. The Clinton administration's original mission was humanitarian, with a focus on protecting United Nations food supplies intended for famine victims. Increasingly, however, the United States got drawn further into the internal conflicts, and the humanitarian mission quickly shifted to restoring order. As the American military was dragged deeper into the conflict, pundits fell back on the Vietnam-era word "quagmire," and political cartoonists began drawing Somalia in the shape of Vietnam.

America's involvement continued to grow in Somalia until October 1993, when a botched attempt to capture a local warlord in Mogadishu resulted in the deaths of eighteen U.S servicemen. When photos appeared in the American press of dead U.S. soldiers being dragged through the streets of Mogadishu, Congress demanded that the troops be pulled out. Clinton quickly withdrew.

The event itself was terrible enough, but the most tragic aspect of the situation was that American soldiers had died because the commanders on the ground had been refused the tanks and air support they had requested. That failure seemed to expose the new president as gun-shy and indecisive. Fearful of a Vietnam-style escalation, Clinton responded to the events in Mogadishu by pushing out his secretary of defense, Les Aspin, at least in part because Aspin was perceived as indecisive on a variety of military issues, including Somalia.[2]

Just ten days after the mess in Mogadishu, events in Haiti made the United States again appear weak and indecisive. In 1991, a *coup* had driven the democratically elected Jean-Bertrand Aristide from power in Haiti and into exile, resulting in chaos in the capital at Port-au-Prince. Clinton planned to send in two hundred noncombat solders to help train the Haitian police force, and then to restore Aristide to the presidency.

But as the soldiers prepared to come ashore at Port-au-Prince, a mob formed on the docks, and began chanting "Somalia, Somalia." Clinton blinked, and ordered the troops to return to the United States.[3]

Perhaps the greatest military challenge of the 1990s came with the dissolution of Yugoslavia. Created after World War I as a patchwork of ethnic regions and nations, Yugoslavia began to disintegrate in 1990 when the Soviet Union dissolved and could no longer control Yugoslavia's economy, social structure, and politics. Slovenians and Croats in the north were Catholic and (as they saw it) European by nature. In the south, Serbs dominated. They considered themselves the purveyors of Slavic culture, and they held strongly to Russian culture and the ancient Serbian Orthodox Church. To the Serbs, the Croats and the Muslims (mostly in Bosnia and Herzegovina) were enemies. The capital of Yugoslavia had been the old Serbian capital of Belgrade, and the prominent political figure in the region was the Serb Slobodan Milosevic.

Much of this began with the secession of Slovenia from the carcass of Yugoslavia in 1991—and the subsequent recognition by much of Europe. Almost immediately, Croatia followed and a civil war broke out between Croatia and Serbia. The Croats drove the Serbs out of their country, and then allied themselves with the Muslims. The Yugoslav-Serbian army then struck back at Croatia and the Muslims and forced them into a ceasefire in January 1992. Bosnia-Herzegovina, then, declared its own independence. In response, Serbia invaded. By the end of 1992, Yugoslavia was gone, plunged into a series of battles between the Bosnians and the Serbs. The victorious Serbs, then, began a policy of "ethnic cleansing" with the goal of removing Croats and Bosnians from what they called a "Greater Serbia."

It was NATO (led by England and France) that moved to restore order in the region. George H. W. Bush insisted that the United States would not again intervene in the affairs of Europe. Bill Clinton, then a candidate for president, criticized Bush's insensitivity toward the victims of the Bosnian War, and Bush responded to Clinton's criticisms by sending relief supplies to the war zone. In August 1995, Clinton, now president, sent in U.S. air forces against the Serbs. Later that year, he finally committed U.S. troops to a NATO peacekeeping force in Bosnia in an attempt to force the Serbs to stop the killing. In November 1995, the United States brokered a ceasefire agreement (the Dayton Peace Accords) that included sending in sixty thousand NATO peacekeepers to enforce the agreement.[4]

Polls made it immediately clear that the American people were opposed to getting militarily involved in areas of the world where the nation's national interests were not directly at stake. At the same time, Clinton seemed to handle the war in a haphazard, almost arbitrary, manner. The same polls also showed that the American people did not want their president to appear indecisive and apprehensive in the face of events.

Whatever apprehensions or inexperiences Clinton may have exhibited in the Bosnia incident, he was better able to deal with the situation in Kosovo—perhaps because of his experiences in Bosnia. In 1999, the Serbian president, still Milosevic, unleashed a new round of "ethnic cleansing" in the Balkans, this time against ethnic Albanians in Kosovo. Kosovo was another old Yugoslav province, inhabited by 1.8 million people. When Milosevic revoked Kosovar autonomy within the Yugoslav state, the Kosovar Albanians formed their own breakaway state. Led by the Kosovar Liberation Army (KLA), the Kosovars insisted on independence from the Yugoslav federation—and eventually political union with Albania. The KLA militiamen attacked Serbian soldiers and policemen inside Kosovo, which quickly escalated into a full-scale rebellion. Milosevic responded by attacking the Kosovar Albanians, forcing as many as 800,000 to flee into the countryside and into neighboring states. Clinton, along with the heads of other NATO countries, ordered the bombing of Serbia in March 1999 in an effort to force Milosevic to end the persecution of the Kosovars. Milosevic responded by stepping up his "ethnic cleansing" in Kosovo. Within weeks, the entire situation turned into a disaster. Thousands of Kosovar Albanians were slaughtered; another 100,000 remain unaccounted for and are presumed dead.

Finally, after seventy-eight days of bombing, Milosevic relented and signed a ceasefire. By then, however, he had achieved most of his goals of consolidating his power in Serbia and pushing the Albanians out of Kosovo. NATO troops were sent in as peacekeepers and to aid the Albanians in their return home. The KLA continued to operate, demanding independence for Kosovo (but that was never a part of any agreement). Milosevic was voted out of office, then captured and arrested. He died in 2006 while standing trial for war crimes before the United Nations War Crimes Tribunal in The Hague, Netherlands. Kosovo declared its independence from Serbia in 2008. Its independence is recognized by the United Nations, but not by the state of Serbia.[5]

During the two administrations of Bill Clinton (January 1993 to January 2001) the United States tried to keep Saddam "in his box," mostly through a no-fly zone imposed over portions of Iraq. In his 1998 State of the Union address, Clinton told the nation that Saddam was in the process of building an arsenal of chemical, biological, and nuclear weapons. Later that year, Clinton signed into law the Liberation Act of 1998, which called for "regime change" in Iraq. But to do that Clinton needed the support of Congressmen, most of whom opposed U.S. military intervention in the Middle East. To win congressional support, the bill expressly stated that the process of regime change would not include military ground forces. Clinton then followed up with Operation Desert Fox, a three-day bombing campaign in mid-December. Before Clinton left office, U.S. and British aircraft hit hostile Iraqi air defenses nearly 250 times.

George W. Bush was elected to the presidency in 2000, and took the oath of office in January of the next year. There seems little doubt that when he came to the presidency he was intent on starting a war with Saddam. He seemed to believe that the 1991 war had not been resolved, and that in April 1993 Saddam had tried to assassinate his father, George H. W. Bush, while Bush-the-elder was visiting the Middle East. According to Seymour Hersh (in a now-famous article in the *New Yorker*) the George W. Bush administration created the Office of Special Plans (OSP) for the expressed purpose of finding evidence that Saddam had close ties to terrorism in the Middle East and to al-Qaeda. The organization was also designed to show that Iraq had at its disposal a large cache of nuclear, chemical, and biological weapons—weapons of mass destruction, or WMDs. If such weapons were not immediately available to Saddam, it was assumed that he was in the process of developing them. The OSP was originally created by Paul Wolfowitz and Douglas Feith at the behest of Secretary of Defense Donald Rumsfeld. The organization only existed for about a year, from summer 2002 until June 2003.[6]

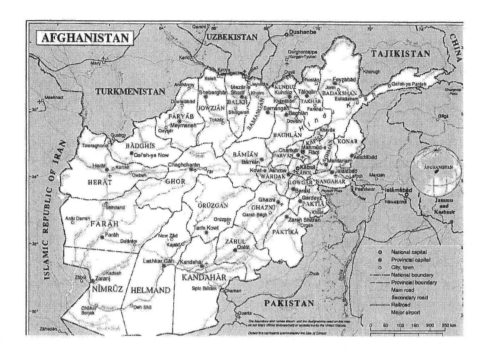

As the situation in Iraq escalated, the situation in Afghanistan was developing almost simultaneously. Most Americans believed that their war in Afghanistan began with the 9/11 attacks against the United States in September 2001. But in fact, the situation in Afghanistan had been smoldering at least since the early 1970s. In 1973, King Zahir Shah was overthrown by his cousin Mohammed Daoud Khan, in a bloodless political *coup*. Daoud Khan had been Afghanistan's prime minister since the early 1950s, and he is best known for his attempts to modernize the country. He also worked to maintain a close relationship with the Soviet Union, his closest neighbor to the north.

Despite Daoud Khan's ties to the Soviets, he was murdered in 1978 by members of the Afghan Communist Party in a *coup*. This People's Democratic Party of Afghanistan, or PDPA, attempted to put Afghanistan on the road to a Marxist-Leninist-socialist regime that was intent on undermining the traditional tribal order of Afghanistan. The result was that a significant opposition arose in Afghanistan to combat the new order. This Mujahedeen fought to end control by the PDPA, but they only succeeded in destabilizing the regime. The Soviet

Union refused to sit back and allow one of their client states to fall into the hands of anti-Communists on their southern border, so they intervened militarily and installed a PDPA faction in Afghanistan. Afghanistan was renamed the Democratic Republic of Afghanistan—a Soviet client state.

The Soviet invasion of Afghanistan plunged Afghanistan onto the cold war stage. America's only visible reaction was to pull out of the 1980 Moscow Olympics. But behind the scenes, the United States, Pakistan, Saudi Arabia, and even China worked to bring an end to what most saw as the blatant Soviet invasion and occupation of Afghanistan.

Through much of this period, Afghanistan continued to be a land of local warlords and tribal leaders. The Soviet military maintained control of the major cities in Afghanistan, but the countryside remained under the control of the fiercely Islamic Mujahedeen. And through Pakistan's Inter-service Intelligence (the Pakistani equivalent of the CIA) the United States armed the Mujahedeen against the Soviets. The war also attracted a large number of non-descript fighters known as "Afghan Arabs." Among this group was Osama bin Laden.

American-made, shoulder-fired surface-to-air missiles played havoc with Soviet helicopters, and finally the Soviet military decided to cut its losses and pull out of Afghanistan. This was in May 1989. By most accounts, the ten-year Soviet adventure in Afghanistan was an expensive, closed-ended quagmire with no light at the end of the tunnel—a Russian Vietnam. The PDPA regime limped along on its own in Afghanistan until it collapsed with the final disintegration of the Soviet Union in 1992. With the Soviets and the socialists out, and the cold war mostly over, the United States lost interest in events in Afghanistan. And what followed was an era of warlordism, with the various warlords of the nation competing for power. Osama bin Laden, by then, had also left Afghanistan. Burhanuddin Rabbani, a Mujahedeen commander, became president of the Islamic State of Afghanistan, although significant warlords continued to control certain parts of the country.[7]

In 1994, Mullah Omar, a Mujahedeen fighter, moved from Pakistan to Afghanistan and founded the Taliban. His followers were called *Talibs*, and they intended to end the warlordism in Afghanistan through a strict application of Islamic law. They quickly captured Kandahar and then, in

1995, they marched on Kabul. After some initial setbacks, the Taliban (with military support from Pakistan and financial support from Saudi Arabia) seized Kabul and then founded what they called the Islamic Emirate of Afghanistan. They imposed a strict interpretation of Islamic law on the people of the country—or at least on those areas they controlled.

In opposition, several enemies of the Taliban pulled their disparate forces together to form a military force commonly known as the Northern Alliance. This Northern Alliance was made up of Tajiks, Uzbeks, Pashtuns, and even a large number of defected Taliban soldiers. All agreed to fight under the direction of the exiled Afghan king, Zahir Shah.

The civil war (fought between the Taliban and the Northern Alliance) was particularly bloody. The Taliban used terror and murder in their attempts to control northern and western Afghanistan, and to impose onto the Afghan people their brand of Islamic law. By 2001, the Taliban, with the assistance of Pakistan, had succeeded in controlling almost all of Afghanistan. The Northern Alliance continued to exist, but their power was confined to the northeastern corner of the country.

Osama bin Laden formed al-Qaeda in the late 1980s to assist the Mujahedeen in their fight against the Soviet occupation of Afghanistan, but the infighting and warlordism of Afghanistan had disillusioned him a great deal. He then moved his operation to eastern Afghanistan, where he began training fighters, importing weapons, and plotting international terrorism. Most of his recruits were sent to fight with the Taliban against the Northern Alliance. A smaller number of specialized fighters was retained and enlisted into al-Qaeda.

In late summer 1998, following al-Qaeda attacks on several US embassies in east Africa, Bill Clinton ordered a series of missile strikes on al-Qaeda and Taliban training camps in Afghanistan. Clinton also insisted that the Taliban capture bin Laden and turn him over to the United States for prosecution. In each case, the Taliban refused the demands. The Clinton administration followed up with several CIA operations into Afghanistan to kill or capture bin Laden. Several times these CIA operatives were near success, but they did not receive orders from the White House to proceed with bin Laden's capture.

In August 2001, the new administration of George W. Bush presented the Taliban with an ultimatum: either surrender bin Laden (and other al-Qaeda operatives) or the United States would begin aiding anti-Taliban groups—particularly the Northern Alliance. This Northern Alliance had talked of democracy, and its leaders had even signed the Woman's Rights Declaration. A large group of Afghan civilians (those considered the Taliban to be oppressive) escaped from several Taliban-held areas for the north, and the protection of the Northern Alliance. To Americans, and their leaders in Washington, the Taliban in Afghanistan were suppressing a young democracy with the bludgeon of Islamic fundamentalism.

While these events were taking place in Afghanistan, and immediately following the September 11 attacks in the United States, President George W. Bush sent a warning to Saddam that the United States would undertake military action if UN inspectors were not allowed to continue their inspections of Iraqi sites. Through 2002 and into 2003, President Bush insisted that Saddam comply with several United Nations Security Council Resolutions that required weapons inspections—and to bring an end to Iraq's production of weapons of mass destruction (WMDs). As early as 1999, UN weapons inspectors made it clear that they had found evidence that Saddam was manufacturing WMDs—clandestinely, at various places throughout Iraq. In late 2002, UN weapons inspectors, however, finally had to admit that despite their best efforts and assumptions, they had found no WMDs. They did, however, mistakenly identify two mobile weapons laboratories as WMD-manufacturing facilities.[8]

Iraq had agreed to these weapons inspections, mostly in accordance with UN Security Council Resolution 1441. As part of that agreement, Iraq was required to submit a report to the UN Security Council. In the report (that spanned nearly 12,000 pages) the Iraqi government stated unequivocally that it had no WMDs. Almost immediately, the UN sent its lead weapons inspector, Hans Blix, to Iraq. Blix reported (to the surprise of many) that Iraq was cooperating fully with the inspections.

Through 2002, the bombing of Iraq by U.S. and British war planes increased considerably, and by fall of that year the bombing had become a full-on air offensive. In October, seventy-five U.S. Senators were told by the Bush administration that Iraq had the ability to attack the eastern seaboard of the United States with WMDs. A few months later, on

February 5, 2003, Colin Powell told the UN Security Council that Iraq was hiding its WMDs, and that Iraq was prepared (or quickly preparing) to launch these weapons against the United States if given the opportunity. The Senate, then, voted to approve a Joint Resolution that gave the Bush administration the legal basis for an invasion of Iraq—ostensibly to find and destroy Saddam's WMDs.

Years later, Powell admitted that his statements before the UN were inaccurate, even "deliberately misleading." George W. Bush, after he left office, stated that his "biggest regret," as president, was "the intelligence failure in Iraq."[9]

In the growing conflict in Afghanistan, the primary figure in the Northern Alliance was Ahmad Shah Massoud. Massoud was a Tajik Sunni Muslim from northern Afghanistan who might best be described as an Afghani warlord—a member of the Mujahedeen, who had fought against the ten-year Soviet occupation. Just two days prior to the 9/11 attacks, Massoud was assassinated (most likely on orders from al-Qaeda) by two Algerian suicide bombers.[10]

The events of September 11, 2001, are well known. Nineteen Arab men hijacked four commercial passenger airliners. The hijackers were all members of al-Qaeda's Hamburg cell. They intentionally crashed two of the airliners into the Twin Towers of the World Trade Centers in New York City, killing all on board and over 2,000 people in the buildings. Both buildings collapsed. The hijackers crashed a third plane into the Pentagon in Washington, D.C. A fourth plane was forced down into a field in southwest Pennsylvania. No one on board any of the flights survived. The total deaths, including the hijackers, were tallied at just under 3,000.

The Bush administration immediately demanded that the Taliban turn over Osama bin Laden (who was suspected of orchestrating the attacks), expel al-Qaeda from Afghanistan, and shut down all terrorist bases in the country. The Taliban in Afghanistan ignored the Bush ultimatum, only responding by insisting that the United States provide proof that al-Qaeda was involved in the attacks. The Bush administration did not respond, considering the Taliban's request for proof to be little more than a delaying tactic.

The Bush team, headed by Secretary of Defense Donald Rumsfeld and General Tommy Franks, decided that the U.S. invasion of Afghanistan should be immediate. On September 26, just two weeks following the 9/11 attacks, the United States sent into Afghanistan a tactical special forces team that quickly linked up with the Northern Alliance.

Within days, the United States (with the assistance of forces from the United Kingdom) officially launched an invasion of Afghanistan. The offensive was designated Operation Enduring Freedom. The Americans and British were later joined by other counties, and the invasion officially became a NATO operation. The United States and its allies (including the Northern Alliance) quickly pushed the Taliban out of Afghanistan. However, most of the important members of the Taliban and al-Qaeda avoided capture, escaping into the nearby mountains.

In Iraq, in March 2002, Hans Blix again insisted that there was no evidence of WMDs in Iraq, but he also added that Iraq (and Saddam) had stopped cooperating with the inspection process. The Bush administration announced that all diplomatic channels had failed and that the coalition (a "coalition of the willing" as Bush called it) would proceed to remove all WMDs from Iraq. The Bush administration then advised the UN weapons inspectors to leave Iraq immediately.

In December 2001, the situation in Afghanistan took a turn, although the Bush administration was looking the other way—toward Iraq. At a conference in Germany, Hamid Karzai was named by a group of prominent Afghan figures to head the Afghan government. As a young man, Karzai had worked as a fundraiser for the Mujahedeen. When the United States invaded, and the Taliban government was removed, Karzai rose to become a prominent figure in Afghan politics. He was elected to govern Afghanistan for only six months. Then, in 2004, he won a general election for a five-year term, and then again in 2009. His two terms ended in September 2014. Under Karzai's government, Afghanistan was officially known as the Islamic Republic of Afghanistan.

In August 2001, NATO officially joined the fight in Afghanistan, but the United States split its forces on the ground: part fought with NATO, while another part remained under US command and outside of NATO's control. In September 2002, Taliban leader Mullah Omar reorganized and combined the anti-American and anti-NATO forces and launched an insurgency.[11]

In August 2003, NATO assumed control of all operations in Afghanistan. The force had grown to a coalition of some 46 countries, all under U.S. command. By 2006, a multinational coalition had begun to replace US troops on the ground, although the United States (along with the British, Dutch, Norwegian, and French) continued to supply air support. Local Taliban troops were strongest through this period. NATO forces, however, achieved several tactical victories in battles against the Taliban. In summer 2006, the Canadians fought the Taliban at the Battle of Panjwaii. And that same year, the Canadians fought the Taliban at Operation Falcon Summit.[12]

In the first few years of the war, the enemy was formidable. They could expect to field a force of about 10,000 men. Fewer than 3,000 of these, however, could be considered well-trained, full-time Afghan insurgents. By 2007, that dynamic changed. In that year, foreign fighters began to slip into Afghanistan, mostly from Pakistan, Chechnya, the several Arab states, and even Turkey. A few Uyghurs from western China were also included. These insurgents were reportedly more fanatical and better trained than the Afghan insurgents.[13]

In Iraq, the plans for that invasion were set in motion, but here (as in Korea and Vietnam) there was no real exit strategy, no plan for withdrawal, and not even any real objectives for the coming war itself. The joint resolution passed by Congress called for Saddam's removal from power and replacement with a democratic government. But would the United States become an occupying force? In a democratic system, would the majority Shiites govern the minority Sunnis, when the Sunnis had dominated the nation's politics for nearly 1,400 years? There would, of course, be opposition. Would that opposition be strong? How would it be handled? It seemed that no one had considered any of these questions. United Kingdom's Tony Blair jumped on board immediately to become a leader among "the coalition of the willing." But almost as quickly, the UN's Kofi Annan declared the operation illegal.

On March 20, 2003, the invasion of Iraq began—and again, there was no official declaration of war from Congress. The attack (which was a surprise) was code named "Operation Iraqi Freedom," and led by U.S.

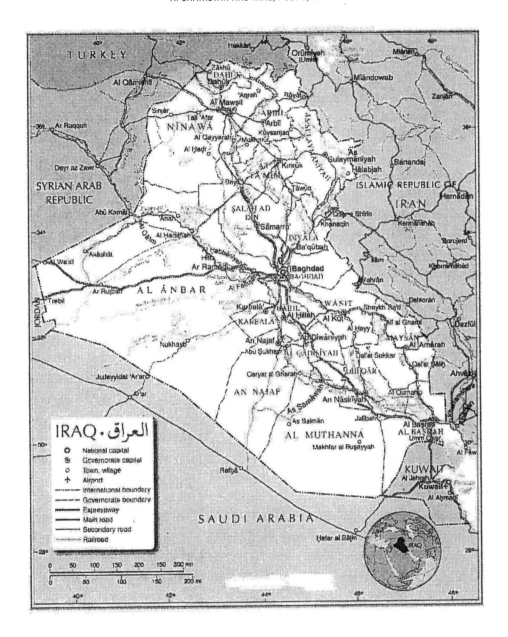

General Tommy Franks.[14] By some accounts, the CIA had been on the ground in Iraq since summer 2002, preparing for a possible invasion, and organizing the Kurds (American allies living in northern Iraq) to be the northern front of an American attack. The first American attack came from Kuwait in the south.[15] Bush's "coalition of the willing" included forces from some forty nations that provided everything from troops to security. The United States, in control at all high levels, provided the vast majority of the soldiers, nearly 250,000. The UK contributed some 45,000 solders, and the Kurds provided about 70,000.

The war itself was generally uneventful, often described as quick and decisive. Unlike the Iraqi forces of the Gulf War in 1991, the Iraqi army of 2003 was eager to take advantage of America's desire to move quickly toward Baghdad. As the U.S. forces moved quickly, the Iraqis reformed behind the U.S. soldiers using fighters dressed in civilian clothes. The strategy surprised American soldiers, but in the end, the strategy was of little military significance. In the south, coalition forces launched massive air strikes, and that allowed coalition troops to capture and control the enemy's oil fields and ports. One major battle was for control of the Talil Airfield. The U.S. Army 3rd Infantry Division crushed Iraqi forces entrenched around the airfield. From there, the 3rd Infantry (supported by the 101st Airborne Division) moved further north. A severe sand storm slowed their progress, but they eventually secured the bridges over the Euphrates River and moved into Baghdad. Farther south, the 1st Marine Division pushed toward the outskirts of Baghdad and prepared to enter the city. Baghdad fell on April 9, just twenty days after the invasion began. Saddam, of course, fell from power, following a twenty-four-year stretch of oppressive rule. U.S. forces occupied the Ba'ath party government buildings along with Saddam's palaces. What followed was one of the most iconic images of the war.

On that same day, April 9, a bronze statue of Saddam was pulled over by what was described as "anti-Saddam Iraqi civilians." The message was clear to America and Americans who watched television: a coalition led by the United States had toppled a tyrant and liberated his people from an unspeakable tyranny. But it became quickly clear that that was not exactly what had happened.

The invasion did produce an outpouring of gratitude for the invaders—the Great American Liberators. But the invasion had also produced a huge power vacuum in Iraq that had, in turn, produced extreme lawlessness, and the United States military refused to intervene. It began with the looting of government buildings, and then a general rise in the city's crime rate. But the crimes quickly expanded to include the loss of nearly 600,000 tons of U.S. ordinance, most of which managed to make its way into the Iraqi insurgency. In the invasion, itself, some 139 U.S. soldiers were killed. Over 9,000 Iraqi soldiers lost their lives in that few days of fighting. Perhaps as many as 4,000 Iraqi civilians were also killed.[16]

In Afghanistan, it was clear by 2007 that a surge in troop strength was necessary if NATO and coalition forces were to be victorious and end the war. Policy makers in Washington feared that to expand the war incrementally might bring about a quagmire similar to Vietnam, perhaps even similar to the Soviet adventure in Afghanistan in the 1980s. But it was finally determined that a big push was necessary if the United States and its allies were to turn Afghanistan into a victory. The problem was, of course, Iraq. The United States was putting its most aggressive foot forward in Iraq, and the situation in Afghanistan was being relegated to a secondary position. But the Bush administration (nearly at the end of its eight-year tenure) began to see a need to focus on the situation in Afghanistan. In 2008, U.S. troop strength in Afghanistan increased dramatically, from about 26,000 to nearly 53,000. That same year, the British increased their contingency to 4,500.[17]

U.S. and Pakistani relations suffered in this period. Through most of the cold war, Pakistan had been something of a reluctant ally, a counterweight to Chinese and even India's influence in South Asia. American special forces attacked and killed a number of Taliban militants inside Pakistan, and the Pakistani government complained bitterly about America's infringement on their sovereign territory. Despite these tensions, the U.S. began using remotely piloted drone aircraft along Pakistan's border regions in an attempt to eliminate Taliban leaders who were hiding in the area. By 2009, U.S. drone attacks had increased dramatically.

By the end of 2008, it became apparent that al-Qaeda and the Taliban were no longer a unified force fighting NATO and the American-led coalition in Afghanistan. It was determined that Pakistani forces on the east side of the Afghan border, together with coalition forces on the west side, were capable of guarding against militants fleeing to safety into Pakistan.

In Iraq, despite the difficulties on the ground, the Iraqi army was defeated—again. Add to that the symbolic destruction of Saddam's statue, and it was time for President George W. Bush to take a victory lap. On

May 1, 2003, he landed on the aircraft carrier *Abraham Lincoln,* just a few miles west of San Diego, and delivered what has become known as his "Mission Accomplished" speech. Under a large banner that declared just that, "Mission Accomplished," the president spoke to the sailors and airmen of the *Abraham Lincoln* and declared victory in Iraq, victory over Saddam. To the American people, that meant the war was over, victory was at hand. It was not.

It seemed only a minor problem that Saddam remained at large. By most accounts, however, he was disarmed and would be picked up by coalition forces soon enough. But there were also substantial pockets of resistance in Iraq, forces left behind by the rapid movement north of the coalition forces. Almost immediately, there was a burst of attacks against coalition forces, particularly in a region known as the "Sunni Triangle." This resistance had its origins among Ba'ath party loyalists, but it quickly expanded to include religious radicals and other Iraqis angered by what they saw as the coalition occupation. These insurgents used old-style guerrilla warfare tactics that were extremely difficult to counter. They often employed suicide attacks, improvised explosive devices (IEDs), car bombs, and snipers. They were well armed with small arms, usually assault rifles. And they were adept at attacking the petroleum, water, and electrical infrastructure of the country.

The objective for the coalition nations in Iraq was to work with the United Nations to establish a stable democratic Iraq, capable of defending itself against any and all opposition forces. The coalition forces (along with the United Nations) recognized that there were several internal divisions in Iraq, and there was a hope that a new democratic government would be able to rise above those divisions—hopefully through some sort of coalition government.[18]

Again, there was no plan for the future of Iraq. There was only hope, and a great deal of confidence in the democratic process. But the United States had learned, most directly from the Vietnam experience, that democracy does not work well in the Developing World; that a working, successful democracy takes years, decades, perhaps even centuries to work out its kinks and evolve into a working plan that includes all sides and opinions. In Iraq, democracy (a brand new governmental system) was expected to solve a series of serious problems just days following the fall of an oppressive dictator.

Until a permanent democratic government could be put in place in Iraq, President Bush, in May 2003, appointed L. Paul Bremer to head the Coalition Provisional Authority (CPA). Bremer immediately issued an executive order excluding all members of the Ba'ath party from any position in the Iraqi government. This proved to be a disaster. Nearly 100,000 Iraqis immediately lost their jobs, including some 40,000 school teachers who had joined the Ba'ath party only for the purpose of keeping their teaching positions. Bremer served as head of the CPA until July 2004, when the organization was finally dissolved.[19]

Also formed in 2003 was an organization designed to capture and eliminate the highest-ranking members of the Ba'ath party. That summer, a raid by members of the 101st Airborne Division killed Saddam's two sons and one of his grandsons. In December, Saddam, himself, was captured near Takrit. To much of the world, Saddam's capture marked a final victory for the coalition forces—the head of the snake had finally been cut off. The U.S. government began the long process of training a new Iraqi security force. The United States also promised $20 billion in reconstruction funds. Iraqi oil revenue was used by the U.S. government to rebuild much of the nation's infrastructure and its destroyed school system. In early 2004, there was a lull in the violence and an assumption that the situation in Iraq had cooled.

But it had not. As the year progressed, violence increased. Foreign fighters from around the Middle East (mostly in opposition to what was perceived as an the American occupation) began to make their way into Iraq, and they coalesced around Abu Musab al-Zarqawi, a Palestinian Arab Sunni. The Bush administration had tried unsuccessfully to use Zarqawi to connect the dots between al-Qaeda and the 9/11 attacks.[20]

Throughout 2004, control of the war in Iraq changed from the coalition forces to the new Iraqi Security force. The insurgency responded immediately with a series of massive bombs that killed hundreds of Iraqi civilians and policemen. In addition, an organized Sunni force began to grow in strength throughout Iraq. They were countered by a growing Shia army that launched a series of attacks on coalition forces. The most significant battle of the war, the First Battle of Falluja, occurred in April—following the murder of several U.S. private military contractors. The Second Battle of Falluja occurred in November and lasted nearly fifty days.

America's role as coalition leader was compromised when abuses and torture of Iraqi soldiers and civilians at Abu Ghraib prison in Iraq were reported in the international media. First reported in *The New Yorker* magazine by journalist Seymour Hersh, and then by the popular television news program *60 Minutes*, the events at Abu Ghraib damaged America's moral justification for the occupation of Iraq. In the eyes of many people throughout the world, especially the Iraqis, the United States was both occupier and oppressor.[21]

In January of the next year (2005), the Iraqis elected the Iraqi Transitional Government and drew up a constitution. In April, an insurgent force attacked U.S. forces at Abu Ghraib prison in one of the largest military events since the Vietnam War. The Battle of Abu Ghraib was followed by a Sunni insurgency against Iraqi Shias that lasted the remainder of the year.

As early as 1999, an organization known as Jama'at al-Tawhid wal-Jihad was formed by al-Zarqawi. This organization pledged its allegiance to al-Qaeda and Osama bin Laden, and participated in the Iraqi insurgency against the March 2003 invasion of Iraq. This organization then joined forces with other Sunni groups to form the Mujahideen Shura Council. In August 2011 (following the outbreak of the Syrian civil war against the Syrian regime of Bashar al-Assad) Abu Bakr al-Baghdadi formed from this and other groups the "Islamic State of Iraq and the Levant," or ISIL. The name of the organization is often translated into ISIS, or the Islamic State of Iraq and Syria. And the American press has often used the acronym IS. In some circles, it is also known as Daesh, which is a crude Arabic acronym for the "Islamic State in Iraq and Syria." In June 2014, al-Baghdadi proclaimed ISIS to be a worldwide caliphate. As a caliphate, ISIS (and al-Baghdadi) claims religious, political, and military authority over all Muslims. At the beginning of 2016, ISIS had succeeded in controlling large amounts of territory in Iraq and Syria, with population estimates at somewhere between three and eight million people. ISIS also claims affiliates in parts of North Africa, Libya, Egypt, Saudi Arabia, Yemen, Nigeria, South Asia, and Afghanistan. The United

States has estimated that ISIS fighters number about 31,000 soldiers. ISIS claims more—about 40,000.

ISIS's success has prompted the United States to renew military action in Iraq, but only in an advisory and air support capacity. In early 2016, Russia entered the war against ISIS, but in support of the Syrian regime. Russia's actions complicated the American effort, which included a war against both ISIS and the sitting Syrian government of al-Assad. As the 2016 election year progressed in the United States, several presidential candidates (particularly on the Republican side of the campaign) insisted that the United States should attack ISIS with all its military might in order to bring an end the ISIS threat.

ISIS is officially designated as a terrorist group by the United Nations, and most Muslims reject the ISIS brand of Islam. Today, over sixty countries are officially waging war against ISIS.[22]

In January 2009, Barack Obama replaced George W. Bush as president of the United States. During his campaign, Obama often pledged to end U.S. involvement in the Middle East. Opposition candidates, however, (particularly Senator John McCain from Arizona, who ran that year on the Republican ticket) complained bitterly that Obama's call for a specific date for a U.S. withdrawal would embolden America's enemies in the Middle East, that they would hold the line in anticipation of a U.S. withdrawal in order to build strength in the region.

America's withdrawal from Iraq was both anti-climactic and barely noticed. Throughout the month of August 2010, the United States had been slowly sending convoys of troops south to Kuwait. By the end of the month, the last U.S. combat brigades left Iraq. But that did not mean that the U.S. adventure in the Middle East was at an end. Some 50,000 U.S. troops remained in Iraq as Advise and Assist Brigades, designed to provide support for the Iraqi military. But even these troops were scheduled to depart by the end of 2011. The new Iraqi government has purchased over $13 billion in U.S. weapons and stepped up its training of Iraqi soldiers. In order to give the new Iraqi government an air of legitimacy, the UN lifted all restrictions on Iraq. Officially, the last U.S. troops withdrew from Iraq in mid-December 2011. What followed was sectarian violence in Iraq—mostly while the world waited for the Iraqi government to form. In summer 2014, President Obama announced the return of U.S. forces to Iraq, but this time only as aerial support, and only in an effort to halt the advances of ISIS and to bring stability to Iraq.

The situation in Afghanistan had not abated. In response to Republican calls for an increase in troops, Obama announced that he would send 17,000 additional U.S. troops to Afghanistan. Several U.S. generals found that number lacking, particularly generals Stanley McChrystal and David McKiernan. By December, Obama had jumped the number again, this time to 30,000.[23] One result of this "surge," as it was called, was that large antiwar protests arose in several major cities throughout the United States. Antiwar leaders emerged. And Americans began to discuss the relationship between America's involvement in Afghanistan and the piecemeal expansion of the war in Vietnam. The word "quagmire" began to be bantered around in the press. And it was determined that the Taliban had as many as 25,000 fighters—perhaps as many as they had in 2005.

In 2009, an election was scheduled for Afghanistan. Despite attempts by the Taliban to disrupt the elections, it was determined that the process was generally fair. Both candidates, Hamid Karzai and Abdullah Abdullah, declared victory, although Karzai was eventually declared the winner by fifty-four percent of the vote—enough to avoid a runoff.

The year 2010 brought a number of peace initiatives, but the year also brought an increase in the insurgents' use of IEDs (Improvised Explosive Devices). By the end of the year, the number of coalition soldiers injured by these devices increased dramatically. The U.S. surge continued into 2010, with another 48,000 U.S. soldiers to be in place by summer.[24]

On May 2, 2011, President Obama announced to the American people that Osama bin Laden had been killed. The covert operation was conducted inside Pakistan by the CIA and US Navy SEALS. It seemed that United States had finally vanquished its foe. But it was made clear to the nation that by 2011, bin Laden was, himself, no longer a threat to the United States, and that al-Qaeda was mostly disarmed and could no longer launch any direct attacks on the United States.

Then on June 11, Obama announced that the United States would withdraw 10,000 troops from Afghanistan, and an additional 23,000 soldiers would be withdrawn in summer 2012. Other NATO countries also began withdrawing troops. Taliban attacks, however, continued.

The Afghan government re-formed the Northern Alliance to oppose any return of the Taliban to power. In May 2012 (one year after bin Laden's death) Afghan President Karsai and U.S. President Obama signed an agreement in Kabul.[25] The agreement called for a long-term relationship between the United States and Afghanistan, and it designated Afghanistan a "major non-NATO ally." By the middle of 2013, all NATO and coalition combat missions were turned over to Afghanistan, and all NATO and coalition combat troops were to be removed from Afghanistan by the end of 2014. NATO would then assume only a supporting role. By June 2013, the transfer of military and security responsibilities was completed.[26] Almost 10,000 U.S. troops were to remain in Afghanistan for two years in support of counterterrorism operations. By the end of 2016, a "normal embassy presence" was all that remained of America's involvement in Afghanistan.[27]

The United States has seldom been at peace in the post–World War II era. At first, in Korea, the United States fought to maintain its role against the forces of world Communism and tyranny, to contain communism. In Vietnam, the United States tried, almost desperately, to convey that same message to the American people and to the world. That plan, however, generally failed, and the forces of world Communism were not abated; by some accounts, they were even strengthened. For almost twenty years, the United States was gun-shy, often unwilling to get involved in international military events for fear of being drawn into another quagmire, another war fought on the wrong side of history. The United States had become what China called a "Paper Tiger." The Gulf War, however, changed all that. With one giant swoop, the United States (at the head of a victorious multi-national force) placed itself, again, into the role of world leader, liberator, and the savior of the weak against tyranny. From then on, the United States continued in that role, the leader of the Free World. Certainly, many Americans were not sure exactly what that meant in the 1990s, but, they believed, it was a good place to be.

The events of the Iraq War (and the corresponding events in Afghanistan) are often derided as unwarranted, unnecessary, even illegal. But the United States brought an end to tyranny, and it transplanted its own brand of democracy into the Middle East. That may prove to be more of a problem than a solution for the future of the region, but at least the United States (and its coalition partners) set an objective and fulfilled it.

In the post–World War II period, the United States did not go to war to preserve liberty or democracy—the concepts and promises for which it often threatens war. At the same time, the United States did not fight to defend areas that figured prominently into its world military strategy. In all its wars, the United States fought to maintain something that is dearer to it in the post–World War II world than anything else: world respect and world leadership. Certainly, the containment of Communism in Korea and Vietnam was the U.S. government's stated purpose in those wars; and the removal of a dangerous destabilizing force in the oil-rich Middle East was the official reason for America's involvement in both Gulf wars. But since World War II, the United States has sought to be the leader of the world. And to maintain that role it has been necessary to show the world that if they are attacked by Communists, the United States will use its powerful military force to come to the rescue. During the cold war the United States and the Soviets, above all else, vied for that role on the world scene by supporting small nations against incursions from the other side. To the victor, of course, went the spoils: world leadership. The question now is whether or not world leadership is worth having: Is it still important to be the world's greatest military power, as it was so important after World War II? Will the nations that lead the world be the world economic leaders rather than the military, political, or cultural leaders? And if so, can the United States maintain its role as an economic leader in the world, or will it lose that war and fall to the wayside? Having achieved its post–World War II goal of world leader, the United States must reevaluate its place in the new world system in the next century.

NOTES

CHAPTER 1

1. Harry S. Truman, *1945. Year of Decisions*, vol. 1 of *Memoirs* (1955; reprint, New York: Signet, 1965), 479.

2. See Arthur Krock, *Memoirs: Sixty Years on the Firing Line* (New York: Funk and Wagnalls, 1968), appendix; see also, Clark Clifford, *Counsel to the President* (New York: Random House, 1991), 124.

3. "X," "The Sources of Soviet Conduct," *Foreign Affairs* (July, 1947), 566–82. See also, George Kennan, *American Diplomacy, 1900–1950* (Chicago, Ill.: University of Chicago, 1951), 89–106.

4. Alfred D. Chandler, Jr., Louis Galambos, *et. al.*, ed. *The Papers of Dwight D. Eisenhower* (Baltimore: Johns Hopkins, 1970—), VIII, 1660.

5. *Foreign Relations of the United States*. 1950, I, 237–39. [Hereafter cited as FRUS, followed by year, volume and page]. NSC-68 was first published in *Naval War College Review* (May-June, 1975), 51–108. George Kennan and Charles Bohlen disagreed with the belligerent wording of NSC-68; John Lewis Gaddis, *The Cold War: A New History* (New York: Penguin, 2005), 164–65, 170.

6. See Dean Acheson, *Present at the Creation* (New York: W.W. Norton, 1969), 355–58; Gaddis Smith, *Dean Acheson* (New York: Cooper Square, 1972), 175–76; *Documents on International Affairs, 1949–1950* (New York: Read Books, 1953), 61–66.

7. Dean Acheson, *The Korean Wa*r (New York: W.W. Norton, 1969), 40n.

8. George Kennan, *Memoirs: 1925–1950* (Boston, Mass.: Little, Brown, 1972), 485.

9. Sergi N. Goncharov, John W. Lewis, and Xue Litai, *Uncertain Partners: Stalin, Mao and the Korean War* (Palo Alto, Calif.: Stanford, 1993). See excerpts in *Time*, 18 July, 1994.

10. Nikita Khrushchev (with an Introduction, Commentary, and Notes by Edward Crankshaw), *Khrushchev Remembers* (Boston, Mass.: Little, Brown, 1970), 370.

11. Robert Ferrell, *Harry S. Truman: A Life* (Columbia, Mo.: Missouri, 1994), 322; Robert J. Donovan, *Tumultuous Years: The Presidency of Harry S. Truman, 1949–1953* (New York: W.W. Norton, 1982), 197.

12. Ernest May, *Lessons of the Past: The Uses and Misuses of History in American Foreign Policy* (New York: Oxford, 1973), 70.

13. *FRUS*, 1950, VII, 157–61.

14. Acheson, *Korean War*, 21.

15. Harry S. Truman, *1946–1952: Years of Trial and Hope*, vol. 2 of *Memoirs* (1955, reprint, New York: Signet, 1965), 382.

16. Donovan, *Tumultuous Years*, 197.

17. Clifford, *Counsel*, 274.

18. Truman, *Memoirs,* II, 379.

19. Truman, *Memoirs*, II, 378–79. Also quoted in William E. Pemberton, *Harry S. Truman: Fair Dealer and Cold Warrior* (Boston, Mass.: Twayne, 1989), 136.

20. Truman, *Memoirs*, II, 379.

21. *FRUS*, 1950, VII, 211.

CHAPTER 2

1. Truman, *Memoirs,* II, 383.

2. Quoted in Allen Whiting, *China Crosses the Yalu: The Decision to Enter the Korean War* (Palo Alto, Calif.: Stanford, 1960), 58.

3. Donovan, *Tumultuous Years*, 121.

4. Robert Ferrell, ed., *The Eisenhower Diaries* (New York: W.W Norton, 1981), 175.

5. *Public Papers of the Presidents, Harry S. Truman, 1945–1953* (Washington, D.C.: USGPO, 1961–1966), 1950, 504.

6. May, *Lessons of the Past*, 71.

7. Kennan, *Memoirs*, I, 489, 500.

8. Quoted in Clay Blair, *The Forgotten War: America in Korea, 1950–1953* (New York: Anchor, 1987), 1987), 168.

9. *FRUS*, 1950, VII, 768–69.

10. Acheson, *Korean War*, 55.

11. *FRUS*, 1950, 953; Truman, *Memoirs*, II, 417.

12. *PP, Truman, 1950*, 672–73.

13. *FRUS*, 1950, VII, 953. For Truman's analysis of these decisions, see Truman, *Memoirs*, II, 426–27.

14. *FRUS*, 1950, VII, 1055–57.

15. *FRUS*, 1950, VII, 1058.

16. Quoted in Acheson, *Present at the Creation*, 465. A portion of this quote is also in Acheson, *Korean War*, 67.

17. *FRUS*, 1950, VII, 1097–98.

18. *FRUS*, 1950, VII, 1107–10.

19. Omar Bradley (with Clay Blair), *A General's Life* (New York: Touchstone, 1983), 587.

20. Acheson, *Korean War*, 68.

21. Quoted in Richard E. Neustadt, *Presidential Power and the Modern Presidents: The Politics of Leadership from Roosevelt to Reagan* (first published in 1960, New York: Free Press, 1990), 107–108. For Truman's own analysis of these events, see Truman, *Memoirs,* II, 395–510.

CHAPTER 3

1. *FRUS*, 1950, VII, 1237–38.

2. Quoted in Blair, *Forgotten War*, 465.

3. Acheson. *Korean War*, 76; Truman, *Memoirs*, II, 441. Truman's entire discussion of the decision is in pages 438–44.

4. *FRUS*, 1950, VII, 1279.

5. Truman, *Memoirs*, II, 450.

6. *FRUS*, 1950, VII, 1320–22; Truman, *Memoirs*, II, 447.

7. Truman, *Memoirs*, II, 489.

8. Truman, *Memoirs*, II, 500.

9. Truman, *Memoirs*, II, 499–501

10. *FRUS*, 1951, VII, 298.

11. Acheson, *Korean War*, 103.

12. Truman, *Memoirs*, II, 502.

13. Truman, *Memoirs*, II, 437.

14. Thomas C. Reeves, *The Life and Times of Joe McCarthy* (Lanham, Md.: Madison, 1997), 370.

15. *FRUS*, 1951, VI, 37, 47–52.

16. *FRUS*, 1951, VI, 33–63.

17. *FRUS*, 1951, VII, 587.

CHAPTER 4

1. Quoted in Blair, *Forgotten War*, 939.

2. Mathew B. Ridgway, *The Korean War* (New York: De Capo, 1986), 192–93. Ridgway's proposal on desegregation of the military was sent to Washington on May 12, 1951. See also, Bernard C. Nalty, *Strength for the Fight: A History of Black Americans in the Military* (New York: Free Press 1986), 255–69.

3. Truman, *Memoirs*, II, 515.

4. Acheson, *Korean War*, 125. See also, Acheson, *Present at the Creation*, 536–37.

5. Acheson, *Korean War*, 124–25.

6. Following the collapse of the Soviet Union in the early 1990s, records surfaced that seemed to show that indeed some U.S. soldiers may have been shipped to Soviet prisons. The number, however, was probably insignificant.

7. Quoted in Stephen Ambrose, *Eisenhower: The President* (New York: Touchstone, 1984), 107.

8. *Cong. Rec.*, 82d Cong., 1ˢᵗ sess., pt. 5: 3600.

CHAPTER 5

1. Maxwell Taylor, *Swords and Ploughshares* (New York: W.W. Norton, 1972), 135–36.

2. *PP, Roosevelt, 1944–1945*, 556–65.

3. Michael Charlton interview with Archimedes Patti (late 1970s) in Michael Charlton and Anthony Moncrieff, ed., *Many Reasons Why: The American Involvement in Vietnam* (New York: Hill and Wang, 1989), 9.

4. Archimedes Patti, *Why Vietnam: Prelude to America's Albatross* (Berkeley: University of California, 1981), 251–52.

5. Charlton interview with Patti, *Many Reasons Why*, 13–14.

6. This is quoted in a number of places. See Jean Lacouture, *Ho Chi Minh: A Political Biography* (New York: Random House, 1968), 153. See also, Stanley Karnow, *Vietnam: A History* (New York: Penguin, 1983), 153; and David Halberstam, *Ho* (Lanham, Md.: Rowman and Littlefield, 1971), 83–84.

7. Patti, *Why Vietnam?*, 393.

8. Vo Nguyen Giap, *Dien Bien Phu* (Hanoi: Foreign Language Publishing House, 1964), 31.

9. *FRUS*, 1950, VI, 747.

10. *FRUS*, 1950, VI, 745.

11. *FRUS*, 1950, VI, 238.

12. *FRUS*, 1950, VI, 711. See also, Allan W. Cameron, ed., *Viet-Nam Crisis: A Documentary History* (Ithaca, N.Y.: Cornell, 1971), I, 141–45.

13. *PP, Eisenhower, 1954*, 245–55.

14. Mathew Ridgway, *Soldier* (New York: Harper and Brothers, 1956), 275–78. See also, George McT. Kahin, *Intervention: How America Became Involved in Vietnam* (New York: Anchor 1986), 46.

15. Ridgway, *Soldier*, 278.

16. Phillippe Devillers and Jean Lacouture Devillers, *End of a War: Indochina, 1954* (New York, Preager, 1969), 123.

CHAPTER 6

1. Kahin, *Intervention*, 89.

2. George Herring, *America's Longest War: The United States and Vietnam, 1950–1975,* 2nd ed. (New York: Knopf, 1986), 55–56.

3. *PP, Kennedy, 1962,* 807.

4. *Vital Speeches* (August 1, 1956), 618.

5. David Halberstam, *The Best and the Brightest* (New York: Random House, 1972), 33. See also, Douglas Brinkley, *Dean Acheson: The Cold War Years* (New Haven, Ct.: Yale University Press), 80–92.

6. Lloyd C. Gardner, *Pay Any Price: Lyndon Johnson and the Wars for Vietnam* (Chicago: Chicago, 1995), 52; Halberstam, *Best and the Brightest,* 167–68.

7. *Pentagon Papers*, Gravel Addition, II, 92.

8. Ibid., 167–68.

9. Ibid., 268.

10. Arthur Schlesinger, Jr., *A Thousand Days: John F. Kennedy in the White House* (Boston, Mass.: Houghton Mifflin, 1965), 997–98.

11. Kenneth O'Donnell and David F. Powers, *"Johnny, We Hardly Knew Ye:" Memories of John Fitzgerald Kennedy* (Boston, Mass.: Little, Brown, 1972), 16. See also, Kahin, *Intervention*, 146–47.

CHAPTER 7

1. Quoted in Walter LaFeber, "Introduction," in William Appleman Williams, *et. al.,* eds., *America in Vietnam: A Documentary History* (New York: W.W. Norton, 1985), 215.

2. *Pentagon Papers, New York Times* edition (New York: *New York Times,* 1971), 277–80.

3. Quoted in Williams, *et. al.* eds., "Tonkin Gulf Resolution and Debate," *America in Vietnam*, 237.

4. Quoted in Kahin, *Intervention*, 226.

5. See Robert Alan Goldberg, *Barry Goldwater* (New Haven, Ct.: Yale University Press, 1995), 214–15; Irwin Unger and Debi Unger, *LBJ: A Life* (New York: Wiley, 1999), 321.

6. See McNamara's sortie numbers in *Pentagon Papers*, Gravel edition, IV, 125–26.

7. Ronald B. Franklin, Jr., *Like Rolling Thunder: The Air War in Vietnam, 1964–1975* (Lanham, Md.: Roman and Littlefield, 2005), 167–71.

8. Memo from Townsend Hoopes to Clark Clifford, in quoted in Larry Berman, *Lyndon Johnson's War: The Road to Stalemate in Vietnam* (New York: W.W. Norton, 1989), 217.

9. *PP, Johnson*, 394–99.

10. *Pentagon Papers*, Gravel Addition, III, 345–54.

11. Ibid., 439–40.

12. Quoted in Doris Kearns Goodwin, *Lyndon Johnson and the American Dream* (New York: St. Martin's, 1976), 251–52.

13. Quoted in George W. Ball, *The Past Has Another Pattern: Memoirs* (New York: W.W. Norton, 1982), 382.

14. Quoted in Kahin, *Intervention*, 339.

15. Quoted in Herring, *America's Longest War*, 178.

16. Quoted in Jonathan Spence, *The Search for Modern China* (New York: W.W. Norton, 1990), 558.

17. *Pentagon Papers, New York Times* edition, 580.

18. Quoted in Berman, *Lyndon Johnson's War*, 93.

19. Quoted in Clifford, *Counsel to the President*, 455.

20. Robert McNamara, *In Retrospect: The Tragedy and Lessons of Vietnam* (New York: Vintage, 1995), 306–309.

21. Lyndon Baines Johnson, *The Vantage Point" Perspectives of the Presidency, 1963–1969* (New York: Holt, Reinhart and Winston, 1971), appendix A. Others in the administration had come to see the war as unwinnable, including Rear Admiral Gene La Rocque, CIA Deputy Director, Richard Helms, and, of course, George Ball, who did not favor a withdrawal from the war but opposed the bombing. See McNamara, *In Retrospect*, 276, 306. See also, Ball, *Past Has Another Pattern*, 404.

CHAPTER 8

1. *Pentagon Papers*, Gravel Edition, VI, 4423.

2. Quoted in James William Gibson, *The Perfect War: The War We Couldn't Lose and How We Did* (New York: Vintage, 1988), 162. For Tet and its significance, see, William J. Duiker, *The Communist Road to Power in Vietnam* (Boulder, Colorado: Westview, 1981), 288–97.

3. William C. Westmoreland, *A Soldier Reports* (New York: Doubleday, 1976), 319.

4. Clifford, *Counsel*, 473.

5. Quoted in David R. Palmer, *Summons of Trumpet: U.S.-Vietnam in Perspective* (San Rafael, Calif., Presidio, 1978), 179; and Palmer, *Readings in Current Military History* (West Point, N.Y.: Department of Military Art, USMA, 1969), 103.

6. Clifford, *Counsel*, 473.

7. Ibid.

8. Polling data cited in Allen J. Matusow, *The Unraveling of America: A History of Liberalism in the 1960s* (New York: Harper, 1984), 391.

9. *Washington Post*, 17 March, 1968.

10. James S. Olson and Randy Roberts, *Where the Domino Fell: America and Vietnam, 1945–1990* (New York: St. Martin's, 1991), 187.

11. Quoted in Walter Isaacson and Evan Thomas, *The Wise Men: Six Friends and the World They Made* (New York: Touchstone, 1986), 690–91.

12. Ibid., 699.

13. Ibid., 700.

14. Ibid., 703.

15. *PP, Johnson,* 1968, 469–76.

16. Quoted in Clifford, *Counsel*, 523.

17. Quoted in Berman, *Lyndon Johnson's War*, 60.

18. Dean Rusk, *As I Saw It* (New York: Norton, 1990), 486.

19. *PP, Nixon*, 1965, 542.

20. Quoted in H.R. Haldeman, *The Ends of Power* (New York: Times Books, 1978), 81.

21. Quoted in George Tindall, *America* (New York: W. W. Norton, 1984), 1403.

22. See Nixon's analysis of all this in Richard Nixon, *In the Arena: A Memoir of Victory, Defeat and Renewal* (New York: Simon and Schuster, 1990), 215–16, 219–20.

23. *PP, Nixon*, 901–99.

24. Quote in Todd, Gitlin, *Years of Hope, Days of Rage* (New York: Bantam, 1987), 378.

25. Henry Kissinger, "The Vietnam Negotiations." *Foreign Affairs* (January 1969), 219.

26. *PP Nixon*, 1970, 405–10.

27. Quoted in Olson and Roberts, *Where the Domino Fell*, 239. See also, "Statement of John Kerry, Vietnam Veterans against the War," in Williams, *et. al.*, eds., *America in Vietnam*, 292–99.

CHAPTER 9

1. Quoted in Karnow, *Vietnam*, 642.

2. Robert Dallek, *Nixon and Kissinger: Partners in Power* (New York: HarperCollins, 2007), 415.

3. Quoted in Richard M. Nixon, *RN: The Memoirs of Richard Nixon* (New York: Grosset and Dunlap, 1978), 718.

4. Henry Kissinger, *White House Years* (Boston, Mass.: Little, Brown, 1979), 1469.

CHAPTER 10

1. *New York Times,* 4 Mar. 1991.

2. The attack was in retaliation for a terrorist bombing of a German disco in which U.S. servicemen were killed. Later evidence has shown that the terrorism was most likely Syrian directed and probably not associated with Ghadafi or Libya.

3. *Newsweek*, 11 March 1991.

4. *New Republic*, 14 Jan. 1991.

5. The quote is by Syrian-born historian Bassam Tibi and is cited in Judith Miller and Laurie Mylroi, *Saddam Hussein and the Crisis in the Gulf* (New York: Three Rivers, 1990), 85.

6. Con Coughlin, *Saddam: King of Terror* (New York: HarperCollins, 2002), 6.

7. Michael Massing, "The Way to War," *New York Review of Books* (28 March 1991), 18. See also, Coughlin, *Saddam*, 255; and Margaret Thatcher, *The Downing Street Years* (New York: HarperCollins, 1993), 817.

8. *US News and World Report*, 20 Aug. 1990.

9. *New Republic*, 3 Sept. 1990.

10. *New York Times*, 4 Aug. 1990.

11. Quoted in *New Republic*, 7 Jan. 1991.

12. A good accounting of the 1968 coup in Iraq is Coughlin, *Saddam*, 66–71.

13. Coughlin, *Saddam*, 72.

14. To the U.S. ambassador to Iraq, April Glaspie (in an interview just a few days before the invasion of Kuwait), Saddam said that U.S.-Iraqi "relations have suffered from various rifts. The worst of these was in 1986 . . . with what was known as Irangate." He then added that mistakes of that sort can "leave a negative effect. . . . Sometimes the effect of an error can be larger than the error itself." See "The Glaspie Transcript: Saddam Meets the U.S. Ambassador," 25 July, 1991, in Micah L.Sifry and Christopher Cerf, ed., *The Gulf Reader* (New York: Three Rivers, 1991), 123. See also, Coughlin, *Saddam*, 250–51.

15. This quote is in several places. See Coughlin, *Saddam*, 247; Miller and Mylroi, *Saddam Hussein*, 12; and the London *Observer*, 21 Oct. 1990.

16. *The Economist*, 29 Sept. 1990. The various quotes are from Saddam's speech of July 17, and from a more detailed letter sent the day before by Saddam to the secretary-general of the Arab League.

17. *Newsweek*, 28 Jan. 1991.

18. *New York Times*, 25 July 1991. Since Tutwiler's widely-analyzed statement, it has been assumed that her reference of U.S. "friend in the Gulf" mean Saudi Arabia. See *Newsweek*, 17 Feb. 1992.

19. "Glaspie Transcript," 122–33.

20. Quoted in Coughlin, *Saddam*, 251. Coughlin cites a *New York Times* article of "late 1990."

21. Walid Khalidi, "Iraq vs. Kuwait: Claims and Counterclaims," in Sifty and Cerf, *Gulf War Reader*, 63.

CHAPTER 11

1. "Glaspie Transcript," 125.

2. Miller and Mylroie, *Saddam Hussein*, 151.

3. "U.S. Senators Chat with Saddam," 12 April 1990, in Sifry and Cerf, *Gulf War Reader*, 119–20.

4. *The Economist*, 29 Sept. 1990.

5. Bob Woodward, "The Commanders," *Newsweek*, 13 May, 1991. The DIA analyst was Pat Lang.

6. Miller and Mylroie, *Saddam Hussein*, 19.

7. *Newsweek*, 28 Jan. 1991.

8. See particularly Bob Woodward, *The Commanders* (New York: Simon and Schuster, 1991), but Powell has been depicted in this vein elsewhere. See Massing, "The Way to War," 17–22. See also, H. Norman Schwarzkopf, *It Doesn't Take a Hero: An Autobiography* (New York, Bantam, 1993), 334.

9. Quoted in *Newsweek*, Gulf War Commemorative edition, spring/summer 1991.

10. Woodward, *Commanders*, 42; *Newsweek,* 13 May 1991.

11. *Newsweek*, 28 Jan. 1991.

12. Woodward, *Commanders*, 26–61. Although Woodward does not name his sources for this information, it seems clear (and *Newsweek* and others agreed) that Powell was his chief source for this material. See *Newsweek*, 13 May 1991.

13. *New York Times*, 9 Aug. 1990.

14. *Washington Post*, 19 Aug. 1990.

15. Massing, "The Way to War," 20.

16. *New York Times*, 9 Nov. 1990.

17. *New York Times*, 30 Nov. 1990. It was UN Resolution 678.

18. *Newsweek*, 21 Jan. 1991.

19. *New York Times*, 10 Jan. 1991.

20. Ibid.

21. *Newsweek*, 13 May 1991.

22. *New York Times*, 10 Jan. 1991.

23. *New Republic*, 7 Jan. 1991. See also, excerpts and comments on Solarz's article in the *New York Times*, 14 Jan. 1991. Solarz told the *New York Times*: "It would be the ultimate tragedy of Vietnam if the mistakes we made then paralyzed us the prevented us from taking action necessary today."

24. *Newsweek*, 21 Jan. 1991.

25. *New York Times*, 21 Jan. 1991.

26. *New York Times*, 17 Jan. 1991.

CHAPTER 12

1. *Newsweek*, 28 Jan. 1991.

2. Ibid.

3. *New York Times*, 12 Aug. 1990.

4. *Newsweek*, 28 Jan. 1991.

5. Ibid.

6. *New York Times*, 15 Jan. 1991.

7. Patrick Buchanan, "How the Gulf Crisis Is Rupturing the Right," *New York Times,* 25 Aug. 1990. This syndicated column was reprinted as "Have the Neocons Thought This Through?" in Sifry and Cerf, *Gulf War Reader*, 214.

8. *Newsweek,* 4 Feb. 1991.

9. Sydney H. Schanberg, "A Muzzle for the Press," in Sifry and Cerf, *Gulf War Reader*, 369. The U.S. military believed they were being open with the press. See Schwarzkopf, *It Doesn't Take a Hero,* 399.

10. *Newsweek*, 4 Feb. 1991.

11. Quoted in *Newsweek,* 4 March 1991.

12. Quoted in *Newsweek*, 25 March 1991.

13. *New York Times*, 19 Jan. 1991.

14. Ibid.

15. *New York Times,* 14 Jan. 1994.

16. *New York Times,* 27 Feb. 1991.

17. *New York Times,* 23 Feb. 1991.

18. *New York Times,* 24 Feb. 1991.

CHAPTER 13

1. *US News and World Report, Triumph without Victory: The Unreported History of the Persian Gulf War* (New York: Three Rivers Press, 1992), ix, 404–406. Sources quoted here were familiar with Iraqi force levels and concluded that the Iraqi army strength was somewhere between 300,000 and 370,000, possibly as few as 200,000. Of that number, as many as seventy percent might be classified as Saddam's "throw-away divisions." They most like deserted or surrendered immediately. The Republican Guard, apparently the only effective Iraqi fighting force, may have numbered as few as 100,000 men. Norman Schwarzkopf had moderately different estimates. See Schwarzkopf, *It Doesn't Take a Hero,* 474.

2. Roger Cohen and Claudio Gatti, *In the Eye of the Storm: The Life of General H. Norman Schwarzkopf* (New York: Farrar, Straus and Giroux, 1991), 278.

3. One hundred forty-eight U.S. soldiers were killed in action in the Gulf War. Thirty-five of those (twenty-four percent) are believed to have been killed by "friendly fire." Another 159 died outside of combat situations. A total of 244 Allied soldiers were killed in action. See *US News and World Report, Triumph Without Victory,* ix. Schwarzkopf makes very few references to war casulties. Schwarzkopf, *It Doesn't Take a Hero,* 528. A good accounting of casualties in the Gulf War is Allan R. Millett, Peter Maslowski, and William B. Feis, *For the Common Defense: A Military History of the United States* (New York: Free Press, 2012), 601.

4. The U.S. Army claims thirteen intercepts of SCUDs over Israel, and twenty-four over Saudi Arabia. See Bruce Watson, ed., *Military Lessons of the Gulf War* (London: Greenhill, 1991), 224–25; Sean McKnight, "The Failure of the Iraqi Forces," in John Pimlot, *et. al.*, ed., *The Gulf War Assessed* (London: Arms and Armour, 1992), 176. *US News and World Report, Triumph Without Victory,* 328–30. The analysis from Arens and Shomron is in *New York Times,* 27 Feb. 1991. Schwarzkopf, in his memoir, *It Doesn't Take a Hero,* has a lot to say about the Iraqi SCUDS. See particularly pages 485–89.

5. Schwarzkopf, *It Doesn't Take a Hero,* 483–84; *US News and World Report, Triumph Without Victory,* 328–30; Mullett, *et. al., For the Common Defense,* 602–603.

6. *Newsweek*, 20 Jan. 1992. Schwarzkopf, *It Doesn't Take a Hero*, 544–45.

7. *New York Times*, 28 Feb. 1991. *Time*, 11 March 1991.

8. *Newsweek*, 11 March 1991.

9. *USA Today*, 26 July 1991.

10. *Newsweek*, 11 March 1991.

11. *Time*, 5 Aug. 1991.

12. *Newsweek*, 13 May 1991.

13. *Newsweek*, 12 July 1993. It is estimated here that before the war, Saddam had nearly one million soldiers, 3,850 pieces of artillery, 5,100 personnel carriers, and 5,800 tanks. See also, *New York Times*, 14 Jan. 1993.

14. *Time*, 5 Aug. 1991.

15. Mullett, et. al., *For the Common Defense*, 604–605.

16. For a discussion of this incident, the validity of the FBI report, and a scathing analysis of Bush's interests in postwar Kuwait, see Seymour M. Hersh, "A Case Not Closed," *New Yorker*, 1 Nov. 1993, 80–92.

17. *New York Times,* 14 Jan. 1993.

18. *Newsweek*, 1 Feb. 1993.

19. Westmoreland, *Soldier Reports,* 119.

20. David Hackworth, in *Newsweek*, 24 June 1991.

CHAPTER 14

1. *New York Times*, 11 Oct. 1993. Anthony Lewis of the *New York Times* quoted the *Economist.*

2. For Clinton's own take on the events in Somalia and Mogadishu, see Bill Clinton, *My Life* (New York: Knopf, 2004), 550–54; Millet, et. al. *For the Common Defense*, 613–16. Taylor Branch, *The Clinton Tapes: Wrestling History with the President* (New York, 2009), 2–5, 304; *Newsweek*, 26 Dec. 1993; Jonathan Stevenson, *Losing Mogadishu: Testing U.S. Policy in Somalia* (Annapolis, Md.: U.S. Naval Institute Press, 1995), *passim.* See also, Mark Bowdon, *Blackhawk Down: A Story of Modern War* (New York: Signet, 1999), *passim.*

3. Clinton recounts the events in *My Life*, 616–19; Millet, et. al., *For the Common Defense*, 616. See also, Branch, *The Clinton Tapes*, 199–201.

4. Ivo H. Daalder, *Getting to Dayton: The Making of America's Bosnia Policy* (Washington, D.C.: Brookings, 2000), *passim*. See also, Branch, *The Clinton Tapes*, 304–305, 307, 309.

5. Millett, et. al., *For the Common Defense*, 617–24. Clinton, *My Life*, 848–52. See also, Ivo H. Daalder and Michael E. O'Hanlon, *Winning Ugly: NATO's War to Save Kosovo* (Washington, D.C.: Brookings, 2000), *passim*.

6. See Hersh's article in the *New Yorker*, 5 May, 2003.

7. Steve Coll, *Ghost Wars: The Secret History of the CIA, Afghanistan, and Bin Laden, from the Soviet Invasion to September 10, 2001* (New York: Penguin, 2004), 176–77, 184–86.

8. *The Guardian*, 15 June 2003.

9. *The Guardian*, 2 Dec. 2008.

10. *New York Times*, 9–10 Sept. 2001.

11. *New York Times*, 13 Nov. 2004.

12. *Washington Post*, 19 Sept. 2006.

13. *New York Times*, 30 Oct. 2007.

14. *New York Times*, 21 March 2003.

15. Bob Woodward, *Plan of Attack* (New York: Simon & Schuster, 2004), 139–44.

16. *Washington Post*, 25 Oct. 2005.

17. *Washington Post*, 23 July 2008.

18. *USA Today*, 30 April 2004.

19. For Bremer's side, see L. Paul Bremer (with Malcolm McConnell) *My Year in Iraq: The Struggle to Build a Future of Hope* (New York: Simon and Schuster, 2006), *passim*. See also, George W. Bush, *Decision Points*, 258.

20. Woodward, *Plan of Attack*, 300–301. George W. Bush generally rejects this point. See George W. Bush, *Decision Points*, 236–37.

21. Seymour Hersh, "Torture, at Abu Ghraib," *The New Yorker* (May 10, 2004).

22. A good source on ISIS is Jessica Stern and J.M. Berger, *ISIS: The State of Terror* (New York: HarperCollins, 2015), *passim*. See also, Andrew J. Bacevich, *America's War for the Greater Middle East* (New York: Random House, 2016), 342–52.

23. *New York Times*, 5 Dec. 2009.

24. *New York Times*, 24 Jan. 2010.

25. *New York Times*, 1 May 2012.

26. *Wall Street Journal*, 18 June 2013.

27. *New York Times*, 27 May 2014.

INDEX

Illustrations are indicated by page numbers in *italics*.

and Saddam-Hitler analogy, 188–9
Bush, George W., 32, 88
    Hussein and, 257–8
    Iraq War and, 262, 267–8
    "Mission Accomplished" speech and, 268
    Taliban and, 260–1

C

Cable News Network (CNN), 226–7
Cairo Conference, 8
Calley, William, 166–7
Cambodia, 93, 109, 113, 144, 146, 159–61,
    165–6, 177–8
Can Vuong, 93–5
Cao Bang, 106
Carter, Jimmy, 138, 183–4, 209
Carver, George, 155
Castro, Fidel, 93
Catholics, 114
Central America, 185
chemical weapons, 194
Cheney, Richard, 204, 206–7, 209, 240
Chen Yi, 51
Chiang Kai-shek, 9, 11, 13, 85, 95
China
    atomic capability of, 142
    civil war in, 9–13
    containment and, 18
    Korean War and, 9–10, 44–8, 51–3, 55–6,
      58–9, 63, 65–7, 69–70, 72–7, 79–81,
      85–6, 141–2
    Nixon in, 168–9
    Soviet Union and, 85
    Vietnam and, 104–6, 117, 133, 141–2
"China Lobby," 25
Chinnampo, 56
Chongchon River, 45, 52
Chosen Reservoir, 53
Chou Enlai, 42–3, 80, 116
Christmas Bombings, 174–5
Church, Frank, 138
Churchill, Winston, 9–10, 107
Chu Van Tan, 95
CIA, 55, 112, 114, 130, 172, 203, 213, 231,
    265
civil war, in China, 9–10, 12–13
Clark, Mark W., 78–80
Clifford, Clark, 14, 134, 137, 147–8, 151–2,
    154–5
Clinton, Bill
    Afghanistan and, 260
    election of, 252
    foreign policy and, 252

    Haiti and, 254–5
    Iraq and, 245, 257
    Kosovo and, 256–7
    Somalia and, 254
    Yugoslavia and, 255–6
CNN, 226–7
Cochinchina, 99–101
Collins, J. Lawton, 55–6, 114–15
Colombia, 93
colonialism, 93–5, 189–90
Commodity Credit Corporation, 192–3
Communists
    in China, 9, 11–18, 20, 22, 24, 41–2, 51
    China Lobby and, 25
    Korea and, 25–7, 30–3, 36, 38, 48, 55, 58,
      61–2, 64–5, 69, 72, 75–85, 87
    Nixon and, 158
    Vietnam and, 95–7, 101, 103–6, 116, 118,
      122–3, 135, 161
Connally, John, 223
Connally, Tom, 32
containment, 14, 18, 21, 32–3, 119
Contras, 185
Counterinsurgency, 120–1
Cronkite, Walter, 145, 154
Crowe, William, 208
Cuba, 93, 122, 184
Cuban Missile Crisis, 118

D

Darlac, 121
Dayton Peace Accords, 255–6
Dean, Arthur, 147
de Cuellar, Perez, 218
De Lattre de Tassigny, Jean, 106
Democratic Party, 13, 41, 47–8, 62, 70, 78, 84,
    118, 157, 172, 217–18
DePuy, W. E., 155
Diem, Ngo Dinh, 113, 115–18, 121–4
Dien Bien Phu, 106–9, 151
Dole, Robert, 194, 202–3
Dominican Republic, 93
domino theory, 103–4
drawdown, 251–2
Dulles, John Foster, 24, 38, 78, 105, 108–9,
    112–13, 115–16, 135

E

Eagleburger, Lawrence, 215–16
"ecoterror," 228–9
Egypt, 270–1; *see also* Mubarak, Hosni
Eisenhower, Dwight, 17
    Diem and, 113–14

ABOUT THE AUTHOR

GARY A. DONALDSON teaches American history at Xavier University in New Orleans, where he is professor of history. He has written a number of books on U.S. foreign policy and politics, including *Liberalism's Last Hurrah*, about the presidential election of 1964, published by Skyhorse Publishing.